Expectant
Fathers

Expectant Fathers

by
Sam Bittman
and
Sue Rosenberg Zalk, Ph.D.

BALLANTINE BOOKS • NEW YORK

For my beloved Maggie. And for my
sons Jondavid, Peter, and Simeon. (S. B.)

For Rich, whose love and continual
support never wavered for even a moment. (S. R. Z.)

Library of Congress Catalog Card Number: 78-54666

ISBN 0-345-31763-7

This edition published by arrangement with Hawthorn Books, Inc.

Manufactured in the United States of America

First Ballantine Books Edition May 1980

6 7 8 9 10

Contents

Preface

Before Maggie was pregnant with Simeon (two and a half years ago as of this writing), I had mornings to myself. Our older boys, Jondavid and Peter (then nine and six) went off to school at eight, and Maggie left for work a few minutes later. I'd go out to the barn and feed the goats (we had two then—now there are eight), and when it was autumn they'd walk with me in our neighbor's stubbled cornfield, where I would sit and lean back on my elbows to watch the sun against the near mountains, while the goats foraged for fallen ears. Sometimes I'd shuck a few and they'd come trotting over to gobble the feed out of my hands. My friend Steve Zimmer, who lives and works in New York City, used to call my morning activity "ecstasy once a day, and that's not bad."

When only the very tips of the corn stubble could be seen through the snow drifting in the field, we became pregnant, and life—subtly but inexorably—began to change. Of course, only a fool would sit in the snow just to watch the sun work its way across the sky for an hour or two, and no sensible goat would venture out chest-high into the drifts of February; so while the daily ecstasy was temporarily canceled, it had nothing to do with the pregnancy. I recall the two different seasons for you only because it seemed to me then there might be a connection. The fact is, that even had we become pregnant in the warm months and I had been able to do my morning goat walks and sun gazing and daydreaming, I would not have enjoyed them as I had before. Even the attempt would only have aroused in me the same guilt and fear I felt as a boy when I stole away from piano lessons to play softball in the schoolyard. I was always too terrified of being discovered to enjoy the game.

It strikes me now how regularly during the pregnancy I found the source of so many feelings in the memories of my boyhood. In fact, I suspect that constant drifting between thoughts of childhood and parenthood at the age of thirty-three had as much to do with writing this book as any other single thing. I was always searching: for clarity in my feelings, for their motivations in my past, for constant support, and at times for what seemed to my family an endless need for love and attention.

Midway into the pregnancy, I remember not finding things very humorous—the thoughts and ideas and jokes that normally amused me seemed unfunny. A note from a journal that I vowed to keep, but which now only contains sporadic and incomplete entries, reads as follows:

> *June 20, 1976.* Five months pregnant now. I feel too somber most of the time. It's not that I can't enjoy things—but nothing makes me smile. Getzoff went into one of her routines this weekend which usually gets me hysterical. I knew she was funny, only I didn't *feel* that it was funny and also I wasn't in the mood to laugh.

Yet the idea that first came to me about writing a book for and about expectant fathers was a funny one: Something like *How to Survive the Insanity of Being a Pregnant Father.* And my first scribblings of a proposal to publishers are dated in that week of June. It was as if, having been unable myself to find some lighthearted information about the experience of expectant fatherhood and thereby relieve much of my tension, I set out to play Pagliacci, the tragic clown—himself incapable of laughter but able to bring joy to the world.

That period of darkness passed without anyone appearing to know the difference—nobody saw a change in me, and I'm sure I would have been in a hurry to cover up any signs of having changed. Nobody told me I would change, or that I even *could* change, let alone *should*. I couldn't make sense of *what* was supposed to be happening. So I just went along.

I thought.

A few weeks later Maggie and I took the canoe out on the lake and paddled to one of the islands to pick blueberries. We talked for hours about intimacy and silence, and sex and about no sex. There were some tears and accusations both ways. In my journal, I wrote:

> *July 10.* Today I learned that intimacy with someone means revealing a lack of it when there is one and not letting someone guess at it. Guessing is for people who believe that closeness means never having to say anything.

I remember a confrontation between the parents of a friend of mine when I was a teen-ager. They'd been quarreling all day:

Her: If you've been so damned miserable, why have I had to wait until now to hear about it?

Him: If you loved me, you would have *known* how miserable I've been!

That dialogue stayed with me for years. I believed *him*; I thought he was right and secretly made myself a disciple of the No-Talk School of Love. For five and a half months of pregnancy I sneaked around my feelings, demanding no response from my wife or anyone else. I asked other men questions about their pregnancies and got small amounts of information—some of it frightening, some of it valuable. Mostly, men told me that their pregnancies had gone very smoothly. That was frightening, since I had a great many unsmooth feelings and fears. Nobody ventured to say to me: "I'll bet that you're scared shitless, but listen, don't worry, I felt the same way when my wife was pregnant."

I never heard anyone admit to feelings of fear, and so I began to think of myself as unstable. What was I afraid of? I was afraid that

I might not be a good father, that I would not have the patience, the *endurance*, necessary to make a successful transition to fatherhood. It is true I had been, by my own standards, a good father to Jondavid and Peter, but they were not my biological children. I had never raised a baby. Jondavid and Peter came all grown up (they were six and three when I met Maggie), so how was I to know whether or not I could handle an infant? I was also out of work and with few prospects: The cartloads of vegetables from our garden and sweet fresh milk from our barn each day did not exactly feel like good paternal providing, and I was afraid I would fail in the role of "head of the household" as well. I wanted to be part of the birth of my child and yet I feared that I would pass out cold in the delivery room and be further emasculated for this great failure. I even feared the deformity of my child. If only I could have heard or read or seen someone else express these concerns, I would have been greatly relieved. But everyone else's pregnancy seemed to be going along beautifully: The men had jobs, they felt confident about caring for their babies, and they had no real worries about fainting during the birth.

I think what turned things around for me (and the thought came to me two hours after Simeon was born and I was under a good hot shower) was the decision Maggie and I had made to have our baby at home. Our obstetrician, Dr. Raymond Haling, had recently attended a national convention of home-birth practitioners and was convinced that home was at least as good a place to have a baby as a hospital. Had we thought about the way we wanted our baby delivered? We had talked very briefly about it before, so I looked at Maggie and said, "I want to have the baby at home." She wasn't so sure. We agreed to join a group of seven other couples all training under a woman from Homebirth, Inc., of Boston, who had relocated in our area and was running classes.

I don't like airplanes; they worry and frighten me. Sue Zalk, my coauthor, recently theorized that I would probably not feel bad about flying if I could be the pilot. I think on some level she is right. I only raise this business about flying because it has a bearing on how the pregnancy changed for me as we entered our sixth month. Having agreed to enter a home-birth training course, we made the decision to *take control* of the pregnancy and the birth too. I had a role. I was still very frightened, but now I was learning how to prepare myself for having something coherent and responsible to do.

In the weeks ahead, I read every book on every aspect of birthing I could lay my hands on. Maggie continued to check out as a perfect candidate at prenatal visits, and the doctor said that we had only one more test to pass, which was to impress his assistant, a nurse-midwife from nearby New York State, that we were "responsible" enough to handle things. It was early in August when Betty came for the interview, and we were approved by and approved of her.

Still almost three months to go. The baby wasn't due until October 14.

A week into October and I still didn't have a job, but I sure thought I could deliver a baby if I had to. In fact, Maggie never *would* read the books about medical emergencies; she would just lie in bed before we turned out the lights, and I would tell her about all the possibilities and exactly what I would do in every case. And don't think I wasn't proud of myself for having memorized everything! And wasn't she proud of me and confident that anything that might go wrong would be handled with savvy and speed!

Then there was little to do but wait. The cradle I had been working on from a shop drawing in an antique furniture book was done. I had made a special trip to Boston during September and my friend Walter and I did the final work on the cradle in his shop—it'll now be for *his* first child with Sharon. Our neighbor Lucia, who'd agreed weeks earlier to take the boys when Maggie went into labor, had wallpapered the baby's room with a beautiful old rose-print paper, and I had painted the floor white. Maggie set up a chest of drawers, painted it, and decorated the top with beautiful dolls of many colors and sizes.

We waited some more. I cut firewood. I went to a produce auction thirty miles away and had fantasies about returning to find the baby had already been born. But that didn't happen. On October 12, Maggie and I drove our truck to a gravel pit on the property and loaded on some limestone chips for a pad we had built for a new woodstove. Twelve hours later, at about 4:10 A.M., I was nudged awake, and Maggie said, "It could be gas, but I don't know." It wasn't gas. And after an hour, when the contractions were still quite mild but obvious and coming regularly every five or six minutes, we called the doctor and Betty, and Maggie went in to shower and wash her hair.

And I was the pilot. In thirty minutes I had everything set up for labor and birth. I boiled water to sterilize the doctor's instruments and thought to myself, "My God, they really *did* boil water back then!" I made a full pot of fresh coffee. Lucia stifled a scream of joy when I called, and then I went upstairs to wake the boys, and they started laughing and crying and came downstairs to see mom who was sitting in the bathroom blowdrying her hair. Jondavid couldn't believe it. "Dad! She's supposed to be having a baby, why is she just sitting there?" Peter, three years younger, thought it was perfectly natural. Both boys were dressed by six and sent up to Lucia's for breakfast. They didn't eat much, I heard that night. Instead, they crouched in her kitchen window and squinted down the hill through the trees toward the lighted window across the room from where Maggie lay in labor, looking for some sign that something was happening.

At eight o'clock the boys grudgingly walked past the house and down the hill to meet the school bus. Every time they looked back over their shoulders, I ducked my head out of sight. I wanted them around and I didn't; I wanted all my close people around, and I didn't. The boys understood: But understanding came a bit more slowly for other friends who felt excluded. We had a strong need to be alone, just ourselves, for the birthing, and so invitations were not extended, even to our very dearest friends. The hurt feelings ran deep for a while, but things have long since been worked out.

Simeon was born at 8:50 A.M. And now, almost two years later, I cannot recall life without him. Even in my recollections of "ecstasy once a day" on the gentle slope of my neighbor's field, facing east to watch the early morning sun against the blazing autumn mountains while the goats browse for grain, I can see Simeon strutting about the way he does, gazing into everything, retrieving evidence of discoveries for me, and I know the feeling of always loving him—then, before then, now, and forever.

S.B.

A Note to the Reader

We began our research for the book by doing an extensive review of professional material written about expectant fathers. Much of the writing we found addressed the issues of extreme adjustment problems as a result of a pregnancy or recent parenthood. The articles and case histories were heavily enmeshed in psychoanalytic theory and concentrated on how stressful the pregnancy and fatherhood can be for many men—even precipitating emotional breakdown in extreme cases. This material was useful, but these men were not typical of the general population of expectant fathers. It was clear that these readings did not provide a sufficient base from which to write a book for expectant fathers. The primary place to go for information, we figured, was to the men themselves. The second best place was to the people who work with fathers, since they would have valuable information to offer and would be able to integrate their many experiences and offer a needed perspective.

We interviewed obstetrician-gynecologists, pediatricians, and people who offered childbirth preparation classes and prenatal parenting classes. We talked to nurses, to nurse-midwives, and to lay midwives, and contacted people at maternity centers. I also sent letters to counselors, psychotherapists, and psychoanalysts asking them to share with me any experiences they might have had while treating expectant or recent fathers. Responses were very positive, and these professionals were enthusiastic about sharing their knowledge with us.

We got information on the experience of pregnancy from men who either were going through it or recently had, in three ways: (1) in expectant and recent fathers' groups, (2) in individual interviews with men, and (3) by sending out questionnaires where the respondent remained anonymous.

Expectant Fathers' Groups

The men's groups and the interviews were conducted in New York's metropolitan area and in northern Berkshire County, Massachusetts, the home bases of the two authors.

At the time we began writing the book, Sam, who was involved in running pre- and postnatal parenting groups at the Visiting Nurses Association (VNA) in Williamstown, Massachusetts, had a ready population of expectant parents. These couples groups met once a week for seven weeks and the participants were usually in the third trimester of the pregnancy. Some of these couples continued to meet after the birth as a postnatal support group. Topics regarding issues and feelings about the various aspects of pregnancy were discussed both by the couples together and in groups of the men alone. These latter were particularly rich meetings, and as the men began to know and trust one another, the sharing and support grew.

A number of "one-shot" expectant fathers' groups were run in New York and Massachusetts as well. These groups were organized both by word of mouth and by the authors contacting professionals who came in contact with expectant fathers.

These groups were quite informal and usually consisted of five or six men who were at different points in the pregnancy. What was most interesting about the groups is that the men participated for no other reason but to talk about their experiences. The topics were feelings and concerns about a broad range of pregnancy experiences—"What kind of a father will I be?"

"How do I feel about my wife now?" "About my own father?" "What are my greatest worries?" "How am I reacting in my gut and in action?"

Three pregnant women's groups also yielded a great deal of valuable information. We felt that this was a needed perspective for our book.

The men who participated in our groups ran a large gamut of occupations and economic levels. They were farmers, factory workers, students, and post-doctoral professionals. Most of the men had at least some college education. Their most notable common feature, however, is that they were all, to some degree, actively involved in the pregnancy.

Interviews with Expectant Fathers

Forty-seven men were individually interviewed (occasionally two friends requested that they be interviewed together). The interviews lasted from one and one-half to four hours, and the longer interviews sometimes had to be spread over two or three sessions. Although we had a very detailed list of topics we wanted to pursue, we were rather flexible during the interviews and dropped our own agenda if the man had other specific issues he wanted to discuss. The men we interviewed were both expectant and recent fathers (with children under six months of age). The recent fathers were questioned on the pregnancy period, the labor and birth, and their parenting experiences. We usually taped the interviews, but if the man appeared uncomfortable or less spontaneous because of the machine (indicated by comments like "Can I play it back?" "Do you think my voice is recognizable?" "I sound terrible on tape"), the recorder was turned off and the interviewer took notes during the session.

Finding men to interview was easy. We were impressed by the number of men who jumped at the opportunity to talk about their pregnancy. They were pleased to find someone who was finally interested in *their* experiences. Occasionally a man would contact us, saying that he'd heard we were talking to men and didn't want to be left out. Our sense from these reactions was that expectant fathers often feel neglected.

The men we interviewed and those in our groups were probably not typical of all expectant fathers in the United States. The very fact that they agreed to be interviewed or voluntarily joined a support group or class makes them quite distinct. Since *you* have chosen to read this book—perhaps an indication of your own desire to become involved in and to understand the changes of expectancy—you may have much in common with these men. Our interest in talking to these men was to get qualitative experiences—what the men were thinking, what they were feeling, what they had to say to other expectant fathers. These men all had very different personalities, different pregnancy experiences, and different interpretations of events. It is likely that you will be able to find yourself in many of the things these men had to say.

The Questionnaire

The third way we directly collected information from expectant and recent fathers was through a detailed questionnaire. We felt that the anonymous nature of the questionnaire might enable men to reveal things they were not comfortable talking about. It would also allow us to obtain some additional specific data on the kinds of attitudes and reactions expectant fathers might share.

We sent out two long, detailed questionnaires: one for expectant fathers and one for recent fathers. We decided to get a lot of information from a smaller number of men, rather than getting many men to answer only a few questions. The questionnaires asked for specific information about the man's personal history and childhood, as well as events and feelings around the pregnancy. The surveys consisted of: (1) multiple-choice questions where a man had to choose one of several possible answers (some questions called for more than a single response) and (2) open-ended questions where a man would write out his response. From the multiple-choice questions we obtained quantitative information. The open-ended questions were used qualitatively.

Recent fathers were asked the same questions about the pregnancy period as expectant fathers (framed in the past, rather than the present tense), and additional questions referred to the labor and birth and the early parenting experience. Many of the questions asked appear in Appendix A.

There was no exact plan for distributing the questionnaires. Anyone who personally knew an expectant or recent father or who had contact with one professionally was given a stack and asked to pass them on with our enclosed, stamped, addressed envelope. Friends posted notices in their places of work. Questionnaires were mailed to friends and professionals around the country for distribution. They were mailed to prepared childbirth instructors, to nurse-midwives, gynecologist-obstetricians, and family-planning groups. Sam put an ad in his local newspaper for men willing to fill them out.

Prepared childbirth teachers were a most helpful source in distributing the questionnaires, which undoubtedly explains why most of our respondents intended to be or were present during labor or delivery. One nurse-midwife from southern Vermont apparently campaigned for us, which may explain why 6 percent of our respondents intended to have, or already had, home births. We do not know what the rate of home births is, but we suspect this is larger than the national figure.

We received back 162 questionnaires before we began the actual writing of the book: 52 were from recent fathers and 110 from expectant fathers. Unfortunately, only 120 were received in time to be processed by the computer (35 recent fathers, 85 expectant fathers). The rest were used for their anecdotes.

We decided to collect information from both expectant and recent fathers, even though the book is primarily for expectant fathers, for two reasons: (1) we wanted information about the labor and birth and early fathering and (2) we were interested in whether men presently going through the experience and men looking back at it had different perspectives. For most of the questions we found no differences in the responses of the expectant and recent fathers, so we combined the two groups when reporting these findings. Occasionally, the expectant and recent fathers' responses were significantly different—for example, expectant fathers report being more nervous than recent fathers recall having been. It may be that the recent fathers forgot what some of the experiences were like, or it may be that they see them more clearly in time. Or, it may just be that the recent and expectant fathers represent two different groups of men who had different experiences.

When we did find expectant and recent fathers responding differently on a question about the pregnancy that we thought valuable to mention, we just reported the expectant fathers' response. It will be clear from the text which respondents we are writing about.

The findings from our men's groups, the interviews, and the questionnaires were all integrated for the writing of this book. For those of you interested in numbers, we have included selected findings from our research in Appendix A.

The Respondents

Although we received most of our questionnaires from the Northeast, responses came from all regions of the country.

The average age of the men responding was 29.8 years. Their wives' average age was 27.6. The range in ages, however, was great. Ninety-five percent of the men were employed as compared to 40 percent of their wives (there was not much difference between the employment of expectant and recent mothers). The couples were married for an average of four and one half years, but they ranged from "not yet married" to fifteen years. A handful of expectant fathers were not married, although most of those men indicated that they intended to (one said he had to get divorced first). Two recent fathers were not married.

Thirty-six percent of the men had other children with their

present wives, while 9 percent of the men had children from previous relationships. Overall, 41 percent of the men had had other children of their own, while 6 percent of the men were living with their wives' children from a previous relationship.

In terms of their own family background, the men had an average of 2.5 siblings. Eighty-five percent of them said their parents were together throughout their childhood and adolescence. The educational level of the men were:

Less than eighth grade	.9%
Eighth grade	0.0%
High school graduate	13.9%
Two years of college	18.3%
Four-year college graduate	33.0%
Masters degree	13.9%
Higher	20.0%

The expectant and recent mothers had the following educational levels:

Less than eighth grade	0.0%
Eighth grade	.9%
High school graduate	21.7%
Two years of college	22.6%
Four-year college graduate	33.9%
Masters degree	15.7%
Higher	5.2%

Expectant fathers were divided into pregnancy trimesters: 13 percent were in the first trimester, 26 percent in the second, and 61 percent in the third. Clearly, the first trimester is underrepresented and the third trimester overrepresented. The reason for the low number of first trimester men seems apparent—many couples are approaching at least the middle of the first trimester before the pregnancy is confirmed. Also, many people who were distributing questionnaires would not have known that a woman was pregnant since she hadn't started to "show." It is easy to explain the high number of third trimester men who responded. Perhaps with the birth approaching they felt a greater impetus to answer the questionnaire. Or maybe they had received the questionnaire earlier, putting it off until they realized they would soon no longer qualify as an "expectant father" if they didn't answer it soon. Most likely it reflects the cooperation we received from childbirth preparation class leaders who come in contact with couples later in the pregnancy. It is important to realize that many of the percentages cited will be heavily loaded with the responses of men who are in later stages of the pregnancy.

Regardless of how representative our respondents may be, we feel certain that many of their concerns, issues, feelings, and reactions overlap with those of all expectant fathers. And we greatly appreciate and acknowledge their real contribution—the willingness to take the time and energy to share their experience with us.

S. R. Z.

Acknowledgments

Loving thanks to Linda White for her constant support and endlessly valuable information; and to Beverly Hertzig and the entire staff of the Williamstown Visiting Nurses Association. We also owe a great debt of gratitude to Dr. Raymond F. Haling, Jr., Dr. Fred Levison, Dr. John Buoni, Dr. Harry Wilson, Dr. Robert Hertzig, Elizabeth Bing, Betty Chludzinski, Dr. William Rashbaum, and the affiliates of the New York Center for Psychoanalytic Training—all of whom were vital to the success of our research.

Special thanks to our research assistants, Rena Repetti and Janice McAdams. We also gratefully acknowledge the support we received from Dr. Frank Dorsky, Barbara Cece, and Linda Radigan of the Northern Berkshire Mental Health Association. Another special acknowledgment to the W. B. Saunders Publishing Company whose photographs in *Before We Are Born* (1974) were of enormous help to our illustrator, F. X. Tobin.

Expectant Fathers

1
Beginnings

Mr. A., a twenty-eight-year-old factory worker with two years of college, reported in an interview with us a great deal of physical discomfort during the first seven months of his wife's model pregnancy. By "model" pregnancy, he meant that Mrs. A. was experiencing no intense physical symptoms, that she never went through morning sickness, had so far gained only fourteen pounds, and was, in short, the absolute picture of health.

She did feel, he said, that their apartment was too small for three people but was concerned about the financial burden a larger place would create. She also requested considerably more help from her husband in handling household chores and had frequent periods when she picked at him for having to be at work so much of the day. She understood that the overtime put in by Mr. A. created income without which the baby's furniture could not be purchased, but still she complained miserably of the isolation forced upon her. This pickiness escalated to the point of her issuing a fierce—although melodramatic—demand that he not come home at all if *that* (his extended absence) was all she meant to him. "Fix yourself a place to sleep in the plant, why don't you?!" Yet Mr. A. calls this a "model" and later an "easy" pregnancy.

Every pregnancy, by virtue of certain invariable events, is as typical as it is unique. And in that sense, some of Mrs. A.'s responses to pregnancy are model, typically human responses. But that is not the light in which Mr. A. presented it. In his utterance of the word *model* was implied the idea of a perfect pregnancy. But what stake does Mr. A. have in projecting an image of perfection? The answer was further complicated by his response to the question of whether he and his wife were having an easy or difficult pregnancy. "Easy," came the unexplained reply. Yet objectively viewed, the shifts in his feelings as well as in hers, the overreactions to stressful events, would hardly create such a portrait.

The mysterious, almost miraculous event we call pregnancy may be infused with the most positive of feelings and actions, but it is almost never *easy*. Feelings, like everything else in this universe, are relatively experienced. A human being feels good about something today, this week, this month, in relation to how he or she felt about it yesterday, last week, last month. "I was terribly worried that my wife would miscarry early on in the pregnancy," one first-time expectant father told us, "but as time went on those same fears disappeared." Ask him now if he's having an easy pregnancy, and he might say yes. But another man might be just a bit more circumspect—like the Georgia farmer who was asked how the weather was so far this year. "Compared to *what?*" he replied with a grin.

Some pregnancies may in fact be easier than others because of an abundance of good health, money, and clear and open communication. But rarely are any *easy*. Ask a woman in her fortieth week how it feels to carry around all that extra weight up front. You will get numerous responses, but rarely will you find "easy" among them. Yet most men readily assert that they and their wives are experiencing an "easy" pregnancy.

Pregnancy, no matter how positive and exciting and un-complicated, is periodically stressful. The process of integrating the pregnancy and the responsibilities of imminent parenthood into the lives of the expectant couple will inevitably create strain. Who could deny that? Who could deny that the drastic changes in body image, hormonal patterns, family patterns, and relationships would create stress? But people do deny it. *What,* one might well ask, could possibly impel them to do so?

Human beings are equipped with psychological defenses, which are an important key to understanding our behavior. Denial, one of many such defenses, has one basic aim: self-protection. If one denies a certain painful reality successfully, he or she will have avoided the pain that this reality—whatever it is—might have inflicted. A thirty-year-old psychiatrist and his wife, expecting their first child, had already survived a miscarriage that caused them both deep grief and anxiety. When she became pregnant for the second time, she was nauseated and sick for three full months. Needless to say, this caused an enormous change in the woman's outlook on life, which, in turn, had to have an enormous effect on the vibrations at home. Looking back on that period, the doctor commented that he was so positive about the morning sickness being a sign that the pregnancy was progressing, he had ignored the great tension it created.

Why do so many expectant fathers discount the reality of stress, and what connection, if any, does this phenomenon have to our Mr. A.'s need to project an image of perfection?

On Top of Things

To grow up male in America is to learn all the rules and definitions of strength and masculine behavior. To be "on top of things" or in control is the cornerstone of the masculine personality. "Wearing the pants" in one's family still means that a man's home is his castle, and he, as Jackie Gleason's immortal Ralph Kramden used to say, is "king o' dat castle!" While progressive changes in male/female roles are evolving these days, ingrained sex-role behavior dies hard. As pertains to pregnancy this is particularly so, since the lines of behavior are, at least in part, physiologically controlled. Cultures will come and go; nations will form and pass into oblivion; but women will always be the pregnant people, and they will never be able to achieve that status without a man's assistance. Since the carrying and nurturing of an unborn fetus is an exclusively female role, it follows that expectant fathers will try to forge their own exclusively male behavior patterns for the pregnancy. Such behavior, however, is much less clearly defined than the woman's, since it does not have the physiological invariables around which it can center itself.

For example, if, in the course of the pregnancy, a woman's breasts become tender and sore to the touch and she requests that her spouse keep his hands off, her decision has the support of her doctor, her friends, her mother, her childbirth instructor, her clergyman, and even her husband—however irritated he might feel at the banishment. Or the woman might experience deep depression in the first trimester of her pregnancy. Once again, the medical community supports the behavior as "normal" since numerous women react in this way as their bodies begin the first in a series of dramatic changes over a three-quarter year's period.

But men have no culturally supportable hormonal or physical evolution during pregnancy to justify depression, loss of appetite, or great nervousness. A man's admission of the existence of such conditions or feelings would hardly evoke limp support, let alone approval. So in order to avoid the threat of unacceptable fantasies, feeling different from the way he imagines any other expectant father does, feeling out of control, he starts denying. For instance, when you ask this man if he and his wife are having an easy pregnancy, the answer is quite often yes, because he sees it his duty to the prescriptives of his role to be a man, not a "woman." "You know women—and especially pregnant women," one man said. "They worry about everything. My wife is even worried about who's going to make the bed at home when she's off having the baby in the hospital!"

From comments such as this last one, it would appear that the only worry most men experience when their wives are pregnant centers around the well-being of wife and baby during the actual birth. Somewhere, way back when, this was deemed an admissible display of feelings. Otherwise, since it is practically written and accepted that a man shall take care of "the little woman," that is what he will do. He will be strong, show no "womanly" fears, and generally stay on top of everything. One can hardly expect an evolving introspection from this enormously "strong" and "perfect" person.

So the sex-role guidelines actually steer the man *away* from his feelings, since to acknowledge stress, particularly to his wife, would not only abrogate his prescribed position as model expectant father, but would cause her undue worry. "I guess," she might surmise, "he's not as strong as I thought he was." Based upon this somewhat oversimplified sense of duty, many couples discover they do not talk about *his* worries, particularly during a pregnancy.

Imagine the irony! A couple conceives a child in love, a joint operation if ever there was one, and then they proceed to isolate themselves from one another and worry alone. "It's so much easier," a university professor and father of two young girls said, "for a woman to be worried and confused in our society than it is for a man." Why does he say this? Not because the confusion causes her any less difficulty over making important decisions for her life, but simply because she is permitted by society to openly declare her confusion. Mr. A., for example, has many concerns that no doubt cause him some confusion. Typically, he does not label them as such, but they are obviously stressful as well as confusing to him. We know, to begin with, that he is short of money, or at least thinks he is or his wife thinks he is, and that this is the reason he must work an additional half shift at the plant every night. With fatherhood staring him in the face, a shortage of money not only limits his ability to buy essential things, it escalates to a much more important question: *Will I be a good provider?* Most men see the role of provider as the most crucial part of fathering, however personally distasteful the specific means to achieve such prized status. Billy Bigelow, the tough hero of Rodgers and Hammerstein's musical *Carousel*, sings about providing for his unborn child. His soliloquy ends, ''I'll go out and make it, or steal it, or take it, or die.''* If that's not stress, what is?

In pursuit of the fulfillment of this important role function, a father sets in motion a chain of events that will have infinite repercussions in his life, each vibrating at its own specific frequency, each with its own real issues. He may spend fourteen hours away from home each day fulfilling his role as future provider, but he could be creating problems in other areas largely because of such extended daily absence. This damned-if-I-do, damned-if-I-don't straitjacket, known as the *double bind*, is a brutal problem for many. Naturally, with every decision to do one thing, something else is given up. And if the expectant father does surrender the fantasy that he can be everything he wants, he will have the bittersweet knowledge that he cannot be, and therefore *does not have to be*, everything to all people! Such is the passage from childhood to adulthood. Such is appropriate defense against unjust demands.

Back to cases. Faced with a lack of funds to adequately furnish the baby's room, Mr. and Mrs. A. have several options: They could borrow the money from a finance company; Mrs. A. could get a part-time job; Mr. A. could find a second job; or he could work overtime if his foreman could guarantee that he would be paid for it. Excessive interest on the loan dissuades them from the finance company route; Mrs. A. has tried to find a job, but no one is interested in hiring a woman due to give birth in five months; Mr. A. finds it too discouraging to look for yet another job after he's waited so long for the one he has presently; so the only feasible option left is for Mr. A. to work overtime.

Once the new routine starts, Mr. A. arrives home at 10:00 P.M., having left his apartment at eight o'clock in the morning. He prepares his own evening meal since his wife is usually exhausted and, more often than not, asleep. If awake, she complains bitterly of the loneliness she has endured and often either sobs herself to sleep, admonishing him to keep away when he attempts to comfort her, or accuses him of not loving her, or both. Rarely is there a coincidence of energy and warmth which would allow the couple to embrace sexually.

So:

1. Mr. A., who disliked factory work to begin with, dislikes it even more now.
2. He earns 50 percent more on paper, but brings home less than that because of additional taxes.
3. He has lost his home-life!
4. He has lost his love-life.
5. He has even lost his dinner.
6. He has no time for himself, since all potential leisure is put into housework his wife can no longer manage alone.

On top of all the tension, anxiety, and general discontent fomented by such a cyclonic turn of events at home, he reports suffering nausea, vomiting, diarrhea and constipation alternately, head and back pain, occasional dizziness, and leg cramps. And this, says Mr. A., is an *easy* pregnancy!

What could induce a man to label such a period in his life as easy? The fears and tensions of the expectant father may be unique, but loyalty to his sex-role behavior is often as devout a religion as exists anywhere and provides the structure for the expression of uncomfortable feelings. And, if "Thou shalt take care of the little woman" implies, as it apparently does, "Thou shalt have no worries," it would be sacrilege—worse, heresy!—to acknowledge that there are. But what price devotion!

Granted, the case of Mr. A. is somewhat extreme, particularly in his physical symptoms; but, given the circumstances, his condition is not at all unusual. Four of his complaints, you may note, are alimentary. Tension, anxiety, nervousness, all tend to disturb our eating habits. Some people overeat when they are tense, others lose their appetites. Constant stomach tension can be expressed in a variety of ways—indigestion, nausea and accompanying sickness, diarrhea, and more. What is of more than just passing interest is that most of these symptoms are commonly associated with pregnancy, as are the headaches, back pain, dizziness, and leg cramps. What are we to make of this? Mrs. A. has cruised through seven months of pregnancy without so much as a headache, and her husband, at various stages, is exhibiting all the classic symptoms of the pregnant woman.

Who's Pregnant

Mr. A., while not necessarily a typical expectant father, is a classic example of a phenomenon that is far more prevalent than even its most devoted researchers first believed. The behavior pattern he manifests has its roots in a primitive charade known as *couvade* (pronounced koo-*vahd*). In certain primitive societies, at the approximate time of their wives' lying-in, men take to bed in a pretense-ritual, simulating the agony of labor and birth. This ritual serves at least two vital purposes: It establishes for the community just who the father is, and, also, it decoys all evil spirits to the father's hut where they can spend their wrath on the mock mother, leaving the actual mother unharmed to go through the birthing of her baby at a safe distance.

What is at work here, on the one hand, is a culturally established, culturally supported behavior which evokes no shame in the participant; and second, but directly related to the first point, there is a magical system of analysis tied in with the omnipotence of thought, i.e., one has only to wish for something and it will be so. In Western societies only children apparently believe in the power of magic, the omnipotence of thought—so much so that young ones often confuse their wishes with what actually can happen, and this can be painful. We will see in a later chapter the lingering effects of this type of thinking when a man confronts expectant fatherhood for the first time. But we can see a connection even now to Mr. A.'s insistence that things are going well. It is an almost childlike blindness to the difficulties he actually faces—as if not putting words to them will cause them to disappear.

The ritual couvade has its repercussions in Western cultures, too, and its manifestations in our society have been of interest to both the anthropological and psychological communities for quite some time now.[1] This system of sympathetic magic was given the name *couvade* by British anthropologist Sir Edward Tylor in 1865. He derived the term from the French verb *couver*, which means "to brood" or "to hatch." Many years later, while serving in the British armed forces during World War II, W. H. Trethowan, a psychiatrist, became fascinated with the couvade. A young warrant officer had complained of severe abdominal pains, which appeared to have no physical cause. Soon thereafter the burly officer received a telegram announcing that his wife had successfully delivered a baby, whereupon the stomach cramps vanished entirely. This *couvade syndrome*, as Trethowan eventually called it, refers to a set of physical symptoms experienced by an expectant father and that disappear almost immediately after his wife has given birth. An early and clear distinction should be made between the ritual couvade, which is an obvious pretense, and the couvade syndrome, where the symptoms are quite real. The degree to which the two overlap psychodynamically makes for fascinating speculation.

In any case, the fact remains that within an annual population of more than three million expectant fathers in this country alone, the reach of the syndrome is extensive. Estimates regarding the number of men affected by the couvade syndrome vary widely, largely depending upon a particular investigator's definition. Some claim as high as one man in two will experience pregnancy-related symptoms;[2] others are more modest. Trethowan and his associate Conlon first thought the incidence of the syndrome was one in nine, or approximately 11 percent, but revised their figures several years later to closer to one in seven, or between 14 and 15 percent.[3] The Trethowan-Conlon definition, however, is an extremely tight one. The couvade syndrome, according to them, involves any number of physical symptoms, whether or not they mimic the pregnancy, which are psychogenic in nature, becoming extremely intense at the end of the first trimester of pregnancy, slacking off, but then recurring with great severity just prior to childbirth. In all cases, symptoms vanish within several days of the delivery of the baby.

In 1965, they conducted a study among 327 expectant fathers at or about the time their wives were due and compared their findings with a control group of 200 men whose wives had not been pregnant for at least one year.[4] All the men were chosen from an industrial area in England and were asked whether they had experienced a certain list of symptoms in the recent past or were experiencing them presently. From this study came these basic results:

1. A greater number of expectant fathers were affected by symptoms than were the control subjects.
2. Expectant fathers suffered from a *greater number* of symptoms than the men in the control group.
3. All symptoms (except for an identical incidence of backache in each group) were more prevalent among expectant fathers, with unquestionable statistical differences with regard to loss of appetite, toothache, nausea, and vomiting.
4. The more anxiety symptoms demonstrated by men over their wives' pregnancies, the greater the physical discomfort they experienced, although the anxiety "*often went quite unperceived by the sufferer*" (authors' italics).[5]

The implications of these findings are potentially far-reaching, although considerably more investigation remains to be done. Each explanation for the existence of the couvade syndrome is as difficult to disprove as it is easy to postulate.[6] And this, of course, virtually forbids one's drawing hard and fast conclusions on the basis of limited data.

These difficulties notwithstanding, it *appears* at any rate that the syndrome is built upon a foundation of anxiety, and we have attempted to establish, by interview and questionnaire, what particular and common causes for anxiety were present across a broad range of men's experiences. One man worried deeply for his wife because his mother had constantly complained of her own painful pregnancy when she was carrying him. He suffered intensely from headaches throughout his wife's pregnancy and then from acute sympathy pains when she went into labor. But another man, whose level of anxiety for similar reasons was equally intense, suffered no physical symptoms during his wife's pregnancy. In some cases expectant fathers who were experiencing little if any anxiety reported nagging physical disorders.

Trethowan placed expectant fathers into three groups[7] with regard to physical symptoms vis-à-vis anxiety.

1. Some felt anxious periodically throughout the pregnancy and saw the connection between their anxiety and their physical symptoms. This group is typified by the young expectant father who had chronic diarrhea and finally understood that his great nervousness over his wife's rocky pregnancy was the probable cause. Sometimes, as in this case, the revelation of the connection dissolves the symptom; in other cases the symptoms persist.

2. In a second group, and a fairly large one at that, the men expressed anxiety over their wives' pregnancies, *did* experience physical distress, but saw no connection between the two. A cautious suggestion that a connection existed would be rejected by these fathers as often as it would be considered.

3. This group of men experienced extremely severe physical symptoms but felt, through an apparently supereffective denial apparatus, no anxiety whatever.

There were, of course, men who experienced anxiety in varying degrees from time to time over the personal and environmental issues related to imminent fatherhood but who reported no physical pregnancy-related symptoms; and a miraculous few reported that they *never* experienced anxiety and *never* experienced physical discomfort. One such man was asked to check on a list the pregnancy symptoms his wife was experiencing. Thirteen symptoms were included. The woman was obviously having a miserable time because her husband checked ten of the thirteen. But when asked to check *his* response to his wife's physical condition, he checked ''No Reaction'' beside each.

This last example points to a source of great clinical controversy. How is the investigator to know if a man reporting no anxiety is actually *experiencing* none? It is almost unbelievable that an expectant father would have ''no reaction'' to his wife's extreme discomfort. We have to look at the man's ability to perceive his anxiety and whether we can accept the fact that there truly have been no episodes in the pregnancy which provoked anxious feelings.

The fact remains that most men will feel *appropriately* anxious about a broad number of concerns that surround expectant parenthood—particularly first-time fathers. And if men tend to hide their tension and anxiety because there has been up to now no acceptable means in our society for expressing it, perhaps we can start to open the entire issue to constructive, warming light. Our initial step will be to identify what things are *naturally* stressful and how fathers in particular are likely to respond to such stress.

Expectant Fatherhood: Feelings and Changes

Stop reading for a minute and think about the myriad of feelings you have experienced since the day you found out your wife might be pregnant. Try to recall the range of emotions and emotional reactions. Feeling light-headed and then getting a rush of tension and a knot in the stomach. Snapping at a friend and then being really open—at almost the same time. Feeling dreamy and yet tense. Wanting intimacy yet pushing people away, sometimes even violently. Getting feedback from co-workers about how bright you look one day and being told the next that you look sad. Feeling loving toward your wife one moment and then shortly after feeling irritated, often furious, punching a wall, throwing something or wanting to—but not sure why. Picking on her to explain your own anger. Maybe crying for the first time in your life at sappy movies. Feeling more attuned to stimuli around you, yet feeling simultaneously dulled.

So many of the questions we asked expectant and recent fathers during our interviews were answered ambivalently or without great assurance—"yes and no," "that's hard to say," "well yes, but not exactly." Yes and no. Up and down. Good and bad. Confused yet sure. The moments of stress and inevitable changes during the expectancy period uncover in all men some of their most basic needs, conflicts, and concerns—the dynamics that make each expectant father the unique product of a lifetime of experiences.

Because the pregnancy signals the beginning of so many major changes in life-style, in relationships, and in feelings about oneself and one's spouse, the expectant father will often experience contradictory and ambivalent feelings. The predominant feelings about the pregnancy and parenthood may be positive, but doubts will still emerge in everyone. Even when the father does not want the child, moments of enthusiasm and excited expectations will creep in, sometimes winning out over the initial disappointment. Pregnancy seems to ignite in all people their greatest fears and spark their most secret smoldering hopes. It will tap vulnerabilities as well as uncover hidden strengths. This is true of all stresses in life, but it becomes particularly acute when fatherhood approaches. The prospect of becoming a father and then being one forces a man to confront parts of his own identity that he may never have considered before. This growing being with half the father's genes is a part of him, yet a separate person. Looking at his wife's belly triggers images of his own childhood, of his parents and the family dynamics, of growing pains and pleasures. It is no surprise then that the pregnancy can elicit so many mixed-up feelings—feelings that men may have expected to experience, but also those they think shouldn't be there.

There is no such thing as wrong feelings. There is no such thing as "you shouldn't feel that way." All feelings are legitimate by their very presence. But most feelings themselves don't cause difficulties for the expectant and recent father. Rather, problems arise when men struggle not to recognize their feelings, to accept them and to try to understand why they are there. This is true for many people, but it is particularly ingrained in men who have been groomed not to be too feeling. Men have been trained to deny intense feelings (except perhaps in outbursts of anger). They have been taught not to react emotionally, exposing weakness instead of exhibiting strength. For our somewhat confused world, a show of emotion is often considered anathema to strength. So what many men do is push their thoughts and feelings into the recesses of their minds where they temporarily lose their terrifying forms. But that's not the end of them. Difficult or painful feelings of threat to the self-esteem, painful memories, fears of past conflicts just don't go away when repressed. They remain in the unconscious and creep out in disguised, backhanded ways. Denying that you have a feeling, even to yourself, doesn't make it nonexistent. The question is, how long will it take to "creep out" and in what form will it manifest itself?

There are as many ways of dealing with stress as there are expectant fathers. And although many men may generally respond in similar ways, every man also reacts in his own style. Each person has his own psychological method for defense against stressful situations. Whatever defense mechanism a man usually employs will become that much more exaggerated during the pregnancy.

We are often unaware of the connection between our behavior and the motivations behind it. So even when we recognize that our actions or reactions to events reflect tension, such as sleeplessness or overeating, or even if we admit that some of our behavior, such as irritability or fear of suddenly getting fired, is not really understandable (although we rationalize it brilliantly), we still must struggle to figure out why it has shown itself at a particular time.

Why bother? Because tension is painful. Because giving stressful feelings some honest expression is less uncomfortable than keeping them in. Because so many of our defensive reactions keep us from the constructive use of our energy. Because so many of these coping reactions are, ironically, self-destructive, creating distance instead of closing gaps. The reluctant expectant father who claims to worry about his ability to provide for his new family calls in sick to work so that he can have the afternoon free to place long-shot bets at the racetrack. Though it appears to him that he is attempting to provide, he actually is running the risk of both losing his job, losing whatever financial cushion he *does* have, and alienating his wife. Is this in fact good providing?

If an expectant father is not clear about how he reacts in times of stress, all he has to do is ask his wife. We all have certain mechanisms that signal our moods to the people who know us well. But even a man's wife may find herself surprised at much of his behavior. Her surprise may be as often positive as it may be negative. For many men the pregnancy reduces certain stresses and meets many needs previously ungratified. The first-time expectant father who always entertained hidden doubts about his ability to father a child may now feel so sexually confident that his wife finds him virtually irresistible. But even those men who never felt more in love, more immortal, and more excited, will still be dealing with areas of concern and worries about the future. Even with the best of pregnancy experiences, the expectant father is on a seesaw.

Some questions an expectant father might generally ask of himself are: How have I been coping? What do I do when my wife snaps at me? (Many men complain of their wives being moody during pregnancy.) How am I responding to the increased presence of my in-laws? What do I do when I suddenly become painfully aware of my own worries? What happens when the pregnancy reminds me of some unpleasant event of the past?

COPING

One of the ways some men attempt to cope with stressful aspects of the pregnancy is to run from it. They literally flee from the situation, actually deserting their pregnant wives or staying away longer than necessary on business trips, with friends, and at work. Some men find themselves frantically running unneccessary errands instead of sitting around the house or helping their wives. This serves the purpose of discharging energy as well as avoiding the increasingly evident pregnancy or some conflict evolving at home.

More often, ignoring the reality of the pregnancy is symbolic, as with J., a man who participated in one of our groups. Throughout the pregnancy J. demonstrated a pattern of behavior that reflected his attempt to deny his wife's pregnancy—a psychological form of escape. Of course, in order to sustain this unconscious denial (consciously he knew only too well she was pregnant), he created ways of avoiding confrontation with the pregnancy. J. found himself daydreaming constantly, wrapping himself in fantasies of becoming a vagabond sailor with excitement and adventure greeting him in every port. His fantasy life became so engrossing and consumed so much of his time that he fell behind on his work, which in turn forced him to work later hours and on weekends. His work load, he explained, was the reason he was unable to help his wife with chores, particularly those related to preparation for the child, but he often found himself so caught up in his dream world that he would forget appointments with his wife and rarely remembered to join her for their prepared childbirth classes. In the time that he actually did spend with his wife he never referred to the pregnancy. When she attempted to talk about the baby he would excuse himself and go to bed or become extremely irritable.

Excessive daydreaming, heavy drinking, forgetting related events, doing things to avoid confrontation with the pregnancy, and having trouble making even the simplest of decisions regarding the pregnancy and birth are all ways of avoiding or fleeing from situations that create anxiety. Well disguised, however, the connection is often invisible to the escaping expectant father. Regressing, or acting inappropriately immature by demanding more attention and care, assuming less and less responsibility, whining, pouting, are all ways of saying that if one were a child again the fears and responsibilities of becoming a father could be avoided. One of the men we interviewed confided that he began to wet the bed when his wife became pregnant—clearly an example of regressed behavior.

Some men, in their attempt to defend themselves against uncomfortable feelings, start to act in ways that are very different from how they feel. When they are furious with their wives but the prospect of expressing that anger is too threatening, they may act particularly loving. Or, if they are feeling irritated at the continual presence of parents or in-laws, they may act especially gracious. It is the exaggeration of the behavior that can usually betray the hidden feelings. One expectant father admitted that he did not want the child, that the pregnancy was an accident. But his wife, for whom he would do ''anything in the world,'' decided that *she* wanted the child, and so how could he feel resentful about the impending birth? This same man went out and spent tremendous amounts of money on elaborate furniture and clothing for the child, considerably more than he could afford. His child, he said, had to have the best. Was he trying to cover up his feelings of not really having accepted the pregnancy?

Some men try to compensate for many of their worrisome feelings about their future fathering skills by reading everything they can find on the subject. This kind of behavior can be constructive—but not all compensation is.

People also attempt to cope with anxiety-producing feelings and thoughts by displacing them. The expectant father who insisted that his wife didn't really want the child and that she was doing things to make herself miscarry was projecting onto his wife his own ambivalent feelings about the child, which were frightening and unacceptable to him. The man who, during each of his wife's three pregnancies, snapped at everyone around him felt he would be excluded from the relationship with his child if he directed his anger where he really felt it—toward the expectant mother. Some men identify themselves with their wives or even their unborn children, as a way of unconsciously disarming their concerns. This is apparent in a variety of physical symptoms experienced by men during their wives' pregnancies. Others, particularly those who are better educated and have become particularly adept at talking around issues (''bullshitting''), will discuss everything but seem to feel nothing. They completely separate their emotional experiences from their intellectual skills and never are in touch with their gut reactions. Nevertheless, the feelings are there.

Every individual has unique defensive reactions—tactics he has learned, developed, even perfected through the years. These mechanisms intertwine neatly with one another and many operate simultaneously. Where there is one defense working, there is probably another nearby. As the mechanisms become more complex and better disguised, they can more adroitly camouflage underlying concerns. But before we make it sound as though defense mechanisms are some kind of disease, let us point out again that they can be functional. Everyone has them—even small children. Everyone needs them as buffers to get by much of the everyday abuse we encounter. If we could not turn off the image of city filth or the discord of nerve-shattering urban noise, our entire lives would seem shadowed with ugliness and tension. The problem is that defenses are often *inappropriately* deployed to help us avoid anxiety-producing thoughts and feelings that really require direct confrontation. To avoid what must be faced is to deny one's responsibility in an adult relationship. And since these feelings rarely dissipate when hidden, they continue to nag at us, pointing an invisible finger of reminder. And we receive little real comfort for having so deftly sidestepped our major concerns.

Many men protest that they do all the ''right'' things. They suppress their own needs because they feel they are expected to be strong. They say what they think they are supposed to say and treat their wives the way they think women "in their condition" should be treated. But they have their *own* needs that are being neglected. Inevitably they feel resentment and anger, and these feelings find expression. Perhaps a man will subtly but pointedly remind his wife of her vulnerabilities or withhold affection. Or say things that can hurt and then assure his wife he was just joking. Or perhaps he will pick on his mother-in-law when it is the expectant mother who is the principal target of his anger. The feelings are there, we repeat, but they are not in the open, so they can not be discussed and dealt with. They cannot help but create tension and distance in the marriage.

The numerous issues, emotional reactions, and attitudes experienced by the expectant father vary in degree, sometimes lying low and other times intensifying—prompted by real or imagined crises. These issues may be triggered by something in particular (e.g., financial losses) or may exist throughout the pregnancy. Real issues and psychological states overlap. "Real" and "fantasy"—or emotionally charged—issues occur simultaneously, one setting off the other. For example, real financial problems may intensify the expectant father's hostility about people being dependent on him. Or the reverse may be true. Feelings about being depended upon may result in behavior (such as heavy gambling) that will cause financial difficulties. Similarly, to be present or absent from the delivery room is a real decision that the expectant father must make. The decision he makes, however, will depend upon his emotional state and psychological makeup.

Each man brings his own unique needs and ways of coping to the pregnancy. In time of stress, and pregnancy is a time of stress, these needs and reactions naturally tend to be magnified and can be understood in terms of the man's own personal history. If we can get rid of the "conspiracy of silence," the refusal to open up and talk about feelings, we can start to gain the needed insights to deal constructively with these feelings and therefore get the greatest pleasure from the pregnancy.

2

The First Trimester

Conception

We have heard from the time of our childhood that what distinguishes us human beings from all other animal life is our ability to *think abstractly*, or to *reason*. We would add to that definition that humans are also the only animals capable of both planning and avoiding their procreation.

This may sound like a circular argument; for, having established that we alone of all animals can plan things out, it would stand to reason that we are capable of figuring out how to undo the most natural and possibly most instinctive of life's phenomena. The conception of life is a good deal more complicated than it seemed some years ago when we were dished out Version Number One of the Facts of Life. The story often went something like this: "Mommy and daddy were very much in love. And when grown-ups are feeling very loving, they like to get as close to one another as they can. As a matter of fact, they get so close that daddy actually gets *inside* mommy. And from his penis comes a little seed which looks like a tadpole, and it swims all the way up the stream to where mommy's seed is sliding down a special chute. And when the two seeds meet, a baby is begun."

Quite poetic, filled with wonderful graphic images which children enjoy and find memorable. That is good, of course. We want our children to remember what we mustered the gumption to teach them. Unfortunately, the story never talks about the tadpole that never makes it, nor about the times when the tadpoles arrive and don't get met.

At least not many of the little boys we know got the R-rated tale. As a result, young male adolescents, as well as females, race through puberty into adulthood and when contemplating the start of a family, they still have the fable firmly planted in their minds that conception, the beginning of pregnancy, is a virtual certainty should they want a child. Intercourse takes place without contraceptive measures, and a baby is on its way.

The point of rude awakening is no news to the tens of thousands of couples who want children but who experience a range of difficulties in getting a pregnancy started. One expectant father called the groundwork for this shocking lack of instant fertility ''the arrogance of the male posture. Here I thought all I'd have to do was stick it in and wham she'd be knocked up. Who the hell would have known that I'd be reading temperature charts and researching the acid level in my wife's vagina!''

We think it is meaningful to note that of the eighty-three men responding to our questionnaire whose pregnancies were planned, the average number of months from the time intercourse was directed toward conception until conception was achieved was 6.3 months with a range of one to sixty months.

In a world so severly overpopulated, it seems hard to believe that conception ever fails. On the other hand, given the great number of variables in the lives of an average American couple and within the reproductive systems of those same two people, one muses how pregnancies ever get under way at all! A universe of physiological and psychological realities holds great sway over the moment new life is, or can be, created.

Most of the men in one survey taken among a group of twenty expectant fathers rated themselves as ''not very knowledgeable'' about the anatomy and physiology of reproduction, particularly with regard to the reproductive system of the female.[2] The ''arrogance of the male posture'' is built, we think, upon a solid foundation of ignorance. These two—arrogance and ignorance— hardly establish a pattern of sexual sensitivity, and this may well

The Female Reproductive System

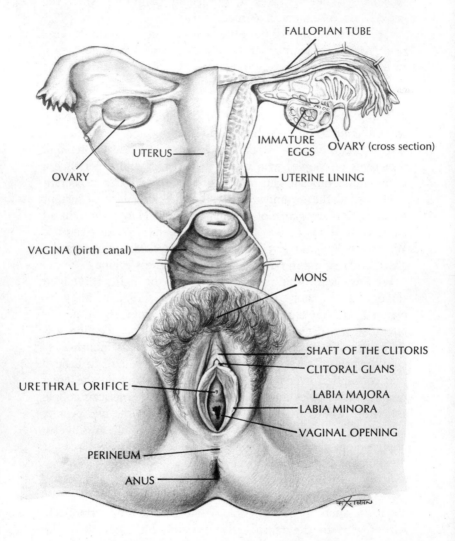

FALLOPIAN TUBE

OVARY

UTERUS

IMMATURE EGGS

OVARY (cross section)

UTERINE LINING

VAGINA (birth canal)

MONS

SHAFT OF THE CLITORIS

CLITORAL GLANS

URETHRAL ORIFICE

LABIA MAJORA

LABIA MINORA

VAGINAL OPENING

PERINEUM

ANUS

The Male and Female Reproductive Systems During Conception

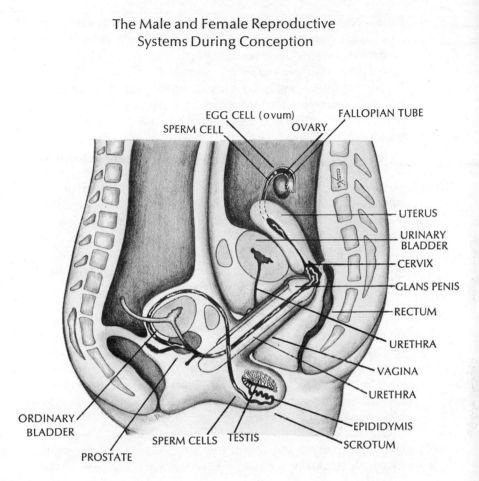

have a bearing on the ease with which conception is achieved. The "stick-it-in-and-wham-she'll-be-knocked-up" attitude precludes any sensitive understanding of psychosexual and biological responses in the male and female. Men and women experience a highly formalized response to sexual stimulation, and these responses play a role in the procreation of the species.

Although our liberated society boasts that it has changed the point of sexual intercourse from having babies to having fun, our sexual responses are biologically geared toward the reproduction of ourselves. The various phases of sexual response consequently play a part in facilitating that end as much as they contribute to the mutual sexual pleasure and gratification of the couple. Vaginal secretions due to a kind of perspiring of the vagina's lining, vaginal distension (widening and elongating), and the pulling back and flattening out of the labia majora, all of which occur when a woman becomes aroused, ease penile entry. When stimulation continues, lubrication from the vagina accommodates penile thrusting, and the engorgement of blood in the tissues of the vagina actually make the vaginal opening smaller, serving as a hold on the penis. The male sexual responses are similarly structured around conception. When aroused, penile blood vessels engorge, causing an erection. Obviously the erect penis will have easier entry into the vagina. Elevation of the testes prior to orgasm increases the pressure with which ejaculation takes place.

Orgasm, a series of muscular contractions, serves as a release of muscle tension and forces the blood out of the engorged tissues. It is usually a euphoric experience and the peak of the sexual experience. For men, orgasm is critical if conception is to occur. The male orgasm is generally accompanied by ejaculation, in which the sperm cells spew out and swim toward the fallopian tubes where fertilization takes place. There is some indication that a woman's orgasm may also assist in the conception process although it is by no means necessary. This assistance may come from the deep vaginal contractions as well as the ever-so-slightly-increased opening of the os (the passageway from the cervix to the uterus).

In addition to physical changes during sexual arousal, there are specific changes that occur in the woman's body at the time of ovulation: body temperature drops a degree or so and then increases several degrees, the cervix, which is normally firm, softens considerably to allow for the passage of sperm cells, and the mucous secretions in the vagina change dramatically in consistency, color, and even smell—going from a sticky, cloudy, yellow or white discharge to one of greater volume that has the consistency of egg white. It is believed to ease the transportation of sperm cells and seminal fluid through the cervix and on toward the fallopian tubes.

The ecstacy of lovemaking and the mystery of reproduction are forever there to be pondered. The original natural order of things may have been for sexual interactions to be so intensely pleasurable that the species yearned to survive, but this takes nothing from the lovemaking and nothing from reproducing. It is simply added testimony of the potential of humanity. Since conception takes time (and timing is everything—the woman must have recently ovulated for conception to occur) the "trying" for many couples can be the most intimate and binding of experiences. *Can be*, we say—for the couple who wants the child, for whom the ambivalences and tensions surrounding parenting are minimal, for whom fears of infertility have not crawled into bed along with the lovers, for whom lovemaking is quite special and who are now unencumbered by the concerns of birth control. Such unity can produce a life that partakes of the spirit of both partners.

But things are not always so. Many couples talk about how the fun, pleasure, and gratification of lovemaking they experienced in the first month of trying steadily decreased as the months passed and nothing happened.

There are a number of physiological reasons why conception may be difficult. Some women cannot ovulate at all or do not very often; others may have internal adhesions that interfere with the flow of the egg down the fallopian tube; in some women the uterus may not be receptive to the implantation of the fertilized egg. The male may have too low a sperm count, poor sperm motility, or something may be blocking the passage of sperm. Many of these problems can be medically treated.

More often, however, the problems of conceiving are elusive. We all hear stories, ad infinitum, of the couple who finally accepted the fact that they would *never* get pregnant and *then* got pregnant. Or the couple whose adoption papers for a long-awaited child were no sooner finalized than the woman became pregnant. Explanations for these cases are attributed to psychological factors or tension. But very little is understood about this phenomenon except, of course, that it does point to the power of the mind's influence over basic biological functioning—a concept with which the medical and mental health professions are well familiar.

The variety of psychological explanations for the inability of a couple to conceive has traditionally focused on the female. This failure is explained in terms of her ambivalence about pregnancy or parenting or even about her spouse; or her excessive fears that she won't ever be pregnant; or that she wants a baby so badly that she tries too hard. She is told by friends and family to go on a vacation (with spouse, of course), to stop worrying about it, to stop thinking about it. If she *could* stop worrying, it might help. But who can?

Studies have been done on infertile males; but only in the case of their inability to ejaculate inside the woman have psychological causes been proferred. Men with a variety of (perhaps) hidden fears and concerns about pregnancy and parenting have been known to experience impotency when they reach the decision to have a child; or they become aroused but lose the erection when they penetrate their wives. Or they may be able to maintain an erection but cannot ejaculate, or they can ejaculate but not during intercourse. Often these conditions are temporary, and it may be helpful to see that they reflect some ambivalence about having a child. Discussing these concerns with his wife (it is not as though she is unaware of the problem) may ease the situation. The anxiety about sexual performance, however, can intensify difficulties. Talking about them with a mental health professional may help solve the problem.

But *can* stress and tension and anxiety have an effect on sperm count and sperm motility? Oddly enough, this is a question that we have not yet heard asked, let alone for which an answer has been hypothesized. Infections like flu or cold as well as chronic diseases like diabetes, which place the body under stress, can have a real impact on sperm count. Other physical disorders may have a bearing on the motility of the sperm cells. If physical stress can influence the number and movement of sperm cells ejaculated during coitus, why wouldn't it follow that stress from emotional causes could have a similar impact?

One might entertain a tentative hypothesis that if a man knows his wife is very fertile certain psychological factors will obviously have a bearing on the nature of lovemaking. The issue of becoming a parent can create an emotionally charged atmosphere which will undoubtedly have its effect on the manner in which the couple relate to one another during intercourse. "Oh my God, this is for real!" is a frequent thought in the minds of first-time fathers-to-be. Some men find themselves virtually exploding into their wives' vaginas with great orgasmic enthusiasm and pleasure, while others feel tentative about ejaculating without contraceptive precautions having been taken. The psychological influences on a man's fertility are certainly worthy of serious research. Considering all of the infinite possible reactions to such a memorable event, it is no wonder few couples achieve conception in the first month of trying.

With regard to problems surrounding conception we have somewhat arbitrarily designated the six-month point (although many obstetrician-gynecologists say "give it a year") as the period beyond which a couple could be said to be experiencing difficulty. Many doctors, however, report encounters with young couples who feel there is a problem when they have not conceived after a single month. These cases notwithstanding, by "difficulty" we mean a variety of possibilities—ranging from mild feelings of self-doubt and self-effacement on the part of one or both would-be parents, to much more intense anxiety at the prospect of infertility.

The issue of infertility places a terrible strain on a couple and their relationship. Often sex becomes tiresome, a chore regulated not by desire, but by time of the month. One couple who had two and a half years of highly disciplined sex (that is, they never missed it when they were supposed to do it), told us how much they looked forward to getting to know one another again sexually. Often, men and women wonder to themselves, "Who's to blame?" and secretly feel guilty for letting their partner down. They may entertain fears that they are being punished for some childhood or adolescent wrongdoing (i.e., masturbating, early sexual play, hateful feelings toward the family). Couples wait out each cycle, frightened, to see if *this* month she is going to get her period. Tension builds as the days pass, and if she does start menstruating, the disappointment is tremendous. Tension usually increases with the passing months and each partner is often fearful of burdening his or her spouse with doubts and fantasies. Yet, in spite of the strain, a number of couples find themselves closer together, united by working together for something they want equally. When conception finally takes place, the child is very much wanted, and few couples question that the effort was worth it.

But for most of our readers we can pretty safely assume that conception has already been achieved. If, on the other hand, for some reading this, there has been difficulty associated with the process of beginning a pregnancy, we suggest consulting an obstetrician-gynecologist for assistance.

Beyond that, try to relax. Try to forget the pressure and appreciate the freedom you both have at last! No more pills to take or diaphragm to slide in or condom to slip on or foams to spray. Just get into bed, or start out wherever you want for that matter, and enjoy. As we've indicated, timing is everything, and one's sense of timing will be enhanced by sound information. Since it is known, for example, that the cervix softens and vaginal secretions become quite viscous during the woman's fertile periods, try to look for those signs, and take advantage of their presence. Both sperm count and sperm motility are increased by allowing a couple of days to pass between ejaculations. This information will allow for good, basic planning; for, if it's Monday and by consensus the couple agrees that Thursday is likely to be prime time, it makes sense to build up the odds.

But there are no rules. Sperm count and sperm motility can both be sufficient one hour after an ejaculation if everything else is right and the moment is appropriate. And a man, on the other hand, can store up for two weeks and no one will guarantee conception because of it.

UNPLANNED PREGNANCIES

Before we go on, we want to mention couples who had not intended to become pregnant but did and who made the decision to have the child. Of the 120 men responding to this question, 32 (or 28 percent) placed themselves in this category of expectant father in an unplanned pregnancy. We say "unplanned" and not "unwanted" because of the genuine enthusiasm often shown by couples who do not consciously plan their pregnancies. Although many often feel that the timing might have been better, they usually agree that a child is one thing they have wanted, at some time in their lives, and so they adapt their plans accordingly and get into the swing of the pregnancy.

Despite the high level of involvement among the expectant fathers in this group, their reactions to actual news of the pregnancy varied greatly in kind and intensity—from the response of one man who adamantly did *not* want the child, would have nothing to do with either the pregnancy or his wife during it, to the man who stated that his *wife* did not want the child but agreed to go ahead with the pregnancy because *he* wanted it so badly.

It is interesting to speculate about the relatively high rate of unplanned pregnancies. There are accidents, of course, but given the sophistication of present birth control methods, their rate seems to far exceed the expected number. Most accidental pregnancies are owing to birth control *risks* taken by the couple (*She*: "Oh, I don't want to put the diaphragm in tonight. Why don't you use a condom?" *He*: "No, they're terrible. Why don't I just pull out?") On the surface it may seem here that a pregnancy is undesirable, but for one or both partners there may be a strong, unconscious desire to have a child. This wish is often strong enough to bring about the pregnancy—and not by magic either. Rather, there is a contriving of events that brings the pregnancy about inevitably. And although it may be easy for one of the partners to point a finger of blame, the pointer might well ask himself or herself about the kind of vibrations he or she may have sent out that sanctioned such "carelessness."

There are, of course, men who struggle to, and perhaps never do, accept the pregnancy. They are often extremely resentful of their wives and occasionally deny that the child is theirs. They may even become violent. If open discussion between the couple fails to resolve the issues, then counseling should be sought and perhaps the couple should even consider terminating the pregnancy.

Whoever may have been more directly responsible for the pregnancy, the decision has been made to allow the pregnancy to continue, and we dedicate this book to making that a most gratifying experience.

New Roles

After all the study and all the reading and all the talking and planning, and *trying*, conception becomes a reality. The pregnancy has begun! The knowledge that a new life has been created brings excitement and even incredulity to many men. For couples who have planned for it, the news is almost always greeted by celebration. A night on the town, a swarm of long-distance telephoning, perhaps a quiet rejoicing over a corned beef sandwich at a delicatessen. The congratulations come roaring in from the family and from friends. Men are likely to slap their newly expectant buddies on the back and say things like "I didn't know you had it in you," or "Are you sure it was you?" or "Do you think it was the mailman?" Later in the pregnancy, the expectant father may well kid about the same things, except that he will be referring to himself. Comments like these, aside from being fun, are also statements describing a man's own potency. The friend from work who asks "Are you sure it was you?" is probably asking himself if he is capable of fathering a child. But then again all locker-room or "jock" talk tends to be a boyish affirmation of sexual realities and roles. Pregnancy is, after all, proof positive of a man's virility, and many men, whether their pregnancies were planned or not, respond with pride and a sense of relief.

By and by, though, the jokes stop along with the congratulations. An expectant mother becomes the Madonna, magazines and books and boutiques praising her, encouraging her attention, offering theirs. Friends call and ask, "How is *she?*" The expectant father's own parents call and ask, "How is *she?*" One man told us, "God, I used to be Numero Uno with my own mother. Firstborn son and all. Then my wife became pregnant and I was number two. And when my daughter was born, I swear my mother hardly knew I existed when we came to visit." This man was awaiting his second child. No wonder he was filled with anger and trepidation about being rejected by the very people who ordinarily showered him with love and attention. This same man, a teacher, reported that he had been unable to resist stealing a small piece of hardware at a department store. And stealing is something he normally would never do. He was thoughtful when we suggested that such an action could have been a response to feeling deprived of love and support during his wife's pregnancy. Had he been caught by the store detective, he'd have had more than his share of attention.

Children who feel deprived of loving attention have very direct techniques for arousing their parents' anger, if they feel that is all they are capable of getting. Adults who are not in touch with what they are feeling and unable to verbalize their needs may, like children, seek negative attention. Stealing for a child is one thing; for an adult, however, it can have serious consequences. A man's reputation is at stake; he is risking a fine or even time in jail.

Obviously, not everybody who experiences rejection resorts to such potentially self-destructive behavior in order to dramatize their needs. But if we don't express such feelings verbally, we may resort to a charade or to some other, more indirect means for gaining attention or enacting the pretense that all is well. Since most men do have difficulty in admitting that their feelings have been hurt, they are naturally hesitant about opening a discussion around the real issues. It might appear simpler to pout and wait to be asked: "Gee, honey, what seems to be the trouble?" But, in the long run, it is no less difficult thrashing about the house in a deep funk, picking at one's mashed potatoes, ignoring your wife's sexual requests, and waiting for your mind to be read than it is to say, "Hey, listen. You know, I've been feeling rejected by all the phone calls *you* get these days, and nobody has really been asking about me. When I'm home from work, you seem to spend more time on the telephone with our friends than you do with me. At least that's the way it *feels*."

What's the worst response you can expect after taking a risk like that? Let's play it out together.

Him: Say, I'm feeling very isolated from you these days.

Her: (pretty coldly) How come?

Him: Well, you seem to be giving everyone besides me your attention these days.

Her: Maybe that's because everybody *but* you seems to be concerned about how lousy I've been feeling.

Him: I'm concerned about you, but why don't you ask me about *me* sometime?

Her: Why should anyone ask about you? You're not the one walking around feeling nauseous all the time, are you? You're in the peak of health! You're slim. You're not going to get fat like I will.

Him: I feel bad about that, but I've got needs too. How are we going to solve this problem?

Her: As far as I'm concerned, there is no problem. If

you've got worries, talk to your mother about
them. I've got all I can handle. And besides, what
are you anyway—some kind of sissy!?

Some kind of sissy! That's the worst of it right there. Less than
a man for being worried. A sissy. A homosexual, even. Could
there be anything worse for a man than to expose some latent
nonmale-isms in his behavior? So instead of discussing his fears,
he plays it close to the chest. A voice within whispers, "I may
not know what I really should be doing during this time, but at
least I know what I read in books and see in the movies. And
those guys seem straight, so how far off can I be if I do as they
do?"

This, then, is the springboard for stereotypical behavior—that
is, molding one's actions to a fixed and almost cartoonlike mental
picture that one's peers will agree is the standard way of
responding to a given situation. Now, conformity is some of the
cement that binds our culture, and we are not knocking its values
and necessity. The conflict arises, however, when a person, in
this case an expectant father, puts aside, debunks, and otherwise
forsakes his individual responses to a great experience in his life.
Instead, he cops out and takes society's acceptable route.

Here again, we see the social directive: "Thou shalt take care
of the little woman." Because it has been around for so long, we
may assume that it reflects a sociobiological function in our
species for the male to protect the female during expectancy. It is
his way of contributing to the preservation of the race; nor is this
type of behavior limited to humans. Among mammals who enter
into prolonged paired relationships, we find the male fox and wolf
providing for the female during and after gestation.[2] But the male
plays other roles as well. Among certain species of marine life,
most notably the sea horse and the pipefish, the male actually carries and nourishes unhatched eggs. Some male frogs brood the
eggs in their own vocal pouches, and the young emerge alive at
the end of the incubation period.[3]

We are not trying to do away with this specific role directive, but we think it could use some elaboration. While it may be vital for the human expectant father to assume the role of protector, it is equally vital that he assume other role functions as well. The protection urge is millions of years old. The pregnant female is no longer considered an easy target for some wild predator because she is slower, less able to escape the onslaught of a saber-toothed tiger or a charging mammoth or a snarling brontosaurus. A pregnant female is safe in our culture with or without a man. Notwithstanding her own evolved strength within a changing culture, she is also being kept safe by the magazine publishers and clothing manufacturers and obstetricians who have made a professional and financial specialty of her.

We would like to see the role of the expectant father expand, especially since we are convinced that such a broadening will bring the father-to-be directly into the developing family; will have a positive lasting effect on the marriage; and will prove to be a period of recognized growth in the lives of men who have felt up to now that pregnancy was *just* a waiting period.

Finding out how a new life develops within the cloistered uterus of the expectant mother is the first stage of an expectant father's figuring out just who he is in relation to his new family.

A New Life

For most men, particularly those awaiting fatherhood for the first time, the beginnings of embryonic and fetal life are abstract and take a form that is neither pleasing nor recognizable. It is as though whatever is happening ''in there'' is all going on in some distant country.

The distance and abstraction are understandable—they exist for the pregnant woman as well, particularly first timers, or *primipara* (pri-mih-parah). After all, it is difficult to identify oneself with a one-sixth inch, amphibious, betailed sea horse of a creature at four weeks of life. So the expectant father begins the wait in the wings, as it were, shortly after pregnancy has been confirmed. His time for warm and loving congratulations is past, and the void left is filled with the attitude of "well, it's her trip now."

This appraisal of things is partially accurate: After all, a woman carries and is the source of direct nourishment for the growing fetus. Nature has built her for the job. But the "it's-her-trip" posture is very much like the "you-can't-fire-me-I-quit!" defensiveness that is spurred by feelings of painful exclusion.

Yet, this defensiveness, this anticipated rejection from the developing family, comes from an incomplete understanding of that new life tumbling and swimming in its sea of amniotic fluid. Our present assumptions about early fetal life are that since the life is so new, so alien, and so remote, and because it is invisible and impalpable and only viable *in utero* (within the uterus), it follows, therefore, that it is cut off from and impervious to outside stimulation. Or, if the fetus is susceptible to stimulus, *only* the mother has input. These ideas underlie the belief that the fetus is not really human until much later in the pregnancy, since it is not at all like any human being we have ever seen. That is, however, very much like saying that the first species of *homo sapiens* of however many millions of years ago was not human because we know of nobody similar.

But now try this on for size, as have scientists and philosophers for centuries: *Ontogeny recapitulates phylogeny*—by which is meant that the development of the species as a whole is repeated in the fetal development of each individual specimen. The breathtaking hypothesis here is that each phase of fetal growth reflects and receives signals across millions of years, audible only to the genes of the baby in utero. What a powerful creature this is, then, not simply as testimony to the miracle of life, but also in its role as the chronicler of our phylogenetic past.

As a race we have developed as the only species with the ability to entertain abstract thoughts, and this may be due to the primacy of head and brain development in early fetal life. Unlike many other animals, we develop from the head downward, rather than from the extremities upward. The fetal head is, therefore, disproportionately large relative to total body size in order to accommodate the early mass of gray and white nerve tissue that will soon be the brain, spinal cord, central and peripheral nervous systems. Even in its early shapelessness, the brain is the prime mover of fetal growth, sending out shoots, the way strawberry plants send out runners, that will become the buds of future organs and systems. And each stage is programmed to occur at a specific time on the developmental clock, all preset, precise, and often dazzlingly fast.

It is ironic that the father, feeling himself more and more outside the new family triad, is experiencing this exclusion at precisely the moment his child is creating sense organs with which it will reach out to him. At six weeks of age, the beginnings of the eyes and ears are there, and the hands and fingers are almost perfectly formed by eight weeks, although the feet are somewhat later in development.

We would like to suggest that the expectant father participate in this early stage of his child's development—not just in an academic and meaningless way but in a genuine cause-and-effect relationship, albeit through the expectant mother. Skeptics will say, of course, that we are attempting to build a viable and reciprocal relationship for the expectant father where one does not, indeed *cannot*, exist. But at eight weeks the brain of the fetus is already exhibiting recordable electrical activity. Tap on the amniotic sac and you will see the fetus make a quick arm movement; touch gently in the region of the mouth and the eight-week-old will turn its head away. At nine and a half weeks it will squint and swallow, scowl and retract its tongue, registering its first facial reflexes. As early as eleven weeks, rhythmical respiratory movements are detectable. Even the presence of taste buds has been clinically established through experimentation with sweetening of the amniotic fluid, which the fetus often drinks in.[4]

Now when we talk about a cause-and-effect relationship between expectant father and his child, we obviously do not mean that for every stimulus introduced by the father, the fetus will respond or that the father will be ''communicated with'' by an eight-week-old fetus. But a relationship can exist, and this is by

Development of Fetus in First Trimester

NUMBER OF WEEKS FROM CONCEPTION	DESCRIPTION OF GROWTH
1st week	Egg cluster travels down fallopian tube and on the 3rd day enters the uterus as a blastocyte (a ball with an outer cover of many cells and a liquid center) where it continues to divide. Approximately 1/100 inch in diameter.
2nd week (beginning)	About 10 days following conception, the blastocyte implants itself in the wall of the uterus, doubling in size every 24 hours. Placenta begins to form where the blastocyte has burrowed into the uterine wall.
3rd week (beginning)	Now termed embryo. First signs of spinal cord in the form of a minute streak of nerve tissue. Embryonic sac containing the embryo is 2/5 inch in diameter.
3rd week (end)	Early formation of spine. Central nervous system and spine canal in early formation. Rudiments for brain and entire nervous system established, along with dents for eyes. A tubular heart has begun to beat. Length of embryo: 1/12 inch.
4th week (beginning)	Head starts to form. Still externally located, the heart beats visibly. Early formation of intestinal tract. Mouth still closed. A tail is visible as an extension of the spinal column.
4th week (end)	Entire backbone established and spinal canal closed. Brain size increasing rapidly. Arm and leg buds are apparent, as are buds for eyes and ears. Length: 1/4 inch.
5th week	Heart now inside a completed chest and abdomen. Eyes visible through closed lids. Mouth now open. Lung buds appear. So do big toes. Tail disappearing. Body movement possible. Brain is huge. Length: 1/2 inch; weight: a fraction of an ounce (1/1000).
6th week	Facial features forming: jaws well formed; teeth beginning to form. Fingers and toes forming primitively. Genitalia becoming apparent. Skeleton beginning to firm up. Length: 3/4 inch; weight: 1 gram (1/30 ounce).
7th week	Face completely formed. Extremities partially formed. Abdominal musculature developing. Sex determinable. Length: 1 inch; weight: 2 grams (1/15 ounce).
8th week	Eyes have moved from side to front of head. Face highly developed. Heart taking four-chamber configuration and beats 115–155 times each minute. Roof of mouth almost completed. Scrotum appears in the male. Major blood vessels developing final form.
13th week (end of 3rd month)	Extremities fully formed. Finger- and toenails appear. Ears complete. Legs can kick, toes can curl, arms bend at elbows, and fingers can grasp. Closed eyes seem to squint. Length: 3 inches; weight: 1 ounce.

no means an imaginary one. And with it comes an ordered and coherent role for a man during the nine months of expectancy, a relationship previously denied him by our culture.

Life is more than just an individual organism that happens to be alive; it is also a force within the organism that affects and absorbs things outside itself and can be conversely affected and absorbed. Such life force is palpable not only among animals, but many believe among plant organisms as well. Certainly one feels in the presence of budding life when standing beside a pregnant woman, particularly as the months pass. A three-month-old fetus, after all, has eyes, ears, extremities, internal organs, a rapidly developing brain, and a heart that pumps its own blood at approximately one hundred and fifty beats per minute. An expectant father can opt to be there emotionally with his own newly developed life, or he can choose distance. The first choice creates a sense of inclusion in the family; the second reinforces the traditional idea that only the expectant mother can relate to the baby and the father is outside their relationship.

Keeping Close

If the expectant father takes on the role of outsider, *he is really going to feel like an outsider*. Unfortunately our culture reinforces this feeling, and so does his wife—despite (as we saw in the case of Mr. A.) the problems this choice creates. He is alternately related to as father and child. He is either expected to hold everything together for everybody or he is being shooed out from underfoot. ''I wish he'd just go out more often with his friends,'' a primipara of thirty said. ''He's always getting in my way. He is so nervous.''

After the baby was born—and it was a difficult baby in the first weeks—this outburst took place during one of our postpartum groups, in response to an inquiry about the changes in the family since the arrival of the new child.

> *Mr. M.:*   Well, my wife and I are at each other's throats all the time.

Mrs. M.:	(who was walking the baby to keep it quiet) What!?
Mr. M.:	I said, we're at each other's throats all the time. We can hardly stand each other anymore.
Mrs. M.:	That's not true.
Mr. M.:	Oh, yes it is. You just don't know it yet.
Mrs. M.:	Is that why you're always pacing up and down when you come home from work at night?
Mr. M:	I can't stand staying home so much. I just can't stand it. I have all this energy and I don't know what to do with it. I keep pacing up and down the hallway like a caged cat.
Mrs. M.:	I keep telling him, why don't you go out and leave us alone? You get me so nervous with all that pacing. Really, I tell him to go out.
Mr. M.:	I can't go out, for God's sake! I feel too guilty about going out. She's with the baby all day, and it cries all the time, and she's so demanding, and then if I went out at night she'd be stuck with the baby all alone again.
Mrs. M.:	It would be better than watching you pace. Really, I just tell him, why don't you go out?

So Mr. M. was both pre- and postnatally shooed away. Show us an expectant father able to find himself a niche in that monumental nine-month period in his life, and we will show you a father who can easily find a gratifying relationship with his child once it is born. Since the culture in which we live gives no specific role responsibilities to the father in terms of the physical care and nurturing of his own child, he will be excluded from as much of that relationship as he is willing to be.

A man cannot jump into fatherhood. It simply won't let him. Relationships are too complex. Therefore, expectancy provides a much needed transition from life arranged one way to life of a totally different shape and rhythm. Yet, sitting back and passively awaiting the baby's arrival on the presumption that there is nothing else to be done is to miss nature's offered opportunity for smoothing the way to parenthood. And this is all too often the case in our society. Professionals talk about the crisis and trauma of new fatherhood; they imply that the father is almost always unprepared for his role responsibilities and shifts in life routines. Like the child who is tossed into a pond by a well-meaning uncle and ordered to swim without ever having had instruction, the new father flounders.

Although the survival rate in most sink-or-swim experiences is high, for our species is extremely adaptable, there is a great deal to be gained from a few patiently administered swimming lessons. The uncle would never dream of throwing his niece into the drink (''She's just not built for it''), but a man is supposed to be able to survive. But the expectant father has no instructed, coherent range of behavior and responsibilities. Further, his masculine ego is jerked to attention by the suggestion that any true-blue, all-American he-man is damned well ready for anything and, by God, hell bent for leather. Regardless, preparing for difficulty of a sex-role nature is like admitting that you don't know if you're really a man or not. Any man who admits that fatherhood is creating turmoil in his home and in his life is threatened with emotional emasculation. Why in the world do men think that they have to know everything about everything even when they haven't been trained?!

Classes in prepared childbirth over the past several years have boomed into popularity. Men who would have sooner registered for an evening class in needlepoint are now enthusiastically enrolling in the so-called Lamaze courses for what is now referred to as the ''husband-coached birth.'' Such classes are of huge importance, and we will discuss them further at some length since there are quite a variety. These classes have done much to bring men into an area previously forbidden them and deserve great praise.

Objectively viewed, however, most classes only prepare an expectant father for assisting in and becoming involved in a *single day* in the life of his family. An alarming although inconclusive little study was made in northern California in 1976 to determine whether prepared childbirth courses had a positive impact on the expectant father's sense of inclusion in his new family. The investigators found no evidence that the classes helped to give a stronger sense of belonging. Rather, they speculated that the exposure to the physiology and anatomy of pregnancy, labor, and delivery tended to alienate men, since it pointed up the physical differences and their natural exclusion from the routine of the prenatal family triad. The men in the study reported that while the Lamaze classes were very interesting and informative so far as preparing them for the day of labor and birth, they did nothing whatever to prepare them for what was to come after.[5] In other words, a man's presence at conception and then again at birth does not a father make.

It is vital to mention here again, too, that the physiological information given to expectant fathers during prepared childbirth classes is geared around the expectant mother. "This is what's happening to your wife at such and such a time, and you can expect her to react in these following strange ways." Or, "The fetus at term begins its descent into the birth canal after the cervix has completely effaced. . . ." In short, these classes are so future oriented and so involved with the woman and her physiological changes that the expectant father is of necessity learning to concentrate only on what he will be doing on the birthday of his child. And your ability as a labor partner doesn't always coincide with your skills as a father. Such confusion about the father role will produce a father unprepared for the radical changes that are soon to occur in his life. Still, beyond these classes, little is available on an institutional level to prepare expectant fathers for anything.

DEVELOPING A ROLE

In one study, thirty husbands who attended childbirth preparation classes were interviewed with their wives before and after the birth of their children.[6] The results from this study suggest that developing some kind of coherent role was more important to husbands' adjustment to postpartum family life than actual involvement with the family once the child was born.

It may seem too early to be discussing a coherent role for the expectant father but the first trimester of life is exactly the time when a sensible pattern of responsibilities and expectations for the future of the expectant father ought to be negotiated.

In our culture, the father only begins to assume responsibilities for his child once it has been born. It has often been said that once a baby is born, its parents have the privilege of watching the completion of fetal growth in the nursery—the baby is still quite helpless. A year or more will pass before a complex set of responses can be accomplished that will allow the baby to walk, and almost twice that long in some cases for the child to develop language skills. But if the baby's nursery is in fact an extension of the womb, at least for several months, two possibilities arise with regard to the father-child relationship. A choice has to be made between the two:

1. The father should *not* assume responsibilities for his child until it outgrows its helplessness.
2. Or the father should assume role routines for his baby *from the first moments of its life and thus make himself an "insider" from conception onward.*

We firmly support the second position. Let's think about expectant fatherhood from three points of departure:

1. his role responsibilities to his unborn child;
2. his role responsibilities to his wife;
3. his role responsibilities for himself.

We are all familiar with Newton's law—that for every action there is an equal and opposite reaction. Call it prenatal Newtonianism, but, for every action on the part of fetus and expectant mother, there will be a reaction on the part of the father and the other way around, and these reactions identify involvement. It's like playing on a team. Each player has a specific role for each play. Imagine yourself on the offensive line of scrimmage with the Los Angeles Rams and you hear the quarterback yell a strange list of letters and numbers, followed by "Hut. Hut," and then the ball is snapped. It is a nightmare, because not only don't you know your position, but no one has told you your job, and God knows from that strange language what it is you are expected to do! This is guaranteed to make one tense. And keep one tense.

Free-floating anxiety is a term used to describe a general condition of emotional tension. If, as an expectant father, you walk around knowing that there are things that you feel must be done but you can't for the life of you think what they are, you get the terrorizing sense that important issues are being left unattended to. This does not appeal to our sense of order or calm, nor to our wish for well-being.

The trick, then, is to define early in the game what the plays are and who does what or who *wants* to do what, and who will actually *get to do* what, or which plays will have divided responsibilities and on and on until the most important items in the game plan have been established. A couple can become so used to working with one another that important issues are handled as a matter of course. It's like the quarterback calling what is known as an "audible," an automatic change in plans right at the moment the original play was to have happened, simply because the defense's play has forced a change in the approach to the problem of moving the ball from here to there. Flexibility is imperative here, and flexibility comes from thorough knowledge of your responses and responsibilities so that changes in basic patterns can be made easily and precisely at short notice. Professional athletes rarely leave things to chance; but if improvising is called for, they have the skill to create new opportunities when they have to.

Parenting is not a solo routine, unless necessity forces it to be. It *can* be a team effort, a partnership that requires discussion and even practice to smooth out patterns well in advance of the birth of the baby. If it is decided, for example, that father will be bathing the baby, he ought to start rehearsing that procedure as early in the pregnancy as he wishes. But we will be discussing those skills a little later.

For the moment, let us focus on the more general responsibilities to the growing fetus. There are things the expectant father can do long before he and his newborn lay eyes on one another. In most pregnancies, for instance, nutrition is the sole responsibility of the mother. It is her body, and she has the right to put into it what she wishes. But every single substance that goes into her bloodstream only scant moments later passes across the placenta and enters the baby's circulatory system.

The child is joint property; how, then, can its sustenance be the exclusive responsibility of the mother? If she is a chain smoker, does the father have to sit patiently by and hope for the best? If the mother drinks alcohol beyond the point of moderation or devours chocolate bars as if the Hershey Corporation were about to go out of business or pops pills without a doctor's orders or smokes marijuana more than just occasionally—is the father to remain quiet? Nonsense.

We found it interesting that men responding to our questions *about their right* to have a say in their wives' general physical well-beings answered largely that they did feel they had a right; but when we asked if they actually *told* their wives to do or not do something that they felt would be important both for the mothers and the babies, a much smaller number responded that they had done so. Why is this?

Having a say in one's wife's diet is like making a direct contribution to the baby, and while the expectant father may not be able to see the baby's reaction, he can still get the positive impact on those monthly prenatal visits when the obstetrician says everything is going perfectly. A couple then can glance across at one another with great satisfaction for having taken real joint responsibility for that portion of the pregnancy. There is agreement between the parents on a job well done and, evidently, these responsibilities must have been prearranged. Agreed-upon routines are what comprise a *role*; and a role for the expectant father is what we want to stress.

Diet is only one way a man can participate with his unborn

child. Any positive impact he makes on his wife's well-being will be felt by the child sooner or later and can be a source of pride for both parents. Still, one's notion of what constitutes good health may require education, keeping abreast, for example, of the latest information about how various medications affect mother and baby, the impact of "junk" food on the available vitamin supply to the fetus, and much, much more. Men who read about pregnancy- and parent-related issues during the expectancy period are usually very proud of their new knowledge and think of it directly as proof of their *real* involvement in the family. Gaining information fulfills two slots in the preparenting role, then. First, it supplies information useful in making men *feel like parents*, and second, it provides numerous *role activities* which not only have a solid, positive effect on the fetus, but also on the marriage relationship. It firms up the expectant father's actual place in the family before and after the birth of the child.

Changes in the Expectant Parents

The biggest change in expectant parenthood is pregnancy itself. This sounds suspiciously circular but it's an important issue in the early weeks of the trimester. Just because two people know they have conceived doesn't mean they have accepted the pregnancy, particularly if this was not a planned event.

In any case, even the carefully planned pregnancy will create conflicting feelings for the expectant mother in the first trimester. These feelings center around forming a new identity as a mother. This emotional chore is equally powerful in the multiparous woman (one who has already borne children). When a woman is told that there is a life forming in her uterus and she can't see it, hear it, or touch it, how does she deal with such an abstraction? "How is it possible," she asks, "for something that radical to be going on within me and me have so little sense of it?" Although some women may simply experience unqualified joy at the news of a positive pregnancy test, others are alarmed and confused by what is happening so close and yet across light-years of distance from them.

Then we have the dramatic alteration of the chemical balance in the mother's body. Numerous hormones are actively changing their levels at this time. The catecholamines, a group of chemicals that appear to have some connection with the way in which we experience emotions, particularly depression and elation, are strongly affected by the levels of estrogen and progesterone, two hormones that are produced in much greater quantities during the pregnancy than before. Also, the secretions of the adrenal glands, known as the corticosteroids, which play a powerful role in working emotional changes of a depressive or ecstatic nature, are very definitely altered during pregnancy.[7]

While these chemical and hormonal alterations might tend to explain the emotional volatility of a pregnant woman, we do not wish to suggest that she is a robot held captive by the whims of her chemistry, or that as an adult she has no control over the way she acts. Women in the first trimester of pregnancy, just like men, are teeming with thoughts—racing from one plan to another, from one fear, one dreadful doubt, one overwhelming issue to the next, and then on to something amusing or even silly. In such an emotional sprint she may show anger, sadness, nonchalance, tears, and laughter. Though the hormonal changes undoubtedly are playing their part in intensifying these feelings—establishing the reality of the pregnancy and insisting in a way that the mother pay attention to creating an environment safe for the fetus—the particular issues conjured up momentarily or obsessed on are determined by the personality of the expectant mother and her history before she got pregnant.[8]

It is therefore impossible to generalize about expectant mothers and to say with certainty that *your* wife will probably be feeling such and such and acting in this and this way during this or that stage of the pregnancy. Rather, we have a range of responses and we will attempt an explanation of a variety of possible basic motivations. Somewhere along the line you will recognize your own wife and the way she tends to react to specific concerns.

For both men and women pregnancy is a reminder of childhood. Expectant fathers and mothers frequently describe themselves as being in a fog, walking around in a dream. Expose yourself to enough pregnant people and you will sense that they are often floating somewhere between the present and their early youth, bombarded with flashes of memory, some painful, others calming. As an expectant mother daydreams about the way she and her child will be with one another, she cannot help but focus on the memory of her childhood and present feelings for her own mother. Fear that she will repeat some of the hateful things she feels were done to her can often throw an expectant mother into a momentary panic. The strength of her own growing maternal identity will probably contribute to the length and extent of her upset. Moments later she will be back in control, a look of contentment replacing the one of panic, and this often confuses the people around her. In a nonpregnant state, the same thought would probably have had only passing impact upon her, and her face might never have revealed the tension. But now she has *mood swings*—she goes from one frame of mind to another. These, too, perform a vital role in the pregnancy.

In our bodies, pain serves an indispensable purpose. It is a warning that something is wrong inside. If the pain persists, we try to isolate its cause. A sudden but persistent cramp in your thigh might scare you if you didn't recall that yesterday you played handball for the first time in three or four months. The psychic pain, which often appears and then vanishes at various stages of the pregnancy for both men and women, is a signal that there are uncomfortable issues present which have to be confronted. Why do almost all pregnant people experience ambivalent feelings about becoming parents? Why as expectant parents do we remember either consciously or through our dreams the disturbing thoughts and memories of our own childhood? Why do expectant couples constantly worry about the state of their babies at birth, sometimes to the point of great anxiety? Why is there universal fear of birth defects? Or why do we worry so much about finances, about our homes, our health? Note that there are different kinds of worrying. On the one hand, worry signals us that there are things that must be prepared for. If *you* don't worry about the money problems, the environment in which your baby spends its prenatal months, its earliest days, then no one will. This kind of worry can be alleviated by action. Make a list of items that bother you, then deal with them one at a time.

Another kind of worry tends to make issues more important than they should be. These unavoidable worries stem from your own emotional history and may not last long. They generally focus on the psychological transition from being someone's child to becoming someone's parent. When these worries are exaggerated and lingering and disproportionately painful, you might try giving them a closer look.

The perspective to establish, basically, is that the concerns of pregnancy, which in turn create anxiety and tension and stress and sometimes distress, are *all OK*. What is not OK, it seems to us, is that the concerns are denied. Human capacity to bear emotional pain is limited, and it may be more damaging to repress painful items. If you fill a glass with water, then add more water, and keep adding more and more, the glass overflows. What would you say to the person who insists the glass is not yet full? The same is true of feelings.

No feeling should really be considered as "off the wall" since its roots can always be traced. But if it is so obsessive that it causes enormous anxiety or threatens the marriage relationship, then the couple should seek professional help. In the early stages of pregnancy, a woman often feels that something is likely to go terribly wrong. If, the reasoning goes, she cannot feel the embryo inside, how does she know the baby is not dead? The idea of losing the baby is quite common among pregnant couples, and we ought to note that the fear comes at a time when ambivalent feelings about becoming parents are most intense.[9] If these feelings persist, perhaps they signal the wish to reject the fetus. If this is the case, several alternatives are available. The pregnancy can be medically terminated. Or counseling services can help in resolving the basic ambivalence and accepting the pregnancy. In most cases, though, such feelings pass and the growing fetus becomes the object of its parents' love whether its movements can be felt or not.

Most initial responses to a wanted pregnancy are enthusiastic, though some women are uncertain about sharing the news with their husbands. Often this reticence has good cause. One man in a prenatal parenting class said that on the day he discovered his wife was pregnant, he took an armload of rocks and smashed every window in his house. Another man cried and was uncommunicative for several weeks. And yet another who described his reaction to learning of his wife's pregnancy as "extremely positive," said that on that day he just "kept trying to stay cool and nonchalant."

A wife generally knows how her husband will react to basic issues. If he has not been involved to the extent of knowing that she has had a pregnancy test or that she is going for one on a particular day, then there may be good reason for her reluctance to tell him the news. She might fear that he will reject both her and the baby, though the degree to which her fears are real or fantasy depends a great deal on her own ability to accept the pregnancy. In other words, she is likely to project some of her own feelings of ambivalence onto her husband.

Most men react positively to learning that they are soon to become fathers, particularly for the first time. Expectant fatherhood is a milestone in our culture, and the news is welcomed with all the euphoria of a home-team victory. Upon learning of the pregnancy, most husbands kiss and hug their wives, take them out for a special meal to celebrate, and tell everybody they know and anybody else who will listen.

At least for the first few days, early pregnancy can be the sweetest time of life for the expectant father. Everyone who loves him now loves him more. They are proud of him, without qualification, and he is thumped on the back for having successfully fulfilled this cultural role. There are only few events in his life that can rival this one: his bar mitzvah or first communion, the first night he was married, and perhaps his graduation from high school or college.

But soon the spotlight is dimmed, and what appeared to have been his great success now becomes the comparatively minor beginning of something he has never experienced, filled with huge but indefinite expectations for himself, his wife, and his child-to-be. He thinks ahead toward the end of pregnancy and fatherhood, only he has nothing concrete to latch onto, and he soon discovers that he gets no joy from purposeless waiting.

These early days of the pregnancy trigger great self-involvement for each expectant parent. The only difference between mother and father, and it is a significant one, is that when mother turns inward, she can entertain fantasies about a baby she is relatively sure exists within her. But when a man turns inward, what does he look for? What questions does he ask of himself?

The answer, of course, is that he asks the same things of himself that his wife is asking. Will I be a good parent? What will I be like? Will I treat my child the way my father treated me? Spend as little time with him as my father did with me? Or as much? Or will I be able to give of myself? Men responding to our questionnaire agreed (75 percent) that they would *not* be fathers like their own, who, according to their recollections spent small or moderate amounts of not very fulfilling time with them during their boyhood. Remembrances of the past may conjure up feelings of privation, anger, hatred, or lost love. These memories might raise tremendous fears about his ability to provide adequate support for his family and force him to consider solutions that, as in the case of Mr. A., set other serious problems in motion.

Another startling thing of which an expectant father becomes increasingly aware in the first trimester is that it appears he has nothing to do. This is also true of his wife, who is not yet visibly pregnant enough to go on a shopping spree for maternity clothes, is nowhere near far enough along to be invited to baby showers, and knows it is far too early to ''do'' the baby's room. But she at least is following, if only passively, a physiologic timetable. She will probably be tired and more often than not will experience nausea or some form of morning sickness. She will usually ask for greater attention and love as a way of assuring herself that she and her baby have been accepted; and the first-trimester father will usually be more than happy to comply. Paying attention to her gives him something concrete to do and also takes the pressure off his own anxious thoughts and memories. This is what the books and movies always told him he would be expected to do—to be lovey-dovey, an errand boy, and a ''here-honey-don't-do-that-I'll-get-it'' sort of guy ad infinitum, or at least until mama has delivered.

This is perhaps the most critical time of the pregnancy relative to the formation of coherent roles for each expectant parent.[10] If the father assumes that mothering his wife is his central· responsibility for the duration of the pregnancy, he is likely to neglect his own need to work out a great many anxieties about his future capabilities as a parent. And, while he may enjoy showering some extra love and caring on his wife for a while, he will become sick of it by the end of the trimester. No relationship, not even during pregnancy, can be a one-way affair for very long before enormous resentment is aroused.

For one thing, when a wife demands constant mothering, she is denying the fact that her husband is a person likely to have concerns of his own regarding parenthood. For another, when he gets tired of the continuous nuturing role and discovers he is getting nothing in return, the honeymoon will have truly ended, too often with a bang. The trap, however, is not that he will experience or express his resentful feelings; it is just the opposite. He has been snared into thinking that he must be a constant mother or parent to his wife; and so he therefore feels guilty about his feelings of anger and about sensing his own needs for some attention from the woman who, before this pregnancy, used to be very giving and supportive. It is at this point an expectant father either shouts, ''Hey, listen, this is getting ridiculous! You're a grown woman, not a child, and I have some worries of my own which as my wife you really need to get involved with,'' or he allows himself to be caught in a morass of negative feelings for the next six or seven months, which could influence the climate of his marriage.

It is time for an expectant father to reorder his priorities. By urging men to demand a place in the sun for themselves beside their wives, we are not denying the real phenomenon in the expectant mother which involves her serious examination of mother-child relationships. This is indeed preparatory to her own acceptance of the role of mother. Still, she *is* an adult, and there is no reason why she cannot be rationally approached with issues having to do with more than her own fantasies and reveries. Expectant fathers often point to the enormous gap between them and their wives during pregnancy—"A woman can directly nurture a life and exhibit *real* development at almost every step of the way," they insist. "Nothing grows inside the expectant fathers." But this misses the mark. The *issues* of imminent fatherhood, we sugges , are the brainchildren of the men, and they *do* grow and develop. As the expectant couple can take pride and be thrilled at the development of their baby, its first kick, so, too, can they take enormous pride in the development of their working out of the issues and be equally thrilled when certain stages are reached, then passed.

"Do you remember how worried you were about the possibility of losing your job?" a woman in her sixth month reminded her husband. He smiled bashfully, though one could see his pride. "I had this strange obsession," he told the group of expectant couples, "that I would be fired, and then there'd be no money, and the baby would die of starvation. We used to spend a lot of time talking about that one, and I thought she'd get sick of it after a while. Somewhere along the line, the thoughts just vanished. I don't know why they did, but we sure did celebrate."

Further discussion revealed that the obsession disappeared after a visit to the doctor when the couple was invited to listen to the baby's heartbeat for the first time. The man's own ambivalence about becoming a parent had triggered those early fantasies of the death of his baby—the single event that could *undo* paternity. It took him almost five months to accept the reality of parenthood, and hearing the baby's beating heart was the final input he needed. It's important to note here that he was not dealing with his problem alone, having opened it for discussion with his wife quite early on in the pregnancy. She was able to see him through a real phase of development in his life just as he was committed to seeing her through her own growth.

Choosing the Obstetrician

The physician who administers prenatal care for the expectant mother can have a great bearing on how involved the expectant father will become in the pregnancy. A practitioner who has little use for husbands will soon communicate his or her displeasure and make it difficult for the expectant father to be active. Our culture has bestowed godlike status on doctors, and it is easy for us average mortals to quake and tremble, be totally intimidated, as if their sense of things were absolute, and ours foolish, inappropriate, immature. Doctors are in the habit of setting down sentences of confinement, interpretations of correct behavior, appropriate topics for guilt. They are, in short, parental figures. This, of course, is not all bad, for the compassionate reassurances of a physician are comforting and remind us of the days when our parents could reassure us that everything would be OK, and we believed it simply because they said it was so.

Nonetheless, expectant parents need not be treated like children in order to feel better, need not be patronized about the way they are conducting their pregnancy, need not be threatened if they see things differently from their doctors.

Most women who become pregnant, unless they are very young indeed, have an ongoing relationship with a gynecologist. Most gynecologists are also obstetricians, practitioners of *obstetrics*, the art of helping bring babies into the world (or literally, in Latin, ''he who stands beside the laboring woman''). In many cases a woman who suspects she is pregnant will have the test performed by her own gynecologist, and, if the test is positive, it's likely that she will stick with the doctor she knows. There is a great deal to be said for a comfortable relationship between a woman and her obstetrician. Comfort implies trust, and trust engenders relaxation; and when it comes time to deliver her baby, a woman will and should welcome all the relaxation she can get her hands on.

But having been a gynecologist's patient, even for many years, does not necessarily imply a comfortable relationship. So when pregnancy occurs, a woman may question whether this is the doctor for her.

Choosing the person who will provide quality care for the duration of the prenatal period and successfully deliver your baby depends on sorting out your own needs. For example, how comfortable would you like to feel in the doctor's office? Say you locate an obstetrician who has a fantastic reputation but personally is a tyrant, has no time for expectant fathers, and in fact considers them a nuisance. Do you abandon your need for a compassionate physician in order to have the ''best'' of medical care for your wife and baby? This is a legitimate problem. If an expectant father tends to worry enormously about his wife's health, it might make sense to seek out a ''top'' person in the field regardless of personality considerations.

Let's put off an examination of the specific issues until we've laid a general one to rest, and that is: Do you want to be involved in choosing an obstetrician or do you think it is your wife's role to do so? If you believe this is your wife's business, then you might as well jump ahead to chapter 3, for what follows here are the fine points of the Great and Glorious Art of Selecting an Obstetrician.

If you want to be involved, start shopping around. Ask around. Establish a list of questions whose answers would be important for you to know about anyone handling your wife and baby for several months. Ask them both of the people who are suggesting doctors' names and of the doctors themselves. What follows here is a partial list of such questions that acts as a guide. You and your wife will probably wish to add others.

1. Does the doctor welcome the participation of expectant fathers in prenatal care, as well as labor and delivery?
2. Does the doctor provide ample time for questions following examination of the expectant mother?
3. Are you encouraged to ask questions?
4. Does your wife have a relaxed relationship with the doctor?
5. What are the people in the office like? Are they friendly or

are they very businesslike? Do they make you feel comfortable and welcome, or do their looks signify: ''Oh, brother, here comes another *father*!''

6. Whom do you know who has avoided using this doctor's services? Why have they avoided using him or her? Why may someone have recommended him/her?

7. With which hospital is your doctor affiliated? Is the obstetrical personnel of that particular hospital likely to welcome your participation in labor and delivery? Are they likely to be receptive to complying with specific requests you and your wife make? Whom do you know who has had a baby in this hospital: What are their opinions?

8. Does the doctor share your preferences for the way you feel a baby ought to be delivered? Or does the doctor have preferences for delivering about which you have serious reservations?

9. Which doctor or doctors cover for your doctor in the event he or she is unavailable when your wife goes into labor? Are these other doctors of a similar mind regarding issues vital to you, or are you likely to be unpleasantly surprised in the delivery room?

10. How much does the doctor charge for services, including prenatal care and normal delivery? How much additional is charged if a Caesarean procedure is required?

11. Will the doctor take your wife as a patient if you have no insurance? If so, will arrangements be made commensurate with your ability to pay?

12. What if anything does the local family planning agency think about this doctor?

13. What is the doctor's predilection for routine episiotomy (see chapter 7)?

14. Does the doctor heavily favor use of anesthesia during labor and delivery? If so, which types of anesthesia would he/she be likely to prescribe? Are any of these anesthetics a serious threat to the baby or mother? What about other drugs to relieve pain? At what point during the labor does he/she feel they should be administered?

Some men find these questions of great importance, while others tend to feel only a few are particularly relevant. Regardless of what your own questions are, it pays to make the investment of time and money to get answers. Although most doctors are unused to being interviewed by prospective patients, they will usually submit. Depending upon how long your interview lasts, you can expect to be billed for an amount ranging from five to twenty-five dollars. If you should go beyond two or three interviews, you will have invested a modest amount. Still, finding the doctor who answers most of your questions to your satisfaction will be well worth it, and there is a possibility that insurance companies will accept these bills as part of prenatal maternity coverage. But this depends solely upon the plan you belong to. Check with your insurance agent for details.

If your insurance plan does not presently provide maternity coverage, it will be impossible to secure insurance for this pregnancy, except in the rare case of your changing jobs and joining a company whose group benefits might give you automatic coverage. Most companies require that the policy be in effect prior to conception in order for benefits to be paid.

Should you be uninsured, it will be important to be able to work out a payment plan, not only with your obstetrician, but with the hospital or maternity center where your wife plans to deliver the baby. Some hospitals have special free-service plans for people whose income falls below a certain level. The funds that cover these ''scholarships'' are limited, so it pays to check early with the hospital of your choice to discover what resources are available and the likelihood of your eligibility.

Hospital costs vary tremendously from city to city and depend upon whether they are public or private institutions. Consequently, when selecting their obstetrician, a couple may want to research their candidate's hospital affiliations. For a four-day stay for mother and child, the couple may expect to be billed for approximately eight to twelve hundred dollars. The obstetrician's fee will range from four hundred to eight hundred dollars, depending on how fancy his/her neighborhood is. This figure also includes prenatal care. Additional costs for a Caesarean procedure, if necessary, will range from one hundred to four hundred dollars.

Other alternatives to consider, which will be discussed later, are hospital-based midwifery centers and home birth, both of which are considerably less expensive, although less traditional and you may not be able to get as much information about these methods as you have about hospital deliveries.

Once the money considerations are settled, you can look forward to your first real visit to the obstetrician of your choice. Here again, the routine varies with different men. Many expectant fathers never accompany their wives on prenatal visits; others go once or twice toward the end of the pregnancy in order to meet the doctor before seeing him or her in the delivery room; and others go as often as their wives.

For the man who finds these times important, ways can usually be worked out in advance with an employer to have time off from work. Assuming your wife begins her prenatal care at the beginning of month four, you can expect one visit to the doctor each month through month eight. In the final month the doctor will usually want to see her weekly. So we are talking about a maximum total of nine visits barring unforeseen complications.

Some women run higher than normal blood pressure during pregnancy and a doctor may wish to monitor this more closely than once a month. If your wife is terribly anxious about these problem-monitoring appointments, it makes sense for you to go with her if at all possible. Otherwise, nothing monumental ever happens on these visits other than the slapping on of a blood pressure cuff and a weigh-in. At any rate, these appointments aren't terribly time consuming, and if you speak with your employer or supervisor and explain that you would like to take two hours once a month in order to accompany your wife to the doctor and that you will make up the time, it is highly unlikely that you will be denied the opportunity. You may take some ribbing, but in the end, expect the boss to comply with your request.

THE FIRST VISIT

It is not at all unusual for a man to feel out of place when visiting the office of an obstetrician-gynecologist. Invariably he will be either the only man present besides the doctor (if *he* is a man) or one of two. But that feeling will soon wear off when he notices that the women in the waiting room are throwing admiring glances his way, wishing, perhaps, that their own husbands were present.

You will usually wait until after your wife has been examined to be called into the doctor's conference room. At that time the doctor will probably give you and your wife some literature about general prenatal care, along with a sample of vitamins and iron capsules for her to take during the pregnancy. The doctor will explain his or her ideas about rest, nutrition, weight gain, along with warning signs the woman should watch for that might signal some sort of difficulty. Most doctors will encourage an immedite phone call from a woman who has discovered that she is *spotting* or *staining*—showing some sign of bleeding that is evident on the fabric of her underpants. This would be of particular importance for a couple who have gone through a miscarriage or spontaneous abortion in the past. But if this has been the case, the doctor is undoubtedly going to enumerate several items which would warrant urgent and immediate communication should they occur.

Having a man in the office is not yet a very common phenomenon for many obstetrician-gynecologist practitioners. These are professionals who have chosen to work with women and whose experience in medical relationships has been primarily with women. Their discomfort might show itself through an inability to make eye contact with you or through an evidently patronizing attitude. Or perhaps *you* are the one feeling uncomfortable and you find yourself squirming more and more during the session. Don't pretend this discomfort does not exist or that you have to challenge the doctor on every issue—this will just create additional tension. There are a number of reasons why a man may feel uncomfortable with the obstetrician-gynecologist. He may feel jealous of the intimate relationship the doctor has with his wife; he may feel excluded from the relationship—childlike and helpless. If the doctor is male, he may feel as though he has turned his wife over to a strange man and is now unable to protect her.

The best and most legitimate method for handling this discomfort is the direct approach, though time may not really allow for such an open communication. In any event, you will have a month to sort out some ideas as to what made each of you so uptight and what the most effective means might be for reducing further tension or hostility. If you felt fairly comfortable during your interview, it's pretty certain that the discomfort of the first visit was just due to each individual feeling out the situation. Together, you and your wife will be able to work out a united front for the next visit which at least will not leave you feeling isolated or alone. At that second visit, you might take the opportunity to say something like: ''You know, Doctor Brooks, I was so nervous at our last meeting I forgot to ask you this and this question,'' and you proceed to ask, and she/he goes on to answer, and, with God back in heaven, the world is right for everybody. The doctor might even volunteer that she/he was nervous too. Before long a comfortable, open relationship can be established. We know of one man who even wound up playing handball with the doctor who delivered his son.

3

The Second Trimester

The baby is now about to enter its most dramatic period of growth. Within the next twelve weeks it will increase many times in size and weight, jumping in length from about two inches at the beginning of the trimester and weighing about one full ounce, to more than twelve inches in length and in excess of a pound and a half in weight by the end of the twenty-fourth week of the pregnancy.

At the beginning of the second trimester, the baby has all of his/her internal organs, and they have begun to function well. The hands and feet are perfectly formed. By the end of the fourth month (eighteen weeks) the external genitalia of the infant are quite visible and the child's sex could easily be determined even by the untrained eye. The first body hair, which appeared early in the third month, begins to be replaced by *lanugo*, a downy covering that will be almost completely shed before birth. Eyebrows and eyelashes grow on facial skin which lacks the transparency of the earlier weeks. The fetus has gained five ounces in weight during this fourth month and about six inches in length.

In the fifth month the baby again makes enormous growth strides, increasing from six to sixteen ounces in weight and gaining more than three inches in length—from nine to more than twelve inches. During this time the baby's ears develop to the point where they are able to perceive sounds—the mother's voice, the gurgling of her stomach when she eats, loud noises, and perhaps even the voices of other people in the same room. The eyelids, which fused together in the third month, are still closed and will not reopen until the seventh month. From now on fat will continue to be deposited beneath the baby's skin, although for the moment one could never tell this padding was being laid down.

By the end of the sixth month (twenty-seven weeks), the fetus has gained another whole pound and about two inches in length. As the second trimester draws to a close, there are indications that the baby's eyes will soon be opening. Its body is now covered with *vernix*, a cheeselike coating, which is held in place by the lanugo, particularly in the area of the eyebrows and upper lip region. Only a very small percentage of babies born at twenty-seven weeks will survive, primarily due to respiratory immaturity.

The Placenta

Until now, as we've already indicated, the embryo (what the baby is called technically until the end of the second month) derives its nourishment through cell membranes in the uterine wall. From the end of the third month onward, the placenta is the link between mother and child. Also called *afterbirth*, since it is delivered *after* the baby, the placenta is a flat organ, about an inch in thickness and seven or eight inches in diameter at the end of the pregnancy. It is a fascinating piece of prenatal machinery, filled with thousands of blood vessels going in all directions, bringing fresh blood, food, and oxygen to the fetus by way of the umbilicus and carrying away waste material. Virtually everything ingested by the mother will, only moments later, pass across the placenta and be pumped through the baby's own circulatory system. The placenta functions as a leveler between fetus and mother, much like the locks of a canal: When the mother's blood contains a substance in higher quantities than the baby's, then the maternal excess will "spill over" into the baby's bloodstream until a balance has been achieved; and when the carbon dioxide level of the fetus's bloodstream is raised, the excess amount is passed across the placenta to the mother's bloodstream where it moves along to her lungs and is exhaled seconds later. The fetus is· not directly linked to the placenta, since that would limit its movement considerably. Instead, the baby is hooked up to this organ by way of the *umbilicus* (umbi-*like*-us), or umbilical cord, which is some twenty inches in length and allows for all the swimming and kicking the baby wants.

The baby's heart, which was complete and beating efficiently at eleven weeks, pumps blood to and from the placenta through the umbilical cord. The cord is composed of three blood vessels, sheathed by a greenish jellylike tissue, and coated by an extremely thin, shiny membrane. The largest of the three vessels is a vein carrying fresh blood from the mother. The smaller two are arteries which transport deoxygenated blood and waste materials away to be excreted by the mother. It is a flawless support system, often likened to the lifeline of an underwater diver or to the support systems used by astronauts for space travel.

It is interesting to note that symbols of the umbilical cord are often repeated in the dreams of expectant parents. One man, who later acknowledged the ways in which he had been identifying himself with his unborn child, dreamed he was scuba diving off a reef in the South Seas, carrying two air tanks on his back. When the primary tank became depleted, he swam to a buddy, as is customary for underwater divers, and motioned that he needed assistance in turning on his auxiliary tank. The buddy offered him a mouthpiece that was connected not to an air tank, but rather to what the dreamer called the "mother-lode" on the surface. When the mouthpiece was fixed in place, the sense of freedom and joy he experienced was overwhelming. The man now felt he could swim forever, never again needing to fear for his air supply.

We could offer a variety of interpretations about the content of this dream, but one physiological point was completely accurate. The umbilicus is obviously the direct route to the "mother-lode," and the swimmer's perspective of the glistening surface is probably not at all unlike the view of the swimming fetus who perceives the golden haze of sunshine piercing mother's skin and glowing through the amnion.[1]

Changes in the Expectant Parents

The changes in the fetus during this second trimester are so enormous that they cannot help but create changes in the expectant mother. For one thing, it is only a matter of perhaps days into her fourth month before she can actually feel her baby moving about. And that movement, the proof positive that a pregnancy is actually ongoing, creates a deep impact on both expectant parents. It is a genuine thrill for the mother, particularly a primipara, to "feel life" for the first time. These sensations are often called "kicks," though early in the trimester women have described the experience as something much more delicate—the sweep of an eyelash upon one's cheek or the "brush of a butterfly's wing."[2]

The experience is quite personal for the expectant mother. The fluttering within is so faint only she can perceive it, and no amount of hand placement and general touching seems to be able to allow anyone else, including her husband, to detect the inner activity. Sometimes women can be frustrated by this, but one woman told us that she was secretly delighted the experience was exclusively hers. Generally, these fetal movements are small and tranquil now and not so continual that the mother needs to focus upon them as she will in the months to come. Nor will her sleep be disturbed as it will later in this trimester and most definitely in the final weeks of the pregnancy.

As the baby grows, so do its accommodations. The uterus, which before pregnancy had barely the capacity of a thimble, is increasing in size and strength all the time. It grows in an upward fashion, toward the breasts, and during the second trimester a woman's "condition" becomes obvious to the world. She may be congratulated for the first time by acquaintances who had not been told earlier. And she can actually buy maternity clothing, a sign to the world that she is accomplishing a social goal for which she has broad approval.

For most of the women with whom we spoke, there were also other reactions to their changed body image. Beyond the excitement of finally *looking* pregnant seems to be a sense of dismay and sometimes even of panic as the *fundus* of the uterus (the top or bulged portion of that pear-shaped organ) begins to stretch out the abdominal muscles which in time causes the familiar swelling we associate with pregnancy. The glory of visible maternity, the return of energy, the renewed interest in lovemaking may not be sufficient to stave off the alarm a woman feels at the loss of her nonpregnant figure. She may feel she appears unsexy and that her husband will lose interest in her sexually because of her enormity.

But at the same time that she is feeling more energy, feeling—at least relative to the sluggishness of the first trimester—perhaps more sexual and more womanly, the pregnant woman is still feeling her way hesitantly into her role as mother. And it is at this point that she may come to a difficult turning point not only in the pregnancy, but in her life. Her transformation in one fell biological swoop from child to parent forces the expectant mother to cross a bridge in her emotional life which is an irrevocable step. Having accepted the verity of the pregnancy and therefore having identified *herself* as a parent, she may feel she can no longer turn to her own parents for support. This can create a sense of great emptiness in her life and an awful fear. She will soon realize that she can ask her parents for help, but the fact remains that she is no longer their baby.

The kind of support the expectant mother needs now comes more appropriately from her husband, from whom she might now demand, perhaps with more needfulness, reassurance in the form of love and affection. The pickles and ice cream fetish is less a real issue than it is a question: "Do you love me enough to get out of bed in the middle of the night and drive around until you find an all-night grocery?"

Sometimes a woman will turn to her husband as though he were her parent, as though through him she will recoup some of the loss of her childhood dependency. A man who wishes to be a husband, and not a parent, to his wife will call a halt to the kinds of demands that constantly cast him in the role of protector and her in the part of a helpless girl. He wants and deserves to be seen as he actually is—her husband.

Often, however, husbands tend to gravitate automatically and without apparent displeasure to the role of parent to their wives. Establishing a relationship that is entirely focused on the woman may be a convenient way to dodge their own feelings. Though an expectant mother having some difficulty separating from her own parents may experience no small measure of comfort under this protectorship, she should realize that continuing the marriage relationship this way will only cut down on her individuality.

Usually these kinds of role assumptions are from the past, and the couple seems to mimic roles they saw or played at home as children. At other times, such roles may meet certain emotional needs for one or both expectant parents. For the man having difficulty accepting the pregnancy because he has so many attendant concerns about becoming a father, the assumption of a domineering father role may feel comfortable and may provide the necessary rehearsal (he thinks he needs) to prepare him for his new position in life. Or perhaps his fear of parenthood, based on his own father's inadequacies, may force him into childlike behavior, making of his wife a mother or father. A child, of course, need not be bothered with responsibilities; if he behaves like a child, then, he is safe. While it is true his wife is feeling her way into motherhood, using him as a child substitute is not exactly appropriate training.

What every couple should keep in mind about taking on inappropriate roles is that unless they are temporary, they can turn a relationship terribly awry. If a man is behaving like a child much of the time, what effect might that have on the nature of the couple's sexual relationship? If, on the other hand, the expectant mother faces a father figure in bed every night, the probability of her unconscious perception of sexually relating to her father will likely have a depressing impact on her sexual appetite. What mature, well-adjusted female would welcome the idea of making love to her father?

This problem can also be true for the expectant father, especially during this second trimester of pregnancy and most especially following the first perceived movements of the baby and the obvious growth of his wife's uterus. His wife's maternity is so visible, becomes such a constant topic for conversation, not only between the couple, but with friends and colleagues and even strangers, that the expectant father may not be able to keep from seeing her as ''mother,'' and may find that he cannot think of her as anyone but his own mother.

Among adults the sexual embrace is often a stage for dramatizing the issues, the climate of a relationship. When a man or woman has need for affection and support, it is often expressed sexually. If the expectant mother in the second trimester has such a need—and many of those with whom we have spoken corroborate this—we may have some clue about the origins of the myth of the nymphomaniacal pregnant woman of midpregnancy. In the second trimester she has put aside the fatigue and nausea of earlier weeks; she has become accustomed to the pregnancy emotionally; she is enormously excited over the life within her. At the same time, she is fearful of parenthood, of loneliness, of losing her career, and a great many other things which pass across her mind, and she may require more physical contact with her husband in order to feel reassured. Put the two sets of circumstances together and there are at least the makings of an improved love life.

And there is still more evidence to explain the increase in some women's sexual needs during this period of the pregnancy. As the uterus grows, it requires greater and greater supplies of rich, oxygenated blood for adequate cell growth. With all this new blood circulating in the pelvic area, the genitals become engorged without any direct sexual stimulation. The equivalent for a man would be a constant erection of the penis. One woman we spoke to, Mrs. D., described her insatiable drive for sexual fulfillment during the second trimester of the pregnancy as follows:

> My husband and I always had a pretty good sexual thing together, and I never had any problems with reaching orgasm or anything like that. When I was five months pregnant, what I wanted to do was screw all the time, and that continued for two months or more. All my husband had to do was look at me and I had an orgasm. When we made love I would have one right after the other, sometimes as many as ten or even more in just a few minutes, and yet I never could get to the one that would make me feel emptied out, that would make me feel like I really got off, you know what I mean?

But from what we have gathered from the expectant fathers with whom we spoke and those responding to our questionnaire, Mrs. D. is not as typical as prenatal folklore assumes. According to their husbands, 25 percent of second trimester women showed an increase in libido, while 45 percent remained unchanged in their sexual behavior and 30 percent showed an actual decrease in their sex urge. The point to be understood here is that however dramatic the claims, the fact remains that there are no rules. The woman who approaches her husband one day with sexual needs motivated by a need for her own parenting may come the next day for more physical reasons, and again the following day for other reasons entirely.

Pregnancy is such a changeable, volatile state that a woman in her fifth month can be insatiable one minute and quite disinterested in sex the next. When a man is asked if his wife's sexual appetite has increased over a three-month period from the previous three months or previous year, upon how much behavior does he base his judgment? Statistics are interesting when it comes to human behavior; but the irreducible factor among human beings, which may tend to diminish the force of "numbers," is the uniqueness of individuals. So rather than examine the figures, let us simply stress that during pregnancy all feelings in women, *including* sexual feelings and drives, are subject to very rapid change. And further, when fast changes occur, it is perfectly normal and masculine to ask for time to adjust. If a man first responds to his wife's signals that he be more sexually attentive, more sexually aggressive, what does he do with his feelings two weeks later when she has asked him to stay away from her sexually?

An additional difficulty husbands may experience at this time is that they feel sexually turned off at the same time their wives may be asking for more physical attention. Other men, in contrast, feel alarmed at their own increased sex drive. Resolving temporary problems of this sort by talking and working out the differences can now bring a deepening of the relationship, rather than a distancing. A thirty-four-year-old newspaperman recalled: "My own temporary loss of libido about four months before the birth of my youngest son frightened me into silence, and all the more so when I noted how beautiful my wife appeared, how full her breasts had become, and how generally pleasing I had become in her eyes."

The feeling that "something is wrong with me" is one expressed by many men, who experience a decrease in their sexual drives. Our culture permits the female to "have a headache" when she is not in the mood for making love, but a man better be ready to have intercourse at a moment's notice or else he is not considered virile. Just as it would be insensitive and perhaps cruel if he were to force himself sexually upon his wife, so, too, may the imposition of his wife's sexual will upon him be impersonal. The fact that your pregnant wife may have been waiting all day for you with the fantasy that she would ravish you at the front door does not obligate you to oblige. It would be a mistake to go along with what she wants simply to avoid confrontation. Certainly a wife should be capable of hearing that her husband's difficulties at work, or on the way home from work, or his general concerns about fatherhood have made sex the last thing on his mind. If your wife can cope with her disappointment for a while and focus on your need for support, it probably would create such gratitude in you that, after a meaningful and *helpful* discussion of *your* concerns, you might well turn to her and say, ''To hell with the heavy stuff, let's get into bed!''

In chapter 2, we spoke of the relationship between father and unborn child. It is during the second trimester, when the baby begins to move, when its heartbeat is audible through the doctor's fetascope (an amplified stethoscope), that this near give-and-take relationship can assume a more definite character.

Husbands are usually fascinated by the bumping movements of their unborn babies. Some men can spend hours watching and waiting, touching and caressing the soft skin of their wives' abdomens. Women with whom we have spoken report that their husbands kiss them more on their bellies during pregnancy than they do at other times in their marriages. Often this caressing and tenderness can be sexually arousing, and many couples report that what may have begun as a casual observation of mama's tummy when baby was particularly active, ended in great sexual passion. At these precious times, the baby has actually brought its parents together, and a sense of family for both mother and father will have had its earliest stirrings. It is as if the three had shared an activity of love. And for the father who has chosen to be a closely involved member of the family, whatever he imagines when he feels his baby moving, whatever he chooses to think is happening inside, whatever he dreams he and his baby are saying to one another through their touching, a relationship is being established between the two of them that will last both their lifetimes.

Some men are less imaginative, less willing to extend the kind of psychic energy that will hook them up emotionally with their unborn babies. ''I asked my husband if he loved the baby,'' a six-month primipara, Mrs. W. said. ''But he answered, 'How can I love the baby? I don't know it yet!' He touches my belly whenever the baby moves, but he's more the logical type, and I guess I'm the emotional one.'' It is perhaps unfair that a woman ask that her husband feel the same things for the baby that she does, who is in constant contact with its movements, perhaps even with its *pattern* of movements. Nonetheless, feelings of isolation for women do exist, often with good cause, especially with husbands who really want nothing to do with an unborn child and who grudgingly put a hand on their wives' bellies when asked to do so but pull away as soon as the ''obligation'' has been met. For the woman seeking closer ties with her husband at this time in the pregnancy, such peremptory kinds of relating may seem like, and in fact may actually be, a rejection. And it is not necessarily because a man is callous or insensitive or unloving. More likely his distance comes from a feeling of general inadequacy as with Mr. W.:

> How can I possibly feel what my wife feels? And every time that she calls me over to feel the baby kick, it makes me think I am just feeling nothing more than a cat in a bag bumping this way and that. And when she says something like, ''Isn't it fabulous, or wonderful, or blah-blah,'' I get queasy and feel dishonest when I smile and say, ''Yes, it does feel wonderful; I really *can* imagine what the little bugger is doing in there.'' But I can't, I really *can't*, and it makes me want to run as far away as I can.

But even those men who are genuinely pleased with the experience of feeling the baby's movements can have other reactions. They approach the experience with caution, as if a laying on of hands too heavily will cause some damage to the baby, since one rarely knows if it is a head or a hand or a haunch bumping and weaving under the mother's belly. In a group of sixteen expectant couples, fourteen of whom were in the second trimester of pregnancy, it was the men (talking to one of the authors in a group apart from their wives) who verbalized far greater concern about the well-being of the baby than did the women.[3] The expectant mothers agreed that although they thought about their babies all the time, obsessing on the possibilities of birth defects and other kinds of fetal distress would drive them crazy. They actually tended to focus on these fears less than their husbands and were surprised at the men's concerns since they rarely heard such fears expressed directly. It appears, as we have already strongly indicated, that although expectant fathers worry and suffer, they do so in silence.

Men will sometimes remove themselves from sharing the experience of the baby's first movements because they are angry over their own inability to carry a child. Pregnancy envy is not discussed by expectant fathers very often. Still, it is the rare little boy who does not want to be "like mommy" in everything she does, including when she is pregnant. And, although these feelings may never surface in clear conscious form, it is highly likely that they reappear when the little boy is himself an expectant father. It may be entirely possible that boyhood identification with one's mother may renew itself in an expectant father's identification with his pregnant wife to the point of developing pregnancy, or couvade, symptoms or symptoms of a much less severe nature as in weight gain, something that one in three responding to our questionnaire did in fact experience.

Filling the Void

There is not, or does not appear to be, much to do during the second trimester; and yet the pregnancy is very much the predominating theme in the life of the couple, so worrying may be the expectant father's constant occupation. Reading about pregnancy and childbirth is a rewarding pastime during what has been described as the "quiet months" of gestation. But one can do only so much reading or knitting or crocheting before it becomes abstract or boring.

The idea of making things for the baby seems tenable for women but has not much application for most men. As a matter of fact, men sometimes complain that their wives are often much too premature in their need to have "baby's room" or "baby's things" set up and complete. This is frustrating to an expectant father since it assumes mother is totally in charge and he would not be a principal player if it weren't for his muscle. Despite the stereotyped vision of his role, the pregnant father ironically expects to do what under normal circumstances he would consider his wife's work. The irony, of course, is that along with the expectation of his role as ''gofer'' comes the fear of exclusion from making substantial input during this stage of the pregnancy. It is almost as if he is feeling two conflicting things: ''Look, don't order me around as if I had no say in this project,'' and ''This isn't really man's work anyway.'' This split approach is symbolic of the expectant father's uncertainty regarding his role in these tasks.

But action can of course be taken to undo this kind of second-class status for the expectant father. This is precisely the time when he can begin to make more and more direct contributions to his unborn child. First, it may be appropriate to tell your wife to slow down if she is insisting on a completed nursery in June and baby is not expected until November, unless of course you are of a similar mind. But if not, and if your wife can't understand that her need to have the baby's room completed so far in advance places unreasonable demands on you, try to reach a compromise solution which both quiets her anxiety and allows you some time. You might agree to spend part of each weekend collecting wallpaper samples or paint swatches or toy catalogs and perhaps spend an evening or two each week discussing possible room plans. If a woman is worried about her baby's nursery five months ahead of the birth, she will really need and appreciate her husband's input. And lest it seem that we are counseling men to tolerate a problem, we should add that the room itself may not actually *be* the problem. A great many other concerns are being channeled into the issue of baby's room, chief among them the fear of being an incompetent parent. So while baby's room may be the nail on which other fears are hung, it is entirely possible that with the nursery being attended to, the other fears will diminish as well.

In this working together, the expectant father will have actually placed himself at the heart of the action, doing for his baby and his wife at the same time. And it goes almost without saying that, during pregnancy, what a husband does for his unborn child is seen by his wife as a love stroke given to her.

Still a man doesn't have to be pushed into baby projects. His wife may be perfectly content to wait for a more appropriate time in the third trimester to draw her energies to the creation of a nursery. So many men who are bored with waiting around begin projects of their own, which can be started early and done a bit at a time over several months—such as building cradles or cribs. This allows for creative time alone and even permits an intensification of reveries about the looks of the baby swaddled in a knitted blanket and rocking gently in its cradle.

In some instances, men and *not* their wives are intensely concerned—perhaps prematurely and preemptively—about the baby's environment. They may, in a whirlwind of energy, rent a floor sander, buy a few gallons of paint, drag a tired wife to a half-dozen furniture stores on a weekday night, and completely furnish baby's room in a single week during month five of the pregnancy. This kind of behavior (as with the expectant mother) is almost invariably a sign that there are other pressing concerns at work, perhaps unconsciously. Since being a good provider is so vital to the expectant father, an unspoken fear that he will not be able to take care of his child in the future might compel him to take care of business *now* while he still has the means. A memory of his own childhood poverty might trigger the kind of over-compensating behavior we have seen when an expectant father outfits his baby's nursery and wardrobe with items far beyond his income.

Compulsive behavior is by its very nature somewhat out of the doer's control. The person is compelled to certain action, apparently unconscious of the motivation. In this way patterns of acting are repeated, sometimes creating great hardships. The expectant father who experienced deprivation during his own boyhood and can't resist going daily to the bank to check the balance in his savings account can be said to be acting compulsively.

We have previously mentioned the expectant father's brainchildren, and how, when they are brought out of hiding, they can often find development and resolution during the pregnancy. We call this *talking* things out, as opposed to *acting* them out, which is what compulsive behavior often is—dramatizing, often symbolically, one's psychological conflicts. More often than not the "actor" is unaware of the impact his behavior has on those around him. The gambler argues, for instance, that he is not gambling for himself, but for his family, for the baby soon to come, but he cannot keep himself from the racetrack despite his heavy daily losses. The long shots will set everything right. Chronic gambling, of course, is an extreme kind of acting out, and only with a very few men responding to our questionnaire did gambling activities seem to increase during the pregnancy. The point here, nonetheless, is that irrational fears tend to spur irrational action, unreasonable and unreasoned solutions to problems which perhaps are greatly magnified *because* of the irrational fear. And whether a man drinks heavily or gambles or acts out sexually with other women or men, or whether he gains a tremendous amount of weight or is virtually comatose in his sleeping habits, the fact remains that although these kinds of symptoms temporarily reduce depression and fear, in the long run they produce pain and discomfort. An expectant father carrying on several affairs with much younger women was found out by his wife, who threatened to leave him if he didn't stop. Although he received little pleasure from these women, he could not resist seeing them repeatedly, which nearly ended his marriage. "My God, what am I doing?" he screamed during an interview.

Talking things out instead of acting out can save a man from highly self-destructive behavior. If an expectant father finds himself sleepless for several nights with no apparent cause, a constructive way to open the discussion is: "What is bothering me? Have I been worrying about fatherhood these last few days? Has my wife implied somehow that I have been inadequate?" There are a million questions one could ask, but the process of rational problem solving begins with rational question asking. It puts a hold on runaway panic because it engages that part of the brain that processes information, which leads to a resolution of problems.

Issues that will need resolving in the months ahead demand

exposure now. We mentioned in chapter 2 that worrying can be addressed directly through action. If the macho expectant father continually denies that he is concerned about being actually able to love a baby, but finds himself irritable and nervous and even sleepless, what good is his outward show of strength? But to be able to say, at obviously some risk of disappointing or worrying his wife: "You know, I have a fear that I won't ever be able to accept a child into my life" at the very least exposes the problem or the fear that a problem may in time exist. And chances are great that he might be told: "Nonsense, you are a loving man. It may take time, but you'll get into it." It may be precisely because of this sort of open and loving communication that many couples refer to these middle months as a second honeymoon and can join together to prepare for the stresses ahead.

The second trimester of a pregnancy is much like the second act of a dramatic play: the plot thickens, subthemes, which had been threading their way between the lines in act one, are now surfacing at complicating speeds, characters are brought into conflict with themselves and one another, and all action starts coming to a head. And though these middle months of pregnancy have been traditionally referred to as the "quiet" ones, perhaps a better description of them would be "quietly tumultuous."

Throughout the pregnancy, men frequently ask themselves what kinds of fathers they expect to be. The particular phrasing of these questions is a reflection of each man's past history (i.e., "Will I be mean?" or "Will I be affectionate or patient or attentive?"). Chapter 6 will give special attention to the way a man's past relationships with parents and siblings and other children have a bearing on his probable experience of expectant fatherhood.

Early Birth Preparation

One of the activities in which all expectant fathers can immerse themselves during the second trimester is researching the various birth procedure options open to couples and the preparation required for each. If we could point to three books that have revolutionized the obstetrical experience for men and women they would be:

> *Childbirth Without Fear*, Grantley Dick-Read[4]
> *Painless Childbirth: The Lamaze Method*, Fernand Lamaze[5]
> *Birth Without Violence*, Frederick LeBoyer[6]

We recommend each of these to all expectant parents and will suggest a great many more helpful works in the Bibliography. But these three are basic, virtually required reading for future parents, particularly first timers who have scores of questions about the actual birth experience. The first two on the list focus on what is now popularly referred to as "natural childbirth" and concern themselves with the fundamental idea that pain proceeds not only from physical but from psychological causes as well. Women have heard from the time they are old enough to understand that birthing a baby is painful and difficult business. "Labor pains" therefore is the phrase used to describe uterine contractions. In one of our prenatal parenting groups, a woman took exception to our use of the word "discomfort" instead of "pains" when describing the labor experience and seemed to feel she was being lied to. The true experience, she felt, was going to be quite different, and she thought we might be leaving her unprepared for the event.

The reality is that uterine contractions can be extremely painful. The uterus is a very large and strong muscle capable of intense clamping down. If, on top of the discomfort of these contractions, a woman also anxiously anticipates the arrival of each one (and they will be numerous for most women), then the pain of each contraction will be experienced even more intensely. The more painful a contraction, the more fearful a woman will be of the next one, and so on until the laboring mother-to-be can become terrified that she will lose total control of herself and will have to scream for anesthesia to eliminate *all* painful sensations.

The growing trend toward childbirth without anesthetic medication is largely an outgrowth of the impact of *Painless*

Childbirth. The classes that prepare the expectant couple for this sort of birth experience have routinely become known as Lamaze classes. Other natural childbirth preparations exist which use techniques for reducing pain that are completely different from Lamaze methods. Incidentally, Lamaze's methods are not originally his but were developed in the Soviet Union after World War II, and were later adapted by the now famous French obstetrician.

Another French obstetrician, Frederick LeBoyer, astounded the world with his *Birth Without Violence* several years ago. Here, rather than focusing on the experience of the expectant parents, LeBoyer describes the birth from the newborn's point of view. He draws for his readers the quality of intrauterine life, its softness, its protective and muted beauty. And then he pulls into sharp and horrible contrast the very first moments of life for a baby in a conventional hospital setting—the glaring lights over the delivery table, the loud voices of doctor and nurses, the clanking of metal, the coldness of the steel weighing scale, the traditional turning of the baby upside down to smack its bottom, inducing the first breath. This, LeBoyer says, is violent birth. And many agree, as do the authors.

Couples are now requesting and even *demanding* that certain of their conditions be met before they enter into a relationship with an obstetrician or a hospital. They demand that the lights be dimmed when the baby is expelled so its eyes are not dazzled; they request hushed voices in the room; a warm bath for the baby; no instant and often premature cutting of the umbilical cord. In short, many, many couples are exercising options where they had none in years past. It was not so very long ago that fathers were not allowed in the delivery room and were confined to pacing the floors in waiting rooms (and you ought to see some of these ''waiting'' rooms!). There are probably more hospitals in 1978 that permit men to be present *during a Caesarean procedure* than the number that allowed expectant fathers to witness the birth of their children twenty-five years ago. But now doctors are being forced to listen to parents.

So options do exist. However, people must know of them

before they can be exercised. Several years back information about prepared childbirth classes seemed only available to a more educated, higher-income population. But that is no longer the case. Hospital-based classes in large urban areas are now drawing couples from the total population, largely because the publicity has been so positive about the so-called natural childbirth experience. Prepared childbirth classes are available to couples usually within eight to ten weeks of their due date, and the class will usually run six or eight weeks. Now, during this second trimester of the pregnancy, is the time for plans to be made. Who teaches classes in the area? With which hospitals are the classes affiliated? Who likes which teachers and why or why not? Which teachers tend to be more attentive to the needs of expectant fathers?

Sometimes couples disagree on preferences for birth procedures. The more traditional disagreement pattern—and this is rapidly changing, we might add—is the one that has the expectant mother arguing for her husband's participation in the birth event, and the expectant father expressing great reluctance. Despite their having to be literally dragged to the first husband-coached childbirth session, many men wind up more enthusiastic than their wives by the time the course is half over. More and more often these days men express an interest in sharing the occasion with their wives from early on in the pregnancy. In some cases, as a matter of fact, it is the women who are reluctant to share the experience, and usually this unwillingness is the result of deeply ingrained lessons about how men have no place in the experience of labor and delivery. Occasionally, a young woman expresses some of her own misgivings concerning her husband attending the birth of their child. She does not want to be seen in the highly unflattering position of legs high up in stirrups revealing herself totally. More important, she does not want her husband to see her out of control, if the contractions become so difficult they make her cry out.

Many women have been taught, probably by their own mothers, that husbands are intruders in this woman's business of birthing babies, and they will pass this feeling along to their own children if changes are not made along the way. Men also frequently are told, usually by their own mothers, that it is ridiculous for them to plan on participating during the actual childbirth. It is not at all rare for the expectant father's family to remind him at these times of how squeamish he was as a boy and that he'll probably faint dead away in the delivery room. Mother quips like ''What do you plan to do there, hold her hand?'' may come from her own bitter memories of the isolation she experienced without her husband twenty odd years earlier—a sort of ''what-was-good-enough-for-me-is-good-enough-for-you'' approach. She is not prepared to tolerate the enthusiasm of her children at the imminence of their own parenthood.

Expectant fathers shouldn't be daunted by these put-downs, for they simply reflect the speaker's insecurities. If a man's wife is the discouraging party, however, there *is* a problem. Others can be shrugged off or perhaps even be told to keep their remarks to themselves, but one's wife, after all, is another case entirely. The need for an expectant father to be present at the birth of his child may be another of his brainchildren, and, by bringing up the issue early in the pregnancy there will be sufficient time and space to turn things around. This is true, not only of the makeup of the birth team, but also for other equally pressing and important issues.

Not all men, of course, will want to be present during the birth of their children. Whether they believe they have no right to be there or prefer to wait for the news in the hospital waiting room or at the home of friends or family, such a decision is as legitimate as the decision to be right on hand. Since most expectant fathers tend to develop relationships with other expectant fathers during their wives' pregnancies, it is not unlikely that the man who has opted for the waiting room will get some pressure from those of his friends who are planning to attend the labor and birth or from those men he knows who have already shared the birthing experience. He will hear things like: ''It's the most exciting thing you'll ever experience, '' or ''My wife and I became so close because of our being together," or "I don't see how any father could keep himself away." While such statements may be accurate descriptions of the way the event was perceived by some men, it by no means follows that *all* experience the occasion similarly.

If, however, the decision to stay away from the birth is a result of some fear, which the expectant father has been unable to express, then exposure to the experiences of veteran fathers can prove helpful and provide him with sufficient comfort to change his mind. This happened on more than one occasion in the Williamstown groups.

The issue of *territoriality*,[7] which has been defined as "the taking, possession, use, and defense of territory on the part of living organisms,"[8] is an extremely important one for the expectant father on the day of the birth of his child. One researcher indicates that although sexuality and sexual attraction may be the bond that provides marital stability, "it is the private territory of the breeding couple that provides most reliably that the children will not be neglected."[9] The father in the hospital delivery room is by no means on his own territory. He is expected to stay out of the way of the hospital personnel. Indeed, in the three Williamstown preparenting groups, the expectant fathers, when asked seriously what they felt their major functions were in the delivery room, almost always said, "To provide moral support and comfort for my wife," and "To stay out of the way." This last statement was usually followed by laughter from all. A good deal is being done by more progressive hospitals to address these territorial needs for both expectant parents. But, to some parents, there is no place like home.

It should be recalled that not very long ago, perhaps fifty years, most Americans—most people in the world for that matter—were born at home. Like everything else, home birth has advantages and drawbacks. On the positive side, of course, is the familiarity of the setting. A woman giving birth in an environment that has special meaning to her will no doubt be more comfortable and relaxed. The more relaxed she is, the less fearful she is likely to become when she enters intense labor. The same is true for her husband who, although he does not experience contractions, will be considerably more at his ease and less intimidated by the doctor and/or midwife simply because he is on his own turf.

The risks of home birth are evident. What happens if there is an emergency? If the expectant mother hemorrhages, or if the fetus should experience distress? Is the hospital close enough for the couple to arrive there in time to resolve the emergencies? Are there certain kinds of emergencies that will not tolerate even a moment's delay? Most couples considering home birth spend much time soul searching before arriving at their decision to have the baby at home; and they may have a continual dialogue about their fear of medical emergency during the birth. Complications do occur.

Most couples contemplating a home birth will want to share their concerns with their obstetrician or midwife, or both. No one will ever be able to say, "Now don't worry about a thing; nothing *can ever* go wrong." So it comes down to a responsible decision: Can we accept the responsibility that goes along with our decision to have the baby at home? Could we live with ourselves if anything ever went wrong that could not be subsequently corrected? Or which might have been corrected had the birth occurred in the hospital? Would the pleasure of the experience outweigh any of the possible risks?

Responsible pro-home-birth literature and practitioners are extremely cautious in helping couples reach a decision. They provide documented statistics regarding the safety of home birth against the risk factors in the hospital. They point out how meaningful preparation can go a long way toward avoiding problems. Still, for those couples whose inclination is to have a baby in a homelike setting, but who could not forgive themselves if anything were to go wrong, there is a middle ground in the form of midwife centers, which are located within hospitals.

In several states, the practice of midwifery has been legalized. In most cases midwives must be licensed nurses who have had a

minimum of one year's working experience in a hospital obstetrical unit and a one-year course of study at an accredited
midwifery school.

The increase in the number of midwives (and, incidentally, one
need not be a woman to be a midwife—one of the more famous,
perhaps notorious, midwives is an Irishman who practices ex-
tensively in America) along with demands by couples for a more
natural setting in which to deliver their children have led to a
resurgence of midwifery. These midwife centers are set up to be
much homier than a sterile delivery room. There are no separate
labor and delivery areas: A woman gives birth where she has
labored. Many of the complaints made about hospital procedure
is that just when a woman is ready to give birth, she must resist
the urge to push the baby out while she is being wheeled across
the floor from the labor room to the delivery area.

The midwife centers tend to provide more personalized care,
and women who give birth under these circumstances report that
they and their husbands are treated with great consideration. The
nurse-midwives are generally supervised by physicians, but they
deliver the great majority of babies alone. Doctors still prescribe
medication and are available for emergency service, but they do
not routinely attend the births. The theory is that since most
births are normal deliveries, that is, without complication, a
trained midwife is completely capable of being the one expert on
the scene and the doctors are then available where they are really
needed—in the emergency cases.

Money is a factor in both home birth and hospital-based
midwife centers. Home births, including prenatal care, usually
amount to less than a third (about $650) of the costs of hospital
deliveries and doctor's fees ($2,000). And births at midwifery
centers are approximately half ($1,000) the normal hospital
delivery.

For some couples it is the woman who initially feels more
positive about an alternative to a conventional hospital birth. But
often it is the expectant father who does not want to be ''the jerk
in the surgical gown and mask traipsing after everybody.''

Again, when the issues are raised early enough in the pregnancy, there is room for them to be worked out in time. Certainly, if there is serious ambivalence on the part of one or both expectant parents only days before birthday, it makes sense to reconsider options. In most cases, however, whether a couple plans to have their baby at home or in a hospital, the decision will have been made firmly some time in advance, allowing the couple to try it on, wear it a bit, feel around in it, until it is accepted.

4

The Third Trimester

The final third of the pregnancy is under way. As the seventh month of gestation begins, the fetus becomes covered with a whitish, cheeselike substance called *vernix caseosa*, which functions as a lubricant against the constant exposure to the amniotic fluid. Despite this protection, the baby's skin becomes pretty wrinkled at this time. The fetus has quite a bit of hair on its head now, and the eyes are open. Its length is approximately fourteen inches and it weighs more than two pounds.

Although fat has begun to deposit beneath the baby's skin, the fetus is still quite thin, even gaunt in appearance. It is the final trimester of intrauterine life that allows the baby to fill out. In these remaining thirteen to fourteen weeks, the weight of the fetus will usually triple and sometimes increase fourfold. Increases in length are not quite as dramatic as earlier in the pregnancy, although a growth spurt of six or more inches is by no means a meager achievement. ·

By the end of the seventh month, the child has gained a pound and a half or so and grown a few inches in length. In the male baby, testicles have descended into the scrotum. A baby who is born prematurely at this stage of the pregnancy (approximately thirty-two weeks) will stand better than a one-in-two chance of surviving, given expert care. There is an old myth that the child born prematurely in the seventh month has the survival edge over a "preemie" born in the eighth month. How this myth came into being is unknown to the authors, but medical authorities agree that the longer the fetus remains in utero, the greater its chances for hastening the lung maturity necessary for survival.

When the eighth month of pregnancy is over (thirty-six weeks), the average fetus is more than five pounds in weight and about eighteen inches long. Its chances for survival, should it have to be born now, are better than 90 percent.

At the end of the ninth and final month (forty weeks), the baby is at "full term." Its skin is smooth, though still covered with vernix. Finger- and toenails are edged out past the tips of fingers and toes, almost in need of a trimming. On the average the baby has gained one-half pound and increased in length by one-half inch each week during the last month of the pregnancy. This weight gain is largely due to a depositing of fat beneath the skin. The amount and length of hair on the baby's head will vary, and here again the myths abound. Excessive indigestion during pregnancy, goes one fable, will produce a child with an enormous head of hair. If that were the case, most children would be born longhairs. The reality, of course, is that each baby is different— some bald, some with a great shock of black hair, others with wisps of blond locks. More than 99 percent of babies born at full term survive.

Childbirth

We will talk at considerably greater length in chapter 7 about the onset of labor and the childbirth experience itself. But in this chapter it's probably useful to briefly outline the actual process of the baby's departure from the uterus into the outside world.

FIRST STAGE OF LABOR

What exactly triggers the beginning of this expulsion process is not known, though certain observable phenomena occur in every birth. The *cervix*, a thick disclike apparatus at the mouth of the uterus, begins to *efface*, to stretch and thin itself. This effacement causes the opening in the cervix (the *os*) to open, or *dilate*. This dilatation will be measured manually by the attending nurse and physician in centimeters or inches or "fingers." Maximum dilatation is approximately four inches, or ten centimeters, and is attained through pressure created by the force of uterine contractions against the cervix from inside. There are some statistics on average time for full cervical dilatation, both for first-time mothers and multiparous women, but there can be tremendous variation. Still, the *average* is approximately ten hours for primiparas and six hours for multiparas. There is a phase of this first stage, known as *transition*, during which contractions of the uterus are at their strongest and most frequent. The great force of uterine contractions will now concentrate on pushing the baby down into the lower birth canal, which is the vagina. This transitional phase signals the end of the first stage of labor.

SECOND STAGE OF LABOR

The second stage of labor accomplishes the expulsion of the baby from the birth canal into the light of the world. The contractions of this stage are somewhat less frequent than during transition and are accomplished by the mother's forceful pushing.

THIRD STAGE OF LABOR

The third, or placental, stage of labor, during which the placenta (afterbirth) is delivered, only lasts a few minutes. By this time, of course, baby is either at mother's breast or being weighed or swaddled.

Physical Discomforts in the Third Trimester

The third trimester of pregnancy brings with it a number of physical discomforts which may, depending upon the woman, be very severe in intensity.

INDIGESTION OR HEARTBURN

As the uterus grows, it puts pressure on the expectant mother's stomach. This pressure can force the release of acid upward, through the stomach sphincter, into the lower esophagus. This acrid material produces a burning sensation in the midchest area, and this is what we call heartburn. Uterine compression of the stomach also seems to play a part in slowing down the digestion process, which means that food stays longer in the expectant mother's stomach and in turn produces a mild kind of indigestion.

The major relief from heartburn comes from reducing the intake of fats in the diet, cutting down on gravies and sauces—things that are difficult to digest. It is also helpful for a woman to reduce the size of meals she eats: It's far better to eat numerous, small, frequent meals than three huge ones. And she ought to stay away from over-the-counter antacids because of their high sodium content. Sodium compounds tend to attract and hold water, and the last thing an expectant mother wants is to be retaining fluids. If indigestion is so intense as to require medication, the obstetrician will prescribe one of several which have been prepared with the expectant mother in mind.

CONSTIPATION

Another frequent complaint made by pregnant women is that they are constipated. We are talking not only about infrequent or irregular bowel movements, but also about the passage of a hard and dry stool. There are very special physiological causes that make constipation a normal occurrence in most pregnancies, particularly in the last weeks: pressure on the large intestine, or bowel, from the quite enlarged uterus, a marked decrease of intestinal contractions, and also the superstretched abdominal muscles, which now have a diminished pushing capacity—which is necessary for the regular movement of the bowel.

The condition is far more uncomfortable than it is dangerous.

Increasing the roughage in the expectant mother's diet, in the form of whole grains, fresh, raw fruits and vegetables, and bran cereals will help to soften the stool and thus facilitate its passage. Liquid intake is important and so is daily, unstrenuous exercise, like yoga, stretching and bending, or the childbirth exercises which the expectant mother is reading about or learning in her classes. Some physicians say that regularity of bowel movement can be enhanced by setting a specific time aside each day for this activity. In this way the body becomes conditioned and is ready for each movement at a certain time.

Counsel your wife to stay away from patent laxatives and mineral oils. Mineral oils interfere with the absorption of vitamins. And enemas, though sometimes helpful, should not be taken without prior approval of the obstetrician, simply to see if a flushing of the gastrointestinal tract might be disruptive.

VARICOSE VEINS AND HEMORRHOIDS

Varicose veins are a more frequent discomfort to multiparous women than to first timers. They can range in appearance from a series of fine bluish streaks just beneath the surface of the skin to rather gnarled and bulging eruptions. They occur most frequently in the legs, though their presence in the vaginal area is not highly uncommon, and when they occur around the anus, they are known as hemorrhoids.

Varicosities tend to develop in pregnant women as the increased size of fetus and uterus puts pressure on veins which pass through the pelvic area, past the baby to the lungs. The constriction makes it difficult for the venous blood to run "uphill." The mother's blood supply, which has increased dramatically, tends to back up, causing bulges in the walls of veins which for other reasons unrelated to pregnancy may have a tendency toward weakening anyway.

The level of discomfort experienced can range from modest to extreme. There can be pain, usually dull aching in the area of the varicosities, and little, unfortunately, can be done to relieve much of the soreness. Fatigue can also be a by-product of varicose veins.

The ideal treatment for varicose veins is bed rest with the legs slightly elevated. Obviously it is difficult and frustrating to remain in bed all day, but try to get your wife to avoid standing whenever she can. She will experience some relief if she can sit with her feet raised. A tightly wrapped, inexpensive elastic bandage will give a lot of comfort, and there are also quite expensive surgical stockings available which tightly bind the legs. Before using either bandage or stockings, the obstetrician should be consulted, and he or she will give directions for application.

Veins sometimes begin to protrude from the anus during pregnancy largely due to constipation and the straining that a constipated woman is likely to experience. Here again, patent medicines are to be avoided. Your obstetrician will probably prescribe soothing witch-hazel applications or other similar treatments. Sometimes ice packs can shrink the protruding veins which then can, to the great surprise of many women, be pushed back into place by hand. Diet is also important to alleviate the condition. A high-roughage diet, described earlier as an antidote for constipation, will go a long way toward reducing the need for straining in order to eliminate. Hemorrhoids usually disappear shortly after birth, so most doctors will not recommend their surgical removal during pregnancy.

INSOMNIA OR SLEEPLESSNESS

As if things were not bad enough with these other complaints, the second and third trimesters of the pregnancy may bring on a temporary condition of insomnia. This may be largely due to what seems like a dramatically increased rate of fetal activity as the expectant mother prepares herself for bed. ''It feels as though the baby sleeps when I'm up and is up when I sleep'' is not an infrequently heard complaint of expectant mothers. The baby moves during the day, too, of course, but its movements are not nearly as noticeable as they are in the stillness of the midnight bed.

The temptation to take a sleeping aid, which was previously

prescribed and has been sitting in the medicine cabinet for months, is great, but should be staved off—at least discourage your wife from taking them without prior consultation with the obstetrician. What may have been good medicine for prepregnant mothers can be dangerous to the child she is now carrying. A warm bath or shower followed by meditative exercise can create a state of relaxation which will produce sleep in the midst of any turmoil and with no narcotic dependency for mother or baby.

OTHER MINOR COMPLAINTS

There are numerous other complaints during pregnancy that will have a bearing on the expectant mother's general frame of mind. She might, for instance, experience shortness of breath after only the slightest exercise, perhaps after climbing just a few steps. This is common and is explained by the extreme growth of the fetus and uterus, which are taking up more and more room. As a result, the air capacity of the expectant mother's lungs is diminished since the lungs can no longer easily and fully expand. In the last two or three weeks of pregnancy, but sometimes before, a primipara will experience a "lightening" as the uterus begins to drop and the fetus engages its head in the upper birth canal in preparation of labor. Shortness of breath will likely disappear at that time.

Frequent and very urgent urination is another source of annoyance to pregnant women, and once again this is due to the relatively enormous uterus with the baby inside, having taken up space normally reserved for the bladder. With an appreciably decreased capacity to hold urine, the bladder will have to be emptied much more frequently than normally. The result is a lot of jumping out of bed in the middle of the night and the interruption of daily activities.

No one can seem to explain with great certainty why pregnant women have far more leg cramps than other women. Some say it is because of a calcium deficiency and urge an increase in milk or milk-product consumption. But this would not explain why women who drink a quart of milk each day or consume its calcium equivalent in cheese or yogurt continue to be jerked painfully awake at two in the morning with a knot in their calves that just won't let go. The almost instant cure for a cramp is to flex the foot, that is, point the toes to the ceiling instead of at the wall. It seems to work. Increasing the intake of Vitamin B is also helpful according to some doctors and nutritionists. See what your own doctor suggests.

Other temporary or persistent ailments do occur—such as dizziness or headaches or edema, which is the swelling of tissue, usually of the hands and feet, due to the retention of fluids. There are many possible explanations for these symptoms, and it would be best to speak to the obstetrician about them.

Body Changes and the Psyche

It is often difficult and sometimes impossible for men to understand the depth of some of these changes and the potential effect of the changes on the psychological state of the expectant mother. There is, after all, nothing in a man's life to parallel the kinds of body alterations a woman undergoes during pregnancy. A severe illness or a glandular disorder that blew him out of shape so that he no longer recognized himself is really not a comparable experience, but it does demonstrate the way in which the ego and body image are intertwined.

Just because the visibility of her pregnancy was thrilling to the expectant mother during the second trimester, it does not guarantee her unmitigated enthusiasm for her bulbous shape during these final weeks of gestation. We have enumerated the basic and most vocalized complaints to indicate to husbands that women do begin to feel helpless and frustrated by the inevitability of these annoying and sometimes painful changes. Expectant mothers feel that they may be out of control of their bodies, and this can be a terrifying experience. Men openly speculate in bewildered amazement about the capacity of pregnant women to endure what would have frightened and constantly depressed them.

It is no wonder that a woman's constant physical consciousness during this last trimester greatly diminishes sexual contact with her spouse. Some men are frustrated and rejected by the loss of sexual contact; others accept it maturely as the inevitable result of their wives' physical metamorphoses; and yet others are relieved that the onus of sexual relating has been removed temporarily from the relationship. There are many reasons for this. The most prominent, of course, is the physical discomfort experienced by a woman late in the pregnancy. Another is an essentially irrational fear that the baby will be damaged if the couple has intercourse during pregnancy, particularly during the last trimester. One young first-time expectant father, a physician, said: "I know it is irrational, but I can't help fearing for the well-being of the baby. I don't want to hurt the baby." Another man claimed that a birthmark just below the eye of his first baby was the result of particularly strenuous intercourse with his wife in the eighth month of their pregnancy. "Oh, my God," another man laughed aloud. "*I* was born with freckles!" And the comments and stories go on and on.

The reality, of course, is that a man's penis cannot in any way inflict damage upon the unborn child. It is a physical impossibility. Certainly, a number of real considerations must be given to sexual relating in the last months of pregnancy, but these are more to enhance pleasure by dealing with discomfort for the expectant mother than they are a plan to keep from harming the baby. The conventional "missionary" position, with the man on top, is found by most women to be exceedingly uncomfortable during and after the sixth month or even earlier. One man said, "My wife and I really enjoy a good, pounding fuck, but we've had to give that up for the time being." For the duration of the pregnancy, this couple found gentler sexual activity extremely gratifying. Chapter 5 will treat the entire issue of sexual relating during pregnancy, including some recent research which suggests caution in the final month of pregnancy.

Changes—Large and Small

For women who have careers, and the number is growing, the decision to alter one's professional status from career woman to housewife-homemaker can have alarming and often disorienting effects on both the woman and her marriage. She struggles with a changing identity. Many women work as late into the pregnancy as is comfortable. During the first trimester, some decide to stop work, though they may not actually leave the job until their third trimester. The reactions to leaving work are as numerous for expectant mothers as they are for men and women retiring when they reach their midsixties. Some are absolutely delighted to be able to stay home and give their complete attention to preparing for the baby. Others feel lost and unable to cope with an unending expanse of time on their hands.

Women who have been working for much of their married lives find that they don't have many friends who stay at home. So when they leave their jobs, expectant mothers often have very few people to whom they can relate during the day. For some women who have been awaiting the time when they could put distance between themselves and a world overrun with often meaningless relationships this is a welcomed opportunity. And yet other women dread this time alone. They spend their days aimlessly, trying unsuccessfully to involve themselves in anything, and waiting impatiently for their husbands to return home from work. A five-thirty in the afternoon phone call from the expectant father who has been unavoidably detained at work or whose car has broken down in the middle of nowhere is likely to bring her to tears.

It is an undeniable reality that a woman can handle less and less physical work as the pregnancy advances; she requires her husband's help more all the time. As a result, greater demands are made of the expectant father. While having him keep the house in order may have been premature in the fourth or fifth month of pregnancy, it is certainly appropriate work in the final trimester. This need among expectant parents to put order into the environment is known as ''nesting behavior.'' Possibly, at one time during human evolution, it may have been an instinctive drive, but today this nesting activity produces many chores that the expectant parents, particularly the fathers, may find extremely stressful. For one thing, they are time-consuming items, and most men feel deprived of their leisure and their own private time when asked to contribute to household work.

Some expectant fathers become resentful or even rebellious at their wives' increasing requests for help, and the kind of anger this sets off will often alienate the expectant parents from one another, from their unborn baby, and from their pregnancy in general. Still, both have legitimate points to make. The expectant mother, who has been unable to accomplish certain necessary chores, expects and needs her husband's help when he is home; the expectant father, who works long hours each day, often under difficult conditions, feels he deserves some leisure time when the workday is over.

Some couples battle like adolescents, both asserting their positions. Logic may end a skirmish—one or the other spouse may just be a more convincing talker, a better arguer, successful at forcing the mate into guilty retreat. But feelings, anger in particular, will out. Eventually the same topic will rear its head again and it will be fought out until a more mature approach to problem solving is achieved. After all, pregnancy is a time when being right is not the major issue, when more must be given than can be received. These are critical moments in the life of the couple; some expectant parents now sow the seeds of divorce which will grow soon after the baby is born.

Many expectant parents feel, perhaps for the first time, what seems to be endless, thankless giving and giving and more giving. For the baby has begun to alter life routines before it has made its appearance. What else is the kicking, pressing, physical discomfort-causing *unborn baby* if not *disruptive?* It has to a certain extent limited its parents' sexual contact in the third and even earlier trimesters. It has altered its mother's physical capabilities and forced its parents to spend more and more time around the house at the expense of time spent with friends and a social life. This final trimester of pregnancy is the real beginning of a new way of functioning, and the couple who can appreciate this and not imagine that social, physical, and emotional discomforts will end with the pregnancy will have begun a mature transition into parenthood.

We are not saying, ''Look, you better shape up. Life is filled with tough breaks and the sooner you realize the fun is over the better it's going to be for all concerned.'' The deep sweetness of love between a parent and child has no equal. But the adjustment to parenthood requires an understanding that young children may cannibalize their parents, are able to drain them of their energy to be independent, creative, and self-focused—to be their own people.

The feelings of love are always balanced against the anger and fear we experience when someone, however close, upsets the balance of our lives. This is often true of primiparous couples, principally those who have been married for some time before conception. One such couple in a preparenting group burst into tears after the screening of a film we almost always show called *Are You Ready for the Post-Partum Experience?*[1] When we asked the pair to share their feelings about how they identified with the young couple in the film struggling to adjust to the arrival of a first baby, the expectant mother said, ''Well, we've been married for ten years, and our lives are just so set already. Everything is going to be so different, and I don't know if we are going to be able to make the adjustment.'' Her husband, rather frightened, said, ''I feel pretty much the same way.''

The real issues of coming parenthood race together like storm clouds in the third trimester, and expectant people must realize that within limits being afraid is quite normal—it is not a sign of emotional instability. There are things soon to happen that will transfigure one's life. First, there are the fears of childbirth, an event that can no longer be thought of as far off in the distant future. And there are fears for the mother going through the birth, despite statistics of a great decline in maternal mortality in this country. For the expectant parents who experience constant fear and anxiety, a professional counselor will be able to help. We will discuss this in great detail in chapter 6.

Another worry, which hits expectant fathers in the final weeks of pregnancy more fiercely than ever, is their ability to provide for their families. A large number of first-time expectant couples move to new homes or apartments, often with one or several additional rooms. More space, of course, usually means greater cash outlays, and with a wife and baby at home, some men have terrible anxiety about losing their jobs or having financial set-backs. As if this fear of failing at his primary responsibility were not bad enough (his identity as father and provider is newly formed and still a bit shaky), the expectant father may also dread that his wife will become dependent upon him for everything. There may be no way of knowing whether this will happen, of course, but if the fear is one he can talk about, it would certainly be wise for him to open up the concern to his wife.

Support Groups

This is the time to reach out for support. Preparenting classes, such as the ones we led, are gaining in popularity. Usually obstetricians will know of such courses since it is from their clientele the ''students'' are drawn. If not, a couple can ask at the local family planning organization or visiting nurse association. These classes are not to be confused with prepared childbirth classes, which are not so much for parenting as for the training of labor partners.

We can't stress too strongly the value of preparenting courses. They place couples of all kinds together to discuss pregnancy and parenting, creating a freedom of exchange which may be hard to find outside the supportive group environment. Having worked with such groups, ranging from six to sixteen couples in each, we can vouch for the comfort, reassurance, and enormous support felt by participants.

Other kinds of support groups are becoming available,

although limited usually to urban or suburban areas. They are discussion groups for *either* expectant fathers or expectant mothers, and the issues peculiar to each parent regarding pregnancy and the forthcoming responsibilities of parenthood are explored.

STARTING YOUR OWN GROUPS

If neither preparenting classes for expectant couples nor support discussion groups for expectant parents are available in your area, you can set them up yourselves. A few signs or posters placed strategically in the offices of obstetricians and pediatricians will draw immediate attention. A call to the family planning organization will usually get an enthusiastic response from its staff, and they will be helpful in passing the word to their clientele. Bulletin boards at the supermarket or in Laundromats or in college student centers and bookstores are excellent places for advertising these groups.

Just a few couples can get a group going. Once people have responded to your signs, call a first meeting as soon as possible. This is the time to arrange the number of weeks' duration for these get-togethers and the nominal agendas for each meeting. Often a couples group will want to meet weekly right until the end of pregnancy and continue several weeks later, functioning as a ''new'' parents group. This is a good idea with expectant fathers groups also: The groups can become ''new'' fathers support groups following the birth of the members' children.

Discussion groups formed in these ways do not usually need a specific leader or leaders. Once topics have been agreed on for each of the meetings, the general understanding is that participants who attend the meetings contribute their thoughts and feelings to the other members.

This sort of openness, of course, can be difficult for some. If a discussion of sexual relations, for example, is planned for a particular meeting, but one or two of the couples, or maybe even one person in the group, is against sharing such intimate information, then the group will have to respect their privacy. They may decide to either eliminate sex from the agenda altogether or suggest to the couple that they attend without having to participate. All procedural decisions such as this should be made by the entire group. Since cohesiveness is what gives a group much of its internal strength and the ability to handle business at hand.

PREPARED CHILDBIRTH CLASSES

Couples who have intended to enroll in prepared childbirth classes, or what have come to be called Lamaze classes, named after the French obstetrician who developed the relaxation techniques, usually do so at the beginning of their eight month of pregnancy. Check with the instructors well in advance, however, to ensure that there will be room for you. If the names of local instructors are not available, the hospital in your area will undoubtedly know whom to contact. Most childbirth instructors like to know as far in advance as possible how many couples will be enrolling.

These series of classes usually last six weeks. Some instructors like to leave two or three weeks for the couples to practice on their own, while others arrange the series so a couple will have their last session as close as possible to their due date. There is something to be said for both approaches. Some couples prefer the confidence that comes of independent rehearsal, but other expectant parents enjoy the support they get by being with the class until the very last moment. You can make your choice early in the pregnancy as to which approach you prefer and select the instructor accordingly.

While prenatal parenting classes, such as the ones described on pages 98-99, encourage interaction among class members, prepared childbirth classes focus largely upon breathing and other relaxation techniques. As a result, childbirth classes promote heightened interaction and communication for the couple itself. The goal here is to create a working labor and delivery partnership, and the emphasis is on instruction. The format of the meetings is lecture-demonstration. The teacher instructs, the couples rehearse, and the end result is what has come to be popularly called "husband-coached childbirth." Recently, there has been a move to change the name of the husband's role from "coach" to "partner," since coaching has overtones of competition and the object of an athletic event is winning.

In "natural" childbirth, the hoped-for outcome is a healthy baby and mother, undepressed by anesthetics and analgesics. Women and men in prepared childbirth classes tend to hold the druglessness of the event as somewhat holier than the birthing itself, but those women whose labor discomforts may require a twenty-five- or fifty-milligram dose of Demerol or an anesthetic injection should not feel that they have failed. Pain is pain and people must deal with it in their own way.

Instructors and husbands, in their eagerness and great enthusiasm for the natural method of childbirth, often contribute to the need for stoic perfection, and anything less than perfect is a failure. However, *partnership* is a working relationship which focuses, not on a goal, but on an approach which implies, "We are in this together, and so from moment to moment we will see what the needs are and act upon them. We will get this baby born in good shape."

Prior to their childbirth training, many expectant fathers fear that they will be absolutely useless in the labor and delivery room when it is time for their wives to give birth. Worse than uselessness is the fear of fainting dead away, that they will draw attention to themselves in the most emasculating way. However, these fears begin to vanish once the expectant fathers have some idea of what they can expect. Some men handle their fear by making light of it, joking during relaxation exercises: "I'm practicing to bite my wife's hand to keep me from screaming."

This focus on the anxiety rather than the excitement of the birthing experience is a way of demanding much needed attention. The man who has cracked a hundred jokes on the same topic may be looking more for support than for laughs. Humor can be a wonderfully constructive tool to help people through tight moments—sort of like whistling in the dark. But compulsive joking is often defensive and serves to prevent a man from confronting the nature and depth of his anxiety regarding childbirth.

Men whose inclination is to open up and talk about what ails them, in general, will probably find it easier to discuss their fears of birth, but at this stage of the pregnancy even those men who have been silent throughout group meetings may speak up. These birth-related anxieties, please remember, are completely normal since all men experience them to one degree or another. The man who does not is the exception and we wonder what marvelous internal mechanism could have removed the tension-producing questions: "Will my baby be healthy?" or "Will my wife be safe?" asked by expectant fathers.

While expectant fathers may have fears that they will pass out in the delivery room at the first sight of blood or sign of great discomfort, most wives interestingly enough have no corresponding fears and sense that their husbands' presence will have irreplaceable value for them. This may be difficult for men to grasp: Only the experience itself will determine whether or not they have given what their spouses expected. Almost every woman in our groups whose husband was there for her labor and delivery told us she virtually could not have done it alone. The comfort and encouragement lent by their husbands' presence, their soft, sometimes firm verbal reassurances saw the women through the more difficult moments of birthing.

Preparing for the Baby's Arrival

In the final weeks of the pregnancy, many women are "showered" with baby gifts: toys, clothing, sheets, pillows, and blankets. Those couples who do not receive baby gifts get the real pleasure of shopping for them. Many expectant couples are cautious about selecting colors when buying baby clothes, since by "thinking pink" or "choosing blue" they superstitiously fear they will influence the sex of their unborn baby. At any rate, couples tend to hedge their bets. They get a couple of each and don't worry too much about the sex or they daringly pick yellows and oranges.

Season will influence your choice of items for the newborn's layette. Receiving blankets are always good to have around, as are several undershirts and sleepers. Newborns like to be bundled up, to be bound pretty tightly by their swaddling—it makes them feel secure, perhaps because they were so confined for their first nine months. Suddenly an open world with no physical limits would be terrifying. There are scores of commercial baby products—powders and oils and lotions—which are available but none of which is a necessity. Simple corn starch is as effective as any expensive baby powder, and warm water and a mild soap can clean baby's bottom as well as any commercially prepared lotion. Still, these things smell nice and sweet and agree with babies, and we want our babies to smell like all other babies, so we buy these things.

Although it may seem natural to follow a discussion of the third trimester with one on labor and childbirth, we're going to take a break in chapters 5 and 6 to investigate some issues and activities of pregnancy that do not relate to specific trimesters.

5

Sexual Relations
During Pregnancy

Expectant couples make love much less often than at other times
during their marriage. They may show great ingenuity and
inventiveness, but they show it more seldom. This reduction in
sexual contact is so expected that, when a man announces to his
friends that his wife is pregnant, he may often hear suggestions
about taking a mistress to compensate for not "getting enough"
at home.

The notion is titillating, but we do not have hard, conclusive
data that indicate a trend toward extramarital affairs during pregnancy (although other researchers have indicated this).[1] In our
own study, only eight in a group of one hundred and ten men had
taken lovers, although a considerably larger number reported
that they were spending more time thinking about it than they
had previously. Not surprisingly, men who reported a decrease in
sexual contact throughout the pregnancy also experienced an increase in sexual fantasies about other women. There is no indication at all, though, that a man will have an extramarital, sexual
relationship simply because he and his wife are experiencing a
temporary lull in their passion.

When Paul, a dairy farmer, was urged by his bowling buddies
to "go get laid," he made a point of asking each of his friends if
they had done so when their own wives were pregnant. Only one,
it turned out, had three or four times gone to bed with a woman

he knew from work. Sexual encounters are seldom guiltless or uncomplicated, except perhaps with prostitutes to whom one pays money for not only sex but also peace of mind.

But to *dream* of an exotic and prolonged affair is provocative, adventurous, erotic, and may even feel legitimate for the expectant father who anticipates having to ''go without'' for months on end while his wife just gets fatter and more asexual all the time. This dreaded expectation of prolonged sexual abstinence, except for those couples so advised for medical reasons such as possibilities of miscarriage, is as fallacious and stereotyped a notion as the one that portrays the midpregnant woman as an insatiable nymphomaniac: ''Hey, pal, you better be good and ready for her in the fifth—she's gonna work you to death!'' Neither idea has much foundation in truth, but the fact remains that for a variety of reasons which we'll go into in a moment and for a host of others about which we can only speculate, expectant couples do not spend as much time making love as they did before the pregnancy. And this is both a reflection and cause of change in the relationship.

Sexual Intercourse over Three Trimesters

Let's isolate some of the standard assumptions and misconceptions made about the sexual lives of expectant people:

1. The first trimester is a bad time for lovemaking because pregnant women are experiencing a range of physical discomfort.
2. Sex is fantastic in the second trimester, and these middle months of pregnancy are often referred to as the couple's second honeymoon. Often the sexual cravings of the pregnant woman will wear her husband out.
3. Sex is unadvised in the third trimester because of discomfort and possible harm to the fetus and mother.
4. Expectant fathers' libido remains unchanged during pregnancy while their wives' sex drive fluctuates.

It appears that this pattern of diminished sex in months one through three, increased sex in months four through six, and greatly reduced sex again in the final months seven through nine is upheld by some research.[2] Other data, however, show a steady decline as pregnancy progresses despite apocryphal tales of marathon sex in the second trimester.[3]

It has always been assumed that the sexual desire of an expectant father is totally dependent upon his wife's sexual state of mind. If she is ''on,'' then things will happen; if she is not, television reruns may be the activity of the night. The rather impersonal given here is that the the man is *always* ready, a notion that reinforces the old macho stereotype of the man as a lecherous beast: ''You know as well as I do that men are after only one thing. . . .'' It also assumes that men are so entirely sexual in their approach to life that nothing in the world, not fears, not personal problems, not emotional setbacks—nothing even momentarily alters their inexorable coital drives.

The expectant fathers polled in our survey shared with us that their sexual desires showed considerable fluctuation as the pregnancy advanced, with an overall trend toward decreased libido. Still, a considerable number of men reported an increase in desire, and an even larger number showed no change from prepregnancy. We also asked whose influence was strongest in determining the frequency of sexual intercourse, and we got the following results: 17.5 percent of the men said their choice had resulted in the decision; 19.3 percent said the choice was that of their wives; and 63.2 percent said they had reached a decision together. A two-thirds mutuality on sexual decisions is hardly reflective of a man's submissiveness or his indomitable sexual control!

OVERALL DECLINE IN SEXUAL PLAY

Although there is a good deal of variation, our data indicate that for most couples there is an overall decline in sexual relations throughout the pregnancy. Perhaps this explains the repeated cracks we heard from expectant fathers about sexless married life. We asked them, "What could your wife do to make this pregnancy easier for you?" and got remarks such as: "Have a baby so we can make love again," and "Remember that she's still married." Also, one of the standard answers to our interview question about the quality of their sex lives was, "What sex life?" If these are the hardships an expectant father supposedly endures for three-quarters of a year, no wonder Paul was urged to cultivate an extramarital relationship.

There are numerous physiological and psychological reasons for the changes in a woman's sexual behavior during pregnancy, many of which will result in a decrease of sexual desire. And even though men may understand the physical and emotional bases for changes in their wives' sexual behavior, they can still feel rejected by, "Not tonight, honey." It is usually not so much abstention itself but the resulting feelings of rejection that may prompt a man to seek the embrace of another woman.

Many expectant fathers do have some appreciation of their wives' disinterest in sex, and because they do, they boast more about their sexual exploits than indulge in them. If a pregnant woman were to out and out say: "Hey, I'm just not into sex, now or tomorrow or next week, so don't bother trying me again until you get the green light," then a man might find it easier to look elsewhere for sexual gratification. But if a couple is not in marital trouble, the husband will rarely take a mistress. And while he may spend more time fantasizing about Tahitian maidens or available women in singles bars, he will probably not act just because he and his wife aren't making love as frequently as they did before the pregnancy.

The changes in sexual activity around the house are not all due to the expectant mother's being out of sorts. The expectant father's emotional life can be every bit as volatile as his wife's, and, as long as his emotions are a factor, it can be expected that they will have a bearing on the couple's sex life together. Both husband and wife will have to adjust to a variety of reactions to these changes and try not to take them personally. "Not tonight, honey," from either partner, does not mean "I don't love you anymore.'' Nor should a man believe himself to be sexually inadequate if his wife cannot find deep satisfaction during their sex play. Being aware of the nature and depth of many of pregnancy's changes and their potential impact on the sexual life will create understanding: ''She's not really saying that to hurt me; she's just *saying* that.''

Body Changes and Sexuality

We have talked about the physical changes of the first-trimester woman. It is easy to see how a woman feeling nauseous or vomiting may not be enticed by the prospect of lovemaking. Additionally, the excessive fatigue experienced by many women may leave them with little impetus for sex. Although these reactions usually diminish by the second trimester, some women are plagued with longer lasting symptoms. There are, however, many other physical changes that impinge on lovemaking.

BREAST CHANGES AND ALTERED SEXUALITY

In chapter 4 we briefly discussed the enormous reactions a woman may have to her altered body image and that her sexual and physical images are very much tied up together. Most attention is usually given the expectant mother's expanded belly and waistline, but the changes in her breasts can have a dramatic effect on the couple's sex play.

The increased blood supply to the breast tissue causes sensitivity in the area of the nipple known as the areole. This engorgement increases during sexual arousal, intensifying breast discomfort for most women. The tenderness may limit an entire area of the couple's sex play, often an extremely erotic one. For the woman who had derived ecstatic pleasure from her husband passionately sucking and licking her breasts (a standard part of their foreplay), a new source of stimulation will have to be found. And the husband banished from his wife's bosom might feel considerable resentment and perhaps even fear that he will not be able to find new and easy ways of pleasing her.

We asked expectant fathers if their wives experienced breast tenderness, and if so, what were their reactions. Some answered that they were "irritated." Probing this further in our interviews, we learned that some of this irritation was related to the hands-off attitude which had come with the onset of breast tenderness. This condition tends to be most noticeable during the first and third trimesters of the pregnancy. Of the first-trimester expectant fathers in our survey, 60 percent reported a decrease in both manually and orally stimulating their wives' breasts. This figure dropped to only 30 percent in the second trimester, but was up again to 51 percent in the third.

When a wife asks that her husband not fondle or suck her breasts, it can be as rejecting to some men as "Not tonight, honey." A number of men told us that it seemed the baby was already coming between them and their wives and that this usurper had taken from them a part of their love never again to be regained. One man, apparently angry with this change of events, recited a short pun: "A mother with two tits gave birth to three kids: Tot, Tut, and Tat. And when Tot and Tut were sucking, there was no tit for Tat."

These changes in a woman's breasts are part of the body's preparation for nurturing the newborn. Breasts are no longer just objects of sexual stimulation and play, they are the potential source of the infant's survival. The "mother" function appears to take over, leaving the "wife" role in the background.

Either as sexual objects or as a food source, the breasts of a pregnant woman become larger than they were during prepregnancy. Many women, particularly those who are smaller breasted, feel great joy at this change in size. If tenderness around the nipples is not extreme, a woman may find herself with a brand-new erogenous zone and a husband only too willing to explore it with her. Many expectant fathers are thrilled and aroused by this physical growth and report that some of their increased eroticism can be traced to the experimentation with this new sensation zone. If ''second honeymoon'' is at all appropriate to describe the second trimester, it may well be due in part to not only the increase in breast size, but the changes that are rounding and softening the expectant mother's fertile body.

GENITAL CHANGES AND SEXUALITY

We spoke in chapter 3 of the potential impact of vaginal engorgment on the sexual outlook and attitudes of the expectant mother and their possible effects on her husband. It is interesting to note the great similarity between the genitals of the sexually aroused woman and the nonaroused pregnant woman. During excitation, the female genitals fill with blood. The pregnant woman, with her genitals already engorged, simulates the state of sexual arousal even without direct sexual stimulation. Indeed, many women do experience themselves as feeling more sexually stirred. When the pregnant woman becomes sexually aroused, this engorgement becomes even greater. Many women experience more intense and frequent orgasms.

One study, however, indicated that in the third trimester women had orgasms less frequently, apparently due to the tensions of pregnancy.[4] As the pregnancy progresses into the third trimester and the expectant mother's blood supply increases with the growth of the baby and uterus, the engorgement of her genitals will also continue. Because of this, the resolution phase of her sexual cycle (that period when her body returns to an unaroused state following orgasm or general sexual stimulation) is considerably slower. This is increasingly so with subsequent pregnancies. Some women, even after an orgasm or perhaps repeated orgasms, never achieve full resolution nor experience sexual relief. These women may find this so frustrating that they choose to avoid sexual relations. On the other hand, a woman may experience an increased sex drive which her husband may find threatening.

It may be hard to find solutions to these difficulties, but silence and sexual indifference on the part of the expectant father may only create anger, resentment, and even contempt. The couple simply must remember that this is only a temporary condition: The end of the pregnancy is close at hand. Hold on.

BELLY SIZE AND CHANGING SEXUALITY

The expanding belly is proof positive of motherhood and makes some women feel more feminine, more beautiful, and considerably sexier. Most pregnant women, however, joke about how fat they are. Some take their weight gain seriously—perhaps more so than necessary. Obstetricians are often quite strict about the amount of weight their pregnant patients gain. Over the past several decades, the obstetrical community has shifted its position as to what constitutes the "proper" weight gain for an average pregnancy. The rule, until very recently, seemed to be as little as possible. Now, however, many doctors agree that women should put on about twenty-four pounds. This figure represents the weight of the fetus at term (seven to eight pounds), the uterus (two pounds), the amniotic fluid (two pounds), increased blood (three and one-half pounds), the placenta (one pound), increased breast tissue (one and one-half pounds), and the maternal reserves (six and one-half pounds).[5]

Still, many obstetricians make pregnant women quite concerned about their weight. Judging the stories we have heard from doctors and patients alike, it is not at all uncommon for an obstetrician to warn: "You don't think your husband would want to get into bed with a body like that, do you?" or "Here comes the blimp." When we asked one woman whose doctor seemed particularly hostile if she felt in any way abused by his remarks, she said, "Well, I guess someone has to keep me in hand. I probably have it coming. Just look at me."

It is not surprising that a woman's expanded abdomen can make her feel less than sexual, certainly less than beautiful. But when we asked expectant fathers how they reacted to seeing their wives naked in the full bloom of imminent motherhood, they often became quite poetic. "She is so sweet and round and so soft. I love to see her just walk into a room, naked or not."

Another man: "Her body is like a ripe fruit, dripping with sweetness and ready to be eaten." And yet another: "If she were not already my lover, I would leave home just to be in bed with her one time and that's all." Some men always have sexual thoughts when they see their wives naked, pregnant or not. Others find the change in shape unpleasant: "I just don't find the pregnant body attractive. It looks misshapen, funny. I find it a turnoff." A dentist said: "When she looks like that, I don't think I know who she is, and I try never to make love to a stranger." A writer: "It doesn't get me hot, period."

There is no problem, naturally, for the man who finds his wife sexually alluring during pregnancy. But the man unaroused by his wife's new size will sooner or later communicate his feelings. It's much better to get those feelings out rather than keep them hidden since eventually he is sure to be confronted with a "What's the matter, don't you love me anymore?" kind of question, and he will have to explain himself then. Men who find their pregnant wives unattractive could be reflecting our American obsession with "slim is beautiful," or they may have deeper feelings about the inappropriateness or even immorality of making love to a pregnant woman. Whichever the case, not talking is to withdraw both physically and emotionally. Once the topic has been brought into the open, he can at least assure his spouse that he loves her and explain his problem. Maybe they can come to some kind of understanding together.

On the subject of expanded bellies, we might again point out that many expectant fathers put on weight during pregnancy. Only in rare cases will a man put on as many pounds as his wife, though ten or twelve extra in the old "tire" will certainly make for a midriff bulge. Quite often women, used to trimmer-looking husbands, are turned off by these physical changes in their men. A pregnant woman can probably avoid betraying her true feelings about her man's weight gain through a series of "not-tonight-honey" cop-outs, but pretty soon he will sense the rejection and create a confrontation of his own.

In the final trimester, 73 percent of the expectant fathers in our survey indicated a decline in sexual intercourse, compared with 7 percent who reported an increase. Two-thirds of the men indicated that the change in frequency was a joint decision. Of the remaining one-third, the decision was split more or less equally between husbands and wives. For many considerations intercourse was curtailed for a large percentage of those interviewed; however this does not mean that all lovemaking ceased. As a matter of fact it is during this period, when an expectant mother's belly starts getting in the way, that some of the traditional lovemaking positions are abandoned and new ones enthusiastically tried out.

The one common trait in all the sexual configurations of later pregnancy is that the bellies of expectant mother and father are rarely in direct contact. This rules out the traditional man on top, or missionary position. One of the most satisfying positions, both for its avoidance of belly-to-belly contact and the comfort of its limited penetration, is the side-by-side approach in the "spoon" position (man behind the woman), raising her leg with the help of a pillow or two to allow for smooth entry. In this position a man may reach around and caress his wife's breasts or run his hands over her belly and even reach down to fondle her clitoris while he is gently thrusting from behind.

For those women whose arms and lower backs are in good shape, there is the rear-entry position, with her on all fours. Many expectant fathers are extremely aroused by such an approach, although rarely will the couple who began intercourse in this position wind up in it because of the strain on the woman. Even here, coitus need not be interrupted for the sake of a position change. If done carefully and in unison, the couple simply decides whether they want to go left or right, and then they slowly roll in that direction, sliding into the side-by-side position.

Most couples have usually had experience with the woman on top, and the final weeks of the pregnancy are a perfect time for this supererotic position. Men who are stimulated by their wives enormous breasts are particularly aroused by this opportunity to have them so close to their hands and mouths. And while some men are a little apprehensive in the last weeks of pregnancy about sucking so vigorously that they draw mother's "first milk," or colostrum, they can avoid this by using their tongues and lips somewhat less strenuously. There are a great many variations for the woman-on-top position, and others can always be invented depending on the comfort and ingenuity of the lovers. The expectant father may sit in a chair and his mate straddle his lap, allowing for easy penetration and a rolling penile thrust. From the reports of the expectant fathers in our survey, just about any piece of furniture in the house may be substituted for the chair: toilets with the tops down, edges of kitchen tables (sturdy ones, for certain), ottomans, desks, and even hammocks (if the couple is agile) make exciting locations for sexual exploration.

During pregnancy many previous sexual preferences can change radically. One man who always chose to keep the bedroom dark when he made love to his prepregnant wife, suddenly found himself, as an expectant father, upping the wattage of the electric light bulbs and placing mirrors in any spot he thought he and his spouse might make love. For reasons unknown even to him, he now had to *see* what was going on when he made love and watching stimulated him even more.

A note about sexual acrobatics: Not all couples are fond of them. Partners may have established routines in their sexual relationship and find new ideas disconcerting. Perhaps they feel foolish and self-conscious or fearful that they will be inadequate in new positions. Often a woman may be carrying so large that she feels awkward, unable to maneuver as she thinks she is expected to. Or she may, just as her husband might, think herself unattractive if parts of her body, particularly the anal-genital area, are seen by her mate from a new and unconventionally close perspective. These are real feelings and a whispered "I'm so embarrassed!" from either lover is likely to bring, not only loving giggling, but reassurance as well. If the reassurance is not forthcoming, if both mates are so uncomfortable that it affects their sexual play, then those new positions should be scrapped for the familiar, perhaps more erotic ones. The focus of sex play is fun and pleasure: When it becomes less than that, it's time to experiment.

Noncoital Alternatives

ORAL-GENITAL CONTACT

Although sexual intercourse can usually continue with success and pleasure well into the third trimester, some couples find the total sexual act so tiring or discomfiting—or perhaps they have been discouraged by their physicians—that other avenues of gratification and fun are explored. Of these nonintercourse alternatives, oral-genital play is favored by many expectant couples. Often, couples realize that they had never gotten into this routine in their preexpectant lives together, and they enjoy discovering new circuits to one another's pleasure. To discover, perhaps for the first time, that the mouth and lips and tongue are capable not merely of giving but of receiving sexual pleasure will often spur a flurry of renewed sexual activity along with creating a different sort of intimacy. In one of our questionnaires a man confided, ''Before this pregnancy my wife had never even kissed my penis. But now she puts it in her mouth.''

Other expectant fathers report, nonetheless, that they are not very turned on to making oral contact with their wives' genitals. For one thing, there is considerably more vaginal lubricant and discharge which, they say, has neither a pleasing flavor nor aroma. Some of these men report that they can still partially enjoy oral contact by limiting it to the dryer clitoral area while using their fingers to stimulate the labia and vagina. But this difficulty can be overcome in other ways too. Assuming the lovers know they will be enjoying one another on a given evening, they can shower immediately before, and both expectant mother and father will have fresh-tasting and -smelling genitals. A man may even erotically apply scented oils or creams to the vagina and surrounding area before oral contact, and a woman aroused by certain aromas may do the same for her husband.

There is only one caution with regard to oral-genital play. Some men are fond of blowing into their wives' vaginas during oral activity. Since the uterine tissues are so engorged with blood, air strenuously blown into the vagina may enter the bloodstream, forming an air embolism which can do grave damage to both mother and fetus.[6] There is some indication that this should be avoided with the premenstrual woman as well, but it is especially dangerous during gestation. Aside from that, however, any oral-genital contact that feels good need not be limited.

MASTURBATION

Many expectant couples enjoy the deep, erotic pleasure that is to be had from mutual masturbation, although this activity, along with almost all other sexual play, seems to decline during the final weeks of the pregnancy. Twenty-two percent of our third-trimester expectant fathers reported that their wives were masturbating them more frequently, while 34 percent indicated a decrease.

As compared with first- and second-trimester men, third-trimester men report that their wives masturbated them more frequently. Obviously, there is a connection between the substantial decrease in sexual intercourse of the third trimester (a 73 percent decrease in the third trimester) and the increased masturbation activity. Men in the third trimester only showed a 12 percent increase in masturbating their wives' genitalia, while 56 percent of our respondents reported a decrease in that activity.

One of the patterns almost expected of pregnant women is that, if they are not inclined toward sexual intercourse or orgasm themselves, they will masturbate their husbands. For some of the couples with whom we spoke, this was considered lovemaking, and both partners found it emotionally, if not sexually, satisfying. However, some women find the role of ''servicing'' their husbands to be distasteful, particularly when it becomes a routine.

Perhaps the fact that there is a considerable difference between the rate at which a woman will masturbate her husband and the rate at which he will masturbate her throughout the pregnancy indicates unfortunate attitudes in our culture. These postures are:

1. A man's sexual gratification is generally more important than a woman's.
2. A pregnant woman cares less about having an orgasm than her mate because the pregnancy makes her feel unsexual anyway.
3. It is the role of a woman to see to it that her man is sexually gratified.

None of these postures has any foundation. Women, pregnant or not, care as much about sexual stimulation and pleasure as men. And if an expectant couple holds onto these fallacious attitudes, they may be letting themselves in for problems—intense resentment and hostility are bound to result. And the same is true where this pattern exists in reverse, where the man is "on call" and expected to be sexually aroused when his wife decides she needs someone to "bring her off." And it's not only the partner that does the "servicing" that suffers from feelings of resentment. A spouse who feels sexual giving is gratuitous will also feel resentful. As these emotions build up and become stronger, the relationship suffers. Someone may get to have an orgasm in the middle of all this, but the price!

One of the ways partners meet their sexual needs independent of one another is through self-masturbation. Strangely enough, there is still a taboo in our culture when it comes to self-stimulation of the genitals. But masturbation, as one expectant father put it, "is often the best game in town with the best seat in the house." Our data show that men tend to masturbate more frequently during the first and third trimesters of the pregnancy, for reasons which are probably already apparent, with no increase among our second trimester respondents. This is a legitimate way to release sexual energy, and though a man may miss the greater intimacy and closeness of sexual intercourse with his wife, there's a lot to be said about the pleasure of one's own private fantasies. Naturally this applies to the pregnant woman as well. Some women masturbate more than before, although others, who tend to feel guilty about it, tend to masturbate less than when they were not pregnant.[7] For either spouse, masturbation should be considered normal behavior.

Some husbands and wives feel sexually rejected when they discover their spouses have been masturbating alone. The only time this can be a problem is when a very recent orgasm through masturbation interferes with previously made plans for the couple to enjoy sexual activity together. If this happens frequently, the solitary sexual act for either spouse may point to another problem which should be discussed.

NONGENITAL LOVING

Sexual pleasure, mutually experienced by the expectant parents, creates a sense of stability and security for the couple. We have seen by now the often tremendous need for support that each parent may experience when under stress. The question arises: If the sexual relationship of the couple diminishes radically, and some couples indicate this is so, then what will become the source of well-being?

Not all sexual intimacy is genital in nature. That is, some forms of lovemaking have very little to do with the goal of sexual release and yet are as intimate in their way as the most intense kinds of genital sex. It is fascinating to note that while all genital forms of sexual relating showed an overall diminution during pregnancy, kissing and other nonclimax-directed contact for many couples increase appreciably.

It may seem at times that one partner is overly insistent on getting support from another, but remember that such needs usually stem from fears about parenthood or crucial interpersonal issues. Saying ''I need you'' may be another way of saying ''I need you but you're nowhere to be found.'' A husband who hears this ought to examine the possibilities that he has been withdrawing in one way or another. ''I-love-you's,'' held hands, embraces, and touches on the arm at just the right moment may be the cure. A woman who is not up to having intercourse can have many of her needs met by a soothing massage, with or without scented oils. Rubbing and holding and caressing are wonderful ways to communicate love and support and are often excellent substitutes for and additions to genital love.

It is much easier for expectant parents to have positive feelings about their unborn baby when they are feeling loved themselves. We can't sufficiently stress the fact that pregnancy is a time when expectant parents can turn toward or away from one another. Loving physical and verbal contact are means for opening channels of emotional communication. Extended silences of any kind are likely to make one partner feel deprived of the other's heart. And it is these very feelings of deprivation, of exclusion, that can impel him or her to the (momentarily) more loving arms of another person.

Psychological Issues of Sexuality

Certainly, when it comes to sex, different strokes for different folks is an accurate slogan. Not only do people have their special sexual preferences but special attitudes and interpretations of sexual behavior too. Sex can mean many things to different people and many different things to the same person. Biological sexual release is a basic human drive. How we use our sexuality, however, and what our individual sexuality ultimately means and expresses to each of us are all the result of a lifetime of experience. Sexual behavior can express affection and caring, which is our primary notion of physical love, but it can also be an expression of aggression and a means of attaining power through domination. It can simply fill temporary gaps of loneliness or, on a more permanent basis, provide for great intimacy with another human being.

The complex meanings of sexual behavior will, of course, present themselves during a pregnancy. If a man or woman believes, on a gut level, that sex is only for procreation, then sex, once the pregnancy is confirmed, may seem sinful. And, of course, stories abound. Either partner may have heard stories as a child, folktales, perhaps from their mothers, about the dangers of sex during pregnancy and the memories of them may persist. Couples who have had a miscarriage in the past may feel extra cautious, not wanting to experience the disappointment, perhaps grief, again.

Psychological factors affecting sexual adjustment are many. A man who is concerned about damage to his penis may fear that the fetus can hurt him. Or a woman who never really liked sex may use the pregnancy as an excuse to run away from it.

Most expectant couples have a sexual history together, even those who become expectant parents only moments after or perhaps before the wedding. The couple's history begins with a precoital courtship, followed by a sexual relationship exclusively for the mutual pleasure and excitement of the couple, then on to a relationship that aims at procreation, to one that accommodates itself to the realities of pregnancy, and on finally to a postpartum, nonprocreation sexual relationship totally different from the relationship that existed prior to pregnancy. Each stage brings with it profound changes, and each stage must be eased into carefully and thoughtfully. How smoothly these transitions are made depends on many physical and emotional issues, many of which we have already examined. What is crucial at each stage is the honest and caring communication that takes place between the partners themselves. Issues of sexuality are usually not so large that two willing people cannot figure out ways to resolve them.

TURN ONS AND TURNOFFS

Discussions about sexual issues are always extremely meaningful in our expectant-parents groups. After a number of these talks, we discovered that a lot of the sexual conflict experienced by expectant couples centers on two basic concerns: permission to be turned on sexually and permission to be turned off. Very few pregnant men or women are one-dimensional in their sexuality; they are, like the rest of us, human beings with ups and downs, likes and dislikes. A turned-on couple one week may be ice-cold the next with no apparent explanation. Probing will usually uncover at least some of the motivating forces behind these shifts in sexual moods.

For many men, sex and motherhood seem incompatible, and many expectant fathers experience guilt when it comes to their sexual desires and actions. Perhaps the difficulty most men have in visualizing the sexuality of their own mothers has a dramatic influence on the ways in which they view their pregnant wives, and this is most notably apparent in the final trimester. Men, unfortunately, tend to group women into those "who do" and those "who don't." Mothers definitely don't. The split vision goes even deeper: the whore who does and the virgin who most assuredly does not. In Western culture, the idea of virgin conception and birth no doubt contributes to the guilt many men express when discussing their own sexuality during pregnancy. The psychological deduction (not theologically sound) about the birth of one of the most holy men who ever lived happening without sexual intervention is that sex itself is impure.

These influences are not conscious in most people; we are simply suggesting the possibility that the notion is unconsciously instilled in many. At any rate, making love to a pregnant woman can make many expectant fathers feel quite uneasy. The results of such uneasiness vary broadly. He may be ashamed of the vigor of his sex urge, but he may also feel inadequate if he does not wish to perform. One dictate of our culture says: "You can't be a sissy. You have to be *ready.*" Let's explore some of the psychological pulls a man may experience.

FEARS: REAL AND NOT SO REAL

Men are frequently baffled when their wives suffer from apparently unexplained yeast-type vaginal infections. They are baffled because their wives rarely have explanations for the problem, and often they will secretly or openly feel guilty about possibly having caused the infections. They blame themselves for inflicting on their wives a prolonged bout of medication and soreness and itchiness, all of which makes intercourse virtually impossible. This fear for some men is sometimes uncontrollable when their wives become pregnant. One very young man, a warehouse clerk, was so frightened that he would contaminate the pregnancy through intercourse that he simply refused, openly, to engage in any sexual play from the moment he and his wife received the positive results of the pregnancy test. Clearly, this is a screen that hides other underlying fears.

At any rate, many couples avoid sexual intercourse for fear of infections. For the most part, vaginal or uterine infections are no more of a concern during pregnancy than they were before. The uterus is closed to the vagina at the cervix whose opening is sealed tightly shut by a mucous plug. The fetus is certainly well protected in its amniotic sac housed within the uterine walls. If vaginal infections do occur during pregnancy, they can make genital sex somewhat uncomfortable; however, most infections are easily treated and there need be no concern for the fetus. Sympathy and encouragement are in order for the expectant mother who has yet another physical gripe with which to deal. While waiting for the infection to clear up, the couple might find noncoital alternatives pleasurable.

There is one real caution about infection, however, and it applies to anal intercourse. This warning holds as much for before pregnancy as for during. The bacteria from the rectum can quite easily be transported to the vagina where they can colonize and cause infection. Vaginal intercourse should never follow immediately after the man's penis has made contact with the anal or rectal areas unless a condom is used for one of the acts or a thorough cleansing precedes vaginal entry.

A very recent study has suggested that sexual intercourse in the last month of pregnancy may increase the chances of some women contracting amniotic-fluid infections that may cause risk to the baby.[8] The specifics of this are still unclear and further research will need to address it. Nonetheless, this would still allow for other forms of sexual contact in the ninth month. Since the reporting of this finding is very recent (November 1979) and it is based on data collected in the 1960s, we suggest you consult your obstetrician for the most updated medical opinion on sexual intercourse in the ninth month of pregnancy.

Fear of injuring the fetus during sexual intercourse is unquestionably the most prevalent concern expressed by expectant couples, particularly fathers. Whether this fear is associated with the Judeo-Christian paradigm of good equals sexually pure is difficult to determine, although we feel there is some psychological link. If you ask an expectant father if he can imagine the specific nature of the physical harm (that is, will an arm be broken or a leg or what exactly?), you will rarely get an answer. If anything, the man is likely to admit the possibility of the child dying as a result but from what precise physical trauma he is unable to say. Or he may laugh, which is extremely common, and say, ''I know it is crazy to think what I think, but I really *believe* harm will come to my baby.''

Just because many men and women share this same unfounded fear is no reason to believe that there is one common explanation for it in each individual. In the early weeks of pregnancy some couples may fear the possibility of miscarriage and therefore avoid sex even though there has been no history of miscarriage and the obstetrician has not issued special warnings or precautions. In cases when unfounded concerns over miscarriages persist, the couples may be reflecting some ambivalence about the pregnancy. That is, we sometimes confuse a fear with an unconscious wish. In most instances, the fears disappear in time—usually when the pregnancy and the inevitability of parenthood have been incorporated into the reality structures of each expectant parent's life. Such feelings should never be held in—the longer they are, the more intensely the vital areas of the marriage will be affected. And sex is often the first thing to go: In this case because it is ''unsafe'' for the baby.

In actuality, unless a man is physically brutal in his lovemaking or the woman is experiencing discomfort during sex, there is no danger whatever for the fetus. The only exceptions again are for those couples that have been cautioned by their doctors against sexual relations in order to avoid the danger of miscarriage. A man's penis has neither the length nor the facility to pierce the cervical plug, enter the uterus, break open the amniotic membrane, and strike the baby. It is impossible. However, there are deep-penetration lovemaking positions during which a man's penis may come into direct contact with the cervix and perhaps break some of the very superficial capillaries in the engorged cervical tissue. This may cause some light spotting and conceivably a mild bruise on the cervix. The spotting will stop and the bruise will heal rapidly.[9] Still, this and any other sighting of blood during pregnancy should be reported to the obstetrician immediately. If the placenta is attached low in the mother's uterus, penile thrusting may be problematic in the ninth month. Discuss these issues with your doctor.

Female orgasms are often a cause of fear for both expectant parents and are linked causally with a concern for potential miscarriage. When a woman has an orgasm, the muscle fibers of the uterus contract in rhythmic waves. Medical experts feel that the sensitive uterus, the one prone to spontaneously aborting a fetus, may be triggered into aborting by the orgasm. A woman whose uterus shows a likelihood to abort may be counseled against having sex with her mate either because of the vigor of penile penetration and thrusting or because of the contraction-inducing orgasms. A couple must be certain to have this point clarified by the obstetrician: "Are we just forbidden intercourse or must we avoid the woman's orgasms per se? And for how long?" If the doctor has discouraged sexual relations because of orgasm, then the couple will have to be cautious about all forms of sex play, since any sexual contact could trigger a climax. Some couples who have been so counseled by their doctors often learn to derive enormous nongenital pleasure from body massages and special new ways of embracing and holding each other, daytime or night. But other couples never get beyond the frustration aroused by this limited, seemingly asexual way of relating, and a good deal of bitterness can come between the couple throughout the period of sexual forbearance. She begins to resent that he can have an orgasm and she can't; but at the same time she feels guilty for depriving him of "real" sexual fulfillment. He is guilty that he can experience a climax but angry that everytime he gets some sexual release he must be reminded of *her* privation.

For couples who have been warned to refrain from sex, the end of the first trimester will usually signal also an end to sexual abstinence—the first twelve weeks of gestation are, for most women, the truly high-risk period. And although the expectant parents may enjoy a burst of sexual activity and explore one another with unparalleled elan, it is certainly not uncommon for the fears of miscarriage to continue into the "safe" period. For very rare couples who, for medical reasons, must sit out the entire pregnancy without coitus, we can only urge a spirit of openness and inventiveness: openness to hear one another's feelings whenever they have to come out and inventiveness because with some good luck and ingenuity the couple might discover a new pastime.

Other concerns about the female orgasm persist. One is that the orgasm itself may hurt the fetus or that it will deprive the fetus of oxygen. Some researchers have found that when the pregnant woman orgasms there is a slight and brief decrease in the fetal heart rate.[10] There is no indication, however, that this is in any way detrimental to the fetus.

Another fear about female orgasm is that it will stimulate premature labor in the latter part of the pregnancy. There are mixed opinions about this, but the general medical consensus is that *if* orgasm can stimulate labor, it is only when the pregnancy is full term and the woman is about ready to go into labor anyway. Consequently, it wouldn't matter. We know several women who have unsuccessfully tried this very technique to induce labor in their ninth month in order to get the pregnancy over with.

Another issue that sometimes comes up on the topic of stimulating labor has to do with a hormone in the male sperm called prostaglandin. This substance is also found naturally in the body of the full-term expectant mother. In large pharmaceutical doses this hormone will trigger contractions of the uterus.[11] The amount of prostaglandin in a male ejaculate, however, is exceedingly small, hardly enough to induce labor.[12]

For reasons indicated earlier, some obstetrician-gynecologists are still discouraging sexual intercourse in the last four to six weeks of the pregnancy. The reasoning behind this is not always clear to the couple. Since each pregnancy may have its unique qualities, a couple told to refrain from sexual relations should question the physician about the reason.

PARENTHOOD AND SEXUALITY

In chapter 4 we gave some attention to the ways in which fears of imminent parenthood seem to increase during the third trimester. Certainly these fears and concerns are not just limited to the last twelve weeks of pregnancy. But it is possible that the eleventh-hour panic has a unique impact on the lives of the expectant couple, perhaps offering yet another clue to the report by almost three-quarters of our third-trimester fathers that their sex lives have been tremendously diminished.

But more than the preoccupation with questions of one's adequacy to parent a newborn is the unborn baby itself. As much as a child may be loved and wanted, it may still be an obstruction to relaxed and pleasurable lovemaking. In the final weeks of pregnancy, the movements of the fetus are not only palpable, they are quite visible. And the fetus is becoming more and more responsive to external stimuli—its parents' sexual activities in particular. Expectant fathers often have several reactions to this "presence." Some think the increased activity of the baby after intercourse is a sign that the fetus has been disturbed, and that its quick bumping movements are another proof that sexual love is inappropriate for expectant people. Other men report an eerie sensation, as though someone were watching them, and they feel the need to cover up, just as they presume they will have to when the baby is actually in the house. Sex is certainly improper when a child is around—a child of any age, they argue. One man who was having some severe fears about the closeness of the fetus during intercourse believed that the baby would reach down and pull off his penis. Clearly the pregnancy had stimulated castration fears in this man. And, perhaps along similar emotional lines, two other men both expressed near anger at having had their exclusive place within their wives usurped by their unborn children.

But many other expectant fathers, even some of those who were unnerved and angry, also experienced a glowing and growing sense of family. With the baby still in its mother's body and the father in there, too, a family tableau had been sculpted of one continuous and loving mass of flesh and blood and genes and history. And with the act of love each member of the family had come together as one.

There Are No Rules, Only Individuals

Regarding sexual behavior, expectant fathers fall roughly into four general groups:

1. Those reluctant to make love and who choose to refrain from sex almost entirely during the pregnancy
2. Those whose sex drives are diminished but who keep up some semblance of their former sexual relationships
3. Those who report no visible changes in their sexual desires or activities
4. And those who seem sexually stimulated by the pregnancy and whose aroused libido spurs an increase in sexual contact from their prepregnancy experiences.

None of these were fixed, of course, since feelings and actions always vary. The expectant father who seemed to think about little else beside fondling his wife had days and even weeks when a two-mile run in a downpour would have seemed more enticing than sexual intercourse with his wife. Similarly, the man whose sex urge was notably depressed for considerable lengths of time had periods when he wished for nothing more than to hang around in bed with his wife in constant and ravishing sexual delight.

Men who experience a loss of sexual drive tend to suffer a great many negative feelings which may ultimately even produce a major identity crisis. They come to think of themselves as less than manly if they are not aroused when their wives are. This is just not realistic, however, and men must understand that, not only as expectant fathers, but as human beings they are entitled to shifts in emotion. There are so many reasons why a man will focus less on sex during pregnancy than before. Perhaps, as we have pointed out, he feels it is inappropriate to make love to a pregnant woman. Possibly the specter of incest taboos intensifies as his pregnant wife reminds him more and more of his own mother. It is also conceivable that living with a woman so obviously filled with motherhood makes him feel like a child, inadequate in his role as lover, inadequate in strength and courage compared to his wife who will soon accomplish the incontestable feat of bearing a child, something he could never do.

Some expectant fathers search elsewhere for their lost masculinity. They may find comfort with another woman, where sexual contact may be less important than the proof that they are still desirable men. Sometimes extramarital relationships during pregnancy can help ease some immediate tension and allow the couple to put certain pressures behind them. (In some cultures there is an implicit acceptance of this.) Or a woman may unconsciously condone her husband's taking a lover rather than having him mooning about the house or making sexual demands on her. More often, however, outside affairs can exacerbate existing tensions and put distance between the couple at a time when closeness and support are necessary for a smooth transition into parenthood. These are personal decisions to be made by each expectant parent, and what will work for some will not work for others.

Expectant fathers who experience depression over the periodic loss of their passion may require additional support and understanding from their wives. It would not be fair, however, to expect women to be mind readers: They must be told directly and simply what has been happening. The problem will be hard enough by itself without complicating matters and cutting off communication. But couples should try to keep in mind the fact that sexual problems are not global, that sexual play is only one metaphor, a single pathway to the love bonding with another human being. And if this one avenue is temporarily shut down, love will most assuredly find other means of expression.

We are all sexual beings. We are sexual when we are born and grope after the breast or bottle. The gratification of feeling satiated with food, being held, feeling safe and secure, the pleasure of the sensation are all part of the comfort we require. As the child develops, different parts of the body take on sexual meaning and our sexual focus becomes increasingly genital. But even as adults, genital preeminence doesn't take away our earlier nongenital experiences and expressions of sexuality which still remain a part of us. It is sexual to hug, to hold, to touch, or to massage. We can even be sexual when we are not touching. And throughout, we are having needs met that are every bit as strong as our drive for biological sexual release.

6
Issues of Fatherhood

Long before the expectant father opens this book, perhaps even before the pregnancy is confirmed, a string of questions about fatherhood will flow through his mind:

> What will be my role as a father?
> Will I provide adequately?
> Will I ever learn child-care skills?
> Will I be a *good* father?
> What will life with an infant be like?
> What kind of mother will my wife be?
> What will our relationship be like after the birth?
> In what way will I be like my own father?

Although there are exceptions (the father with an abundant income may worry less about economic issues and more about his relationship with the baby), these queries are so universally expressed that they seem to be an integral part of the psychological state that prompts a man to prepare himself for fatherhood.

Most of these issues have only-time-will-tell answers. Nonetheless, in raising the questions and addressing each, avenues for preparation unfold.

Childhood Memories and Future Fathering

Looking at your own childhood—your relationship with your parents, with your siblings, and the family's interactions with one another—is one of the ways of preparing for fatherhood. These family experiences are a major contribution to the way you will react to the pregnancy and the newborn, and it is often a real help to see a connection with these past occurrences and the fluctuating moods and feelings of expectant and actual parenthood.

One man we interviewed talked about the unexplainable sadness he felt at the prospect of the birth of his second child, something he did not experience with his first. He said, ''I feel real protective of my daughter. Like it's not fair to her to bring another child into the house.'' This man had two younger brothers. He became thoughtful at the suggestion that he might be projecting onto his daughter his own feelings about having had to share his parents with other children. He was identifying with her loss of the only-child status.

The birth of a sibling often means to children the end of being an only child or a youngest child. It almost always means a little less attention. If that was a painful experience for you as a young boy, similar feelings may creep up when your wife becomes pregnant. You may feel a threat that this baby will deprive you of some loving just as the birth of a sibling did. If these feelings emerge, you may be responding to the baby not so much as your child but as a brother or sister. After the baby is born, incidents may arise where you find yourself competing with your child, just as you competed with your siblings. Recognizing this can help you deal with many an unpleasant interaction.

But a man does not have to have had a younger sibling to feel that the pregnancy threatens his special status with his wife. A man who never really got enough loving as a child or got ambivalent loving or who had trouble separating from his mother and remained overly attached to her may well marry a woman who will ''mother'' him. All men marry women who will, to some degree, be mothers to them. When this is the core of the marriage, however, the newborn will really upset things.[1] As these marital matches usually meet both partners' needs, there is a good chance the wife wanted a "little boy" to take care of. When she becomes pregnant she is faced with the prospect of having her own real little child. One can certainly see how this might disturb the balance of their relationship.

Babies are not the only people who can come between a boy and his mother. A father also can—at least in the mind of a young boy. A boy accurately recognizes the special relationship his parents have together. And if the father was a very threatening personality, the son may fear paternal wrath for wanting a relationship with his mother. He may take special precaution to avoid competing like a "man" and choose to stay childlike and passive in his relationship with his father—a safer stance. When his own wife becomes pregnant, she becomes a mother, and now *he does* have a special relationship with her. To have a "mother" may mean that he has replaced his father, and old fears of retaliation as well as guilt about this "incestuous" relationship ("incestuous" in terms of the *feelings*, of course) may unconsciously reemerge. He may question that he can, or even has a right, to be a man.[2]

Of course, all kinds of interactions that you had with your father can affect the way you react to the pregnancy. The pregnancy may reactivate in you many of the feelings you had for your father and you may secretly assume that your child will feel about you in the same way. If you feel love for your father and recall warm moments together, you will probably anticipate positive things between you and your child. If you hated your father, perhaps for the way he treated you and your mother or because he left the family, you may harbor thoughts that your child will hate you too. For this reason some men prefer daughters because they fear having a son may force them to reexperience some of their childhood discomforts.[3] Your own angry and aggressive feelings toward your father may recur during pregnancy and they can be directed at your unborn child, if you're not aware of what you're doing.

Men who never knew their fathers or who never had a model because their fathers were emotionally absent may be concerned about "how to father." Some men model themselves after uncles, friends of the family, older siblings, or their mothers. One expectant father we spoke to who was orphaned at the age of one year had only fantasies of what the perfect father should be—the father he never had. He was determined to become that idealized father and created tremendous and unrealistic pressure for himself.

One study found that men who had an image of themselves as a "good father" had the easiest adjustment to expectant parenthood.[4] Men who achieved self-image of "good mother" or even "good older sibling" had some difficulties when their wives became pregnant but many were able to use these images productively and adapted well to fatherhood. Men who did not have a self-image that included "good father," "good mother," or "good sibling" had the most difficult time adjusting.

EARLY MEMORIES OF PREGNANCY

There are many things you hear and learn about pregnancy as a child that can reappear in your consciousness when your wife becomes pregnant. For example, 62 percent of the men responding to our questionnaire claimed to know that their mothers had had an easy or difficult pregnancy and/or birth while carrying *them.* That means about six out of ten men remember having heard stories about their mothers' pregnancies or births—an experience in which they were directly involved. These stories may well set expectations for their wives' pregnancies.

Seventeen percent of the men who heard such stories said their mothers had had difficult pregnancies or births. If as a little boy you heard that your mother was in discomfort or danger because of *your* birth, you might have felt that you were to blame. In addition, you may go on to extrapolate from this that pregnancy or birth is dangerous, painful, perhaps even mutilating. When your wife becomes pregnant you might feel unexplainably guilty.

If you were already feeling angry or ambivalent toward her or the pregnancy, the guilt would probably be even greater. We often feel guilty for having angry feelings, but during a pregnancy in which your wife really is uncomfortable (or you fantasize she is), these feelings might be even more intense. It's as if you talked about someone behind his or her back and then a tragedy befell the person the following day. You feel guilty for having had the conversation, as though your bad wishes had caused the event to happen. The same thing can happen when you have ambivalent feelings about a pregnancy. You think your wife is suffering because *you* put her in that state—the guilt is painful and disproportionate to the situation.

This connection between guilt and feelings of anger or resentment may also occur if your wife has had a previous miscarriage or abortion. You might somehow feel responsible. If there is something about the pregnancy that elicits consistent guilt in you, there is a good chance you will resent the baby and your wife that much more—not an auspicious way to begin family life.

Many men remember their mothers pregnant with a younger sibling. Sometimes the memories are hazy, at other times clear; they may run the gamut from pleasant to traumatic. Watching the changes or even hearing about them is a powerful experience for a young boy. Even if he has no memories of this time, he will inevitably be struck by the magic of what occurs inside his mother when he learns the "facts of life." As we will discuss in more detail later, a young boy sometimes becomes determined to perform this same magical feat. And he may find no conflict with the fact that he is a boy, will grow up to be a man, and *can still* have a baby. He is identifying with his mother. When this man's wife becomes pregnant, it is certainly conceivable that he will identify a bit with her as well and envy the pregnancy.[5] This pregnancy envy is sometimes referred to as Zeus envy (named for the Greek god who swallowed his wife so that he could bear the child himself).[6]

A man may respond to this envy in many ways. If the feelings are mild, they may assist him in empathizing with his wife and in feeling nurturing toward the child. Envy might prompt him to become more involved in the pregnancy and in early child care, which he might find gratifying. Some men identify much more strongly with their wives, almost merging their personalities with the expectant mother, in order to deeply experience or even control the pregnancy.[7] They almost feel as though they could do the whole thing by themselves. There is even considerable evidence that both the couvade ritual and the couvade syndrome (see the Glossary or chapter 1) are often the result of a man's identification with his pregnant wife.[8][9] Some men who envy their wives' creativity find themselves with increased work energy—as if they, too, want to create something.[10] They may direct energies into hobbies or new interests.[11]

Some men can be very threatened by this feminine identification. They may begin to engage in tradionally masculine activities, like wrestling and car racing, to reinforce their feelings of masculinity. Others may have an affair with a woman who is not pregnant. Some men find themselves struggling with homosexual conflicts. And all of these anxieties will intensify if the man equates ''wife'' with ''mother'' and unconsciously sees the unborn child as a product of incest. If any of these feelings are strong enough, a man may try to deny the pregnancy or the fact that he is the child's father, or he may try to physically escape the situation.

Some men who have tremendous anxiety about these conflicts may act out by involving themselves in antisocial behavior. One study found that in a group of men arraigned in criminal court, sexual crimes were more likely to occur among expectant fathers in that group than among married men whose wives were not pregnant.[12] The crimes included such acts as exhibitionism pedophilia (sexual advances toward a child), rape, and lewd phone calls or letters. These acts probably reflect immature ways of dealing with feelings of inadequacy. Of course, these are not typical reactions; but when detected, they indicate a definite need for immediate psychological help.

The man who is emotionally immature and is still struggling with many of these childhood conflicts may feel tremendous hostility and aggression toward his wife and unborn child. A likely reaction to the guilt for having such strong feelings is severe depression. It is interesting to note that one of the explanations for the couvade ritual and the couvade syndrome, as well, is that they reflect the father's ambivalent feeling for his wife and that the ritual serves to protect the mother and baby from the father's hostility and aggression.[13] [14] The father takes ''to bed'' when the woman goes into labor or performs some other ritual before or after the birth, ostensibly to protect his wife from demons, but in reality it is to protect her from his own aggression.

Men who have less control of their impulses may find themselves becoming physically aggressive with their wives. Physical brutality toward a wife may first appear when a woman becomes pregnant and may become a pattern for the marriage even after the birth. This is aggression, not only toward the wife but toward the child as well, and it can be considered prenatal child abuse as well as wife beating. The unconscious goal may well be to get rid of the child, and it can also be an indicator of the potential for child abuse after the baby is born.[15] Tangentially, child abuse may not involve physical brutality. Sometimes the aggressiveness toward the child is seen in carelessness and neglect, and this abuse can be just as harmful for everyone concerned.

Of course, these last few examples of men's reactions to pregnancy are exceptions. And it is important to realize that pregnancy is not the cause of such disturbed behavior, just the precipitant. Most men do not act out like this. But aggressive and angry feelings may surface even at the thought of your wife in labor pain.[16] Since this aggression feels inappropriate it is usually accompanied by guilt. This may be turned against yourself and experienced as a mild depression, or you might become careless with your own physical health. The hostility/guilt may find expression in oversolicitousness toward your wife or you being ''too worried'' about her being hurt in an accident or dying in childbirth or that the child will be born deformed.

Still, for most men, the rekindling of old conflicts may not create undue anxiety and may give them a chance to rework some of the loose ends from their own childhoods[17] and ready themselves for fatherhood. Once conflicts are laid to rest, pregnancy can be directly experienced as yet another stage of life, bringing with it emotional growth and a new and exciting era.

Determining Roles

Most expectant fathers see their three major roles as breadwinner/provider, nurturer/care giver, and teacher.[18] We were impressed by the number of men in our own survey who emphasized the emotional aspects of child care. Occasionally (although this is still not the common arrangement) a man would indicate that he intended to be the primary care giver since his wife had a higher-paying full-time job. Other men simply wrote, "I'll do everything my wife does." And still other men saw their role as teaching their children "right from wrong" or being a disciplinarian. Finding a coherent and consistent role is more important for your own adjustment to parenthood than the particular parental tasks you perform.[19] Warmth, love, and caring, not the particular tasks performed by their father, are what counts to children.

The transition into fatherhood will be made easier if the parents can decide on complementary roles that allow them to work effectively together. But whether a couple shares each child-care activity or divides them up so that one parent, for example, takes exclusive responsibility for the baby's laundry while the other is responsible for bathing the baby, they will need to talk about these child-care responsibilites during the pregnancy. Of our questionnaire respondents, 60 percent said they discussed the roles they would take in child care with their wives. That leaves 40 percent who didn't! Of those, three out of four claimed they had an unspoken understanding with their wives. But what if they were wrong? And what about the remaining 25 percent?

Times are indeed changing and men are becoming more and more involved in the nitty-gritty of child-care activities. Fathers are finding that the benefits of participating in and contributing to the care and growth of their children are immense. Still, it is usually the woman who stays home in the first few months after the birth and who performs most of the minute-to-minute child-care tasks. The husband usually works and his parenting is confined to evenings and weekends (or whichever days he has off).

But couples are beginning to consider new options. Men are requesting paternity leaves in order to spend more time with their families. Eighty percent of our respondents said they would be willing to take a paternity leave at full pay, 36 percent at part pay, and 17 percent at no pay. Clearly money is an issue here, and most jobs still do not offer this benefit. In families where both parents work, couples may choose to adjust their schedules to minimize the need for day-care or baby-sitting services.

But tradition dies hard. In a family where both partners work full time and make provisions for the child during the day, it is still more often the woman who assumes the majority of child-care responsibilities in the evening. Many men still opt for minimal involvement with their children whether or not their wives are working. They seem to be waiting for the children to grow up so that they can really communicate with them and assume the familiar role of teacher or authoritarian. As a result those men often feel like strangers to their infant children, like outsiders in their own homes. They are not a part of the noisy excitement and secret intimacies that fill a home where children grow.

But even if fathering has to be limited to evenings and weekends, fathers who want to be part of things can have a strong, positive impact on the development of their children. And there is always a way to catch an extra hour of special time alone with your child. One father simply got up one hour earlier than usual each morning and spent that time with his child. Babies are notoriously early risers! The man who feels that his joʋ needs him from nine to nine and on weekends, too, must evaluate what he is sacrificing for his work and whether he is not just using it to escape the family circle.

THE NURTURING ROLE

Many men discard or amplify the traditional father role of provider-disciplinarian by exploring new and different possibilities. Of course, there have always been nurturing, caretaking fathers. Adopting new roles, however, may be more difficult than it seems. Everything was so much simpler when the father's role was rigidly and carefully defined. Everyone knew what was expected of him, and therefore conflict and confusion was minimized. Some men and women who are still very comfortable with the traditional roles of their own parents find it easier to retain them. But many fathers and fathers-to-be are pioneering new roles for themselves—ones that they feel will be more rewarding. Unfortunately, there are few models. If your own father was a traditional provider-disciplinarian, then your most powerful role model may be at odds with the kind of parenting you yourself would like to do. This can cause a lot of confusion since your own ideas about fathering are not in keeping with the model your father provided. It is certainly a lot easier to be nurturing and caretaking if your own father was. But even if he wasn't, your determination and continual self-evaluation will allow you to create new patterns for yourself and your children.

For many men this new role of love giver and caretaker will demand a change of self-image. It is a lot easier for the man who, as a boy, had experience caring for younger siblings or relatives, or earned a little extra cash baby-sitting. If you had these experiences, you will also feel more confident with your caretaking skills and realize that it will be different with your own child. You will probably experience both more pleasure *and* more anxiety. But even if you never before have held a baby in your arms, learning how to perform child-care activities is not difficult. Just like for new mothers, after a little stumbling, it comes easy. The babies manage because the clumsiness is less important than the love that accompanies it.

Still, the fear of inadequacy in child-care skills is a concern often expressed by expectant fathers and a factor that may create distance between them and their children. We should add that first-time fathers are not alone in this. We know many men with school-age children who have never changed a diaper. Their determination to be more involved in the caretaking of their next child has them equally concerned about the how to's of child care.

As in many other areas, child-care activities are learned through doing. Unfortunately, boys growing up have little opportunity to practice these skills. They are rarely offered baby-sitting as a way to earn extra money, preferring paper routes and shoveling snow. When there is a choice, parents are much more likely to require daughters to be responsible for younger siblings. A deep interest in children is acceptable for daughters but frowned upon, sometimes mocked, when expressed by boys. Even the warm, loving expressions that come with taking care of a favorite doll are all too often forbidden a boy. Parents whose unfounded fears that doll playing may lead a son to homosexuality may rob their boys of valuable nurturing experiences. Perhaps your own sons will be spared these unfounded biases; perhaps you are dealing with their effects right now.

We asked recent and expectant fathers about child-care responsibilities they may have had for younger siblings. The responses from our questionnaire were: considerable 10.1 percent; moderate 28.1 percent; little 61.8 percent. Then we asked about other childhood or adolescent experiences with babies, such as baby-sitting for relatives, neighbors' children, and so forth. Look at these figures: frequent 9.6 percent; occasional 34.8 percent; rare 47.0 percent; never 8.7 percent. Given these responses, it is not surprising that so many men express concern about how they will ever be able to diaper, feed, burp, hold, talk to, bathe, and dress an infant. It is not surprising, perhaps because of their lack of familiarity with these functions, that expectant fathers' fantasies about life with baby are usually centered around a child who is at least two years old,[20] while women seem more likely to daydream about infants.

Child-care skills are *not* instinctive, and many women who lack previous experience with babies feel as unfamiliar with performing these daily tasks as their husbands. In fact, a number of women in our groups felt that their husbands took to the chores more easily than they had themselves. Your own wife may be relying on you to help her figure out some of the basics. Ask her if she doesn't ask you. If neither of you is an expert, you can have a lot of fun learning together. It is important to remember that child care is a team effort and your goals are the same: a healthy and happy child and maximizing your own pleasures. Couples often compete for who does what better. If you find this happening, talk about it. Some of us have trouble asking our spouses to teach us. If your wife has had more baby experience than you, she will probably be a patient and enthusiastic teacher. But if you feel she is condescending or putting you down tell her how it makes you feel. Undoubtedly, she will realize that her style is not going to get her what she wants—your involvement.

There are women, of course, who do not want their husbands involved in childrearing; they feel ''you served your purpose, now butt out'' or think children are their exclusive property and want no one interfering. Such a posture gives them a purpose, a sense of control, and feelings of power, or so they think. The women who act in such a proprietary manner are few as compared to the numbers who bemoan their husbands' lack of cooperation. Most women know the frustration of being ''stuck'' with a child. Forty-four percent of the *recent* fathers who responded to our questionnaire said that their wives would like them to be more involved with child care. Most women deeply value a partner with whom they can share the burdens and joys of childrearing and to whom the family as a unit is a high priority. Only 19 percent of the recent fathers in our survey felt that they themselves would like to be more involved in child care, but this may include men who are already deeply involved. Your asking to be taught will most likely therefore be considered an act of love.

When we gave expectant fathers a list of child-care activities and asked them to check off whether or not they intended to be involved in them, we got the following percentages of yeses:

Diapering	97.5%
Feeding (Most of the remainder indicated that their wives intended to breast-feed.)	65.8%
Dressing	94.9%
Bathing	88.5%
Holding	100.0%
Cutting nails	59.7%
Talking to	100.0%
Night wakes	88.0%
Playing	100.0%
Doctor visits	72.7%
Baby's laundry	48.1%
Food preparation	50.6%

These are impressive percentages of men who see themselves in a caretaking role. The reality of what they will do, however, may differ. When we asked recent fathers what caretaking activities they were involved in and compared their responses to the expectant fathers, considerably fewer reported involvement in diapering, dressing, bathing, cutting nails, and night wakes. There may be practical reasons for these lower percentages, but it's certain that for many men, their idealized role was not realized. Nonetheless, men are still involved in many caretaker activities. We doubt that the numbers would have looked like this fifteen years ago.

If you intend to play a much more active role in the day-to-day care of your baby, you may not want to wait until you have the real thing in front of you to start learning the how to's. There are a number of things you can do before the birth of the child to develop child-care skills.

Here are some suggested activities: baby-sit, practice diapering and bathing dolls, watch other parents closely, talk to new parents and ask questions, read books and articles, and practice on friends' children.

TEACHER-DISCIPLINARIAN

Some men define their fathering role as that of teacher. They see themselves as professor of morality and as a means for socializing their children, their connection to the outside world. These are truly parenting functions. Unlike nurturing or providing, which begin at birth, this role becomes more relevant when the child is a toddler (about two) or usually older. Newborns do learn things, of course, but trying to teach them "right and wrong" and the "ways of the world" would be pretty pointless at this time. The "father" who withdraws until he can become a teacher, must also wait to be a father.

A number of men see their chief fathering role as disciplinarian. We usually think of this function as traditionally the father's, although the woman takes this responsibility in many homes. Even men who preferred to think of themselves as principally giving emotional nurture to their children were concerned about their ability to discipline. "I don't want to *spoil* my children" is the oft-stated fear of too much love and not enough discipline. Other fathers fear the results of excessive discipline. Most parents worry about how poorly administered discipline may hurt their children. They may recall incidents in their own childhood that involved discipline—memories that are confusing or painful, where discipline seemed ineffective or harsh. There are a number of good books on the subject of discipline that may be helpful. But the problems with discipline crop up when the disciplinarian is unaware of what his or her real gut feeling is when she/he starts to "lay down the law." Clearly, some rules need to be enforced in every home, but the issue of discipline and rules don't come up with an infant. An infant's sense of him- or herself and his or her separateness from the external world is barely formed. They can't grasp their impact on the people around them, and they are too young to understand the rules. Their needs dominate their behavior, and although infants can be punished, they won't benefit from such treatment. If you find yourself disciplining an infant, it is time to step back from the situation and think about what is going on in yourself and your family. Talking to someone who is a bit more objective will be helpful.

BREADWINNER

Breadwinner-provider is seen by expectant fathers as one of the major functions of fathering, although increasing numbers of women share this function. We asked expectant and recent fathers what plans their wives had made for returning to work after the birth. Twenty-nine percent responded that their wives would be or were presently working either full time (13 percent) or part-time (16 percent). Another 11 percent indicated that their wives planned to go back to work within a year after the birth. Plain and simple, most of these men indicated the reason for these work arrangements was *money*.

The burden of financial support for most families is still on the man. And expectant fathers worry about money a great deal—some say all of the time. They often feel resentful about this responsibility. Many working couples, particularly those about to have their first child, will lose one salary and gain an additional mouth to feed. And babies cost more than just the food they eat. There are doctor bills, the layette, clothes, baby-sitting, and many extras. Frightened of the added burden, many men feel financially trapped. They feel they must give up those old fantasies of leaving work to travel around the world; gone, too, are the dreams of quitting the nine-to-five job complete with pension and medical benefits to open an independent business. Expectant fathers who are unemployed or whose jobs are not secure or who are still students, often feel *panic*. They may resent the baby and the wife for the pressure they feel and the resulting sleepless nights. Money is another very strong reminder that you are an adult and have undertaken a tremendous responsibility.

The constant concern of many expectant fathers has to do with people depending upon them for survival. This is probably one of the main reasons they may entertain thoughts like, ''What would happen if I die?'' and then worry obsessively about dying. He may even unconsciously be saying, ''If I died I wouldn't have to do this,'' or even ''If *they* died I wouldn't have to do this.'' Perhaps this is one impetus to take out life insurance if he has not previously done so. Every life-insurance salesperson knows that an expectant father is an easy mark.

The Real Expenses

When we asked men what new stresses they were under since the pregnancy began, economic themes occurred repeatedly. One related issue, in particular, seemed to come up again and again and that was moving.

Pregnant couples often feel that they need more space now that a baby is going to join them. Couples move from smaller apartments to bigger ones or they make the decision to move into a house, and larger living quarters usually cost more money. Then they need more furniture; again, *money*. As the pregnancy proceeds, the pressure to get settled increases, occasionally causing tensions in the marriage itself. And the issues around moving aren't just money. Couples feel a need to get their ''house in order'' before the birth—part of the ''nesting'' behavior we talked about earlier.

Some couples opt to keep the smaller place and manage with a squeeze. If necessary, living rooms can be set up as nurseries, but then the couple entertains company with diapers, talcum powder, and toys. Other couples use their bedroom for a nursery and are happy to have the baby close to them in the first few weeks, but others hate to tiptoe around their own bedroom and worry about noises. And a baby, even a sleeping one, can be quite a damper on sexual activity. For creative couples with limited space there are ingenious ways of setting up ''nursery corners'' in just about any room that give everyone at least the *illusion* of space.

CUTTING COSTS WITHOUT CUTTING CARE

Couples often shudder when they think about the costs of raising a child. In reality the outlay of money before the birth is greater than the day-in day-out expenses of infant care. Still there are ways of cutting down costs. For example: (1) A good medical insurance plan may pick up many of the prenatal and hospital costs. If you decide you are going to try to conceive, it may pay to look into the available plans around and on the job. Note that most plans will not give any benefits if conception predated joining the plan. (2) There are excellent midwife programs and maternity clinics that can be explored. They are much less expensive and are discussed in chapter 3. (3) If your wife is partially or exclusively breast-feeding, food costs will be low, if not nonexistant. Even if she is not, careful meal planning can always reduce your food expenses. (4) Diaper service is cheaper than disposable diapers at least for the first year. It's even cheaper to do your own diapers if you have a washing machine. The increased work of this last alternative is apparent. (5) There are many ways to cut clothing costs. Shop for maternity clothes carefully. A simple dress in a fashionable boutique might cost you more than an entire outfit elsewhere. Friends may have maternity wardrobes stored in boxes in the closets; so ask around. There is a good chance someone will truly appreciate their clothes getting some use. This is also good advice when it comes to children's clothes, particularly since sizes don't vary as much with children as with adults. There is hardly a community where several children haven't worn the same infants clothes, since children outgrow sizes sooner than clothes wear out. Infant clothing is a popular gift for newborns; so expect to receive some and wait before you indulge in buying a whole wardrobe. (6) Baby furniture can be made or improvised. Numerous books and magazines provide instructions for making cradles. Dresser drawers lined with foam-rubber padding are perfect cradle substitutes. If building things is not one of your strengths, perhaps a handy friend can get you going. If you decide to buy, bargain hunt. Some used furniture is in top shape. And then there are relatives who are between babies and can spare a few items. (7) Even baby-sitting expenses can be trimmed. For example, there is always bartering. What can you offer? What can be exchanged besides cash? Neighbors with a child may welcome a baby-sitting exchange; they sit with the children one night and you reciprocate the next, as needed.

Unless you are economically well-off, you will probably want to start saving money before the pregnancy begins. Many couples often begin a forced saving regimen as one of the ways to prepare for parenthood when they discover they are pregnant. And children do cost money. Of the men in our survey 36.4 percent indicated that they spent more money during the pregnancy than they had been spending before. If money is no object, you will take pleasure in carefree buying. But even the budgeting couple, pressed for money and concerned for the future, can have fun and even feel as if they are making an even greater contribution to their baby through thoughtful and ingenious planning.

To Prepare

There are many things men traditionally do to prepare for fathering during the pregnancy. One study reported the following:

1. providing living arrangements for the baby
2. making financial purchases for the baby
3. attending parenting classes
4. showing an interest in children
5. anticipating changes in life-style (we will discuss this shortly)
6. thinking about their role as father
7. planning father-child activities
8. reading about fathering
9. observing other fathers
10. talking to other fathers

11. dreaming about their baby
12. increasing family income
13. reorienting network of friends
14. baby-sitting
15. practicing infant-care activities.[21]

This is an impressive list and a good way to begin preparation!

Veteran Fathers

One of the major identity shifts for the first timer is from non-father to father. It is not easy. To incorporate father into your self-image takes time, and pregnancy is a man's time to develop this role, to give shape to this new image. The kind of active, meaningful involvement in the pregnancy that we have been suggesting in this book will ease this transition. And a transition to fatherhood is called for whether you are a first timer or a man with five children.

As with almost everything else, the second time is easier. As a rule, most fathers feel more confident during the second pregnancy—as do their wives. Research on the crises associated with expectant fatherhood is usually focused on first pregnancies. Regardless of the number of previous children, however, crises and stresses may still occur, particularly as life situations change.

The veteran fathers with whom we spoke often indicated that it was a different experience for them the first time around. One man wrote on the questionnaire:

> You should have sent this to me the first time my wife got pregnant. Neither child was planned and I wanted my wife to get an abortion for both, but she's too religious. For the first child I was furious and ignored my wife almost all the time. I didn't think I was ready to be a father or that I could love a child or take care of it. It took me six months to accept the baby. I didn't want this one either but now at least I know we can take care of it. I look forward to meeting this one.

Many of the fears that come from simply not knowing what to expect dissipate on the second go-round. Expectant parents have slews of fantasies, but tying them to concrete experiences often helps to diminish excessive anxiety. If you have been through a delivery without a hitch, your fears about entering a delivery room will certainly decrease. And having seen your wife's changes and your own in a previous pregnancy will give perspective to your moods. And child-care skills are no longer problematic. The list goes on.

If a man has survived previous pregnancies without trauma, then he can hold onto pleasant memories to keep his present fears in check. Again and again the men we interviewed said, "You should have spoken to me during my first pregnancy. This one is a breeze compared to the first." One man we interviewed, whose wife was in her ninth month, would only talk about his first pregnancy, now two-and-a-half years past. He remembered fights they had, disturbing dreams, and conflicts with his own father. He said he was experiencing none of those during this pregnancy, "having worked them through once." However, this pregnancy had its own problems. His wife had a very bad back, and she was in bed on doctor's orders for the last four months. She had to quit her part-time job. He was working full time and he was also responsible for much of the child-care and household tasks. He desperately wanted the pregnancy to be over. Still, he said, he worried less than he had during the first pregnancy, focusing a lot more on the earlier, relatively uneventful pregnancy to avoid some of the concerns of this one. Focusing on his past experience was an effective defense for him.

But what if the first pregnancy did not go smoothly? What if memories of a past pregnancy haunt the present one? Nick, another interviewee, recognized that he was treating his third pregnancy a lot differently than his first two. He recalled his first pregnancy of ten years before as uneventful. The second pregnancy, although uneventful, ended tragically—the child was stillborn. The couple mourned the death and a year later conceived again. Although the pregnancy was going smoothly enough, they recognized a considerable decrease in their involvement. They went about their pregnancy chores routinely but with little emotion or excitement. Both knew they were keeping emotionally distant because of the pain of their previous great loss. This is often seen in couples that have suffered through a miscarriage. They recognize a certain amount of restraint in their excitement and involvement until they enter into the middle months of pregnancy, when the risks of miscarriage diminish.

But one pregnancy experience need not be tragic in order to cast shadows over another. One man we interviewed who had recently learned that his wife was pregnant for the second time recalled how she had spent more time with her mother during the first pregnancy than with him. He understandably experienced this as rejection. Even though his wife's energies were presently focused on him and on preparation for the new baby, he still felt extremely defensive. He jumped at her for staying on the phone too long or for seeing her mother at all. He found himself competing with his wife for the affection of their first child, transferring his need for her attention onto their daughter.

And even when an earlier pregnancy and birth go smoothly, a difficult early parenting experience can affect the outlook of expectant parents. John, an interviewee, said jokingly, "I love it when she is pregnant. I just don't want this part of it to end." His first child had colic and was up most nights screaming. There was little relief. The parents were always tired, emotionally drained, and at one another's throats for three months.

How can the second-time expectant father use his first experience to enrich the quality of the subsequent pregnancies? Try to recall your feelings and actions during the last pregnancy, since in all likelihood they will be cropping up again. Just opening them up for discussion with your wife may be the beginning of a continuing communication which will help you to avoid many of the pitfalls of past pregnancies. It may be easier to hear (or say), "Look, you're doing it again and it makes me feel isolated," than to live with silence and get no response.

Men with previous children are no less plagued than first timers with the economic concerns of having a child. If anything, they may even worry more, since the family and the cost of living may be growing more rapidly than their incomes. An expectant father married for the second time may have the additional burden of child support and alimony. Frustrated and angry, some men cut back on those payments.

The role of nurturer, however, may hold fewer surprises for the expectant father who has had previous children. If he had been at all involved in their child care, most of the basic activities will now come easily to him. A little time to practice his rusty skills and it will feel like old times. If he wasn't previously involved in child care, he may want to be now. This may be more common among men starting a family with a new wife or when there has been a big age gap between children. These men may not know how to bathe or diaper or feed a baby. And, like first timers, they, too, will have to learn.

Expectant Siblings

As though there weren't enough going on already, the expectant father may also have other children at home, who, because of the pregnancy, may require additional attention and thought.

Of those men responding to our questionnaire who had other children, 34.6 percent reported that they were spending more time with them during the pregnancy than before. Only 2 percent reported a decrease. These numbers stayed pretty stable when we asked these same questions to men after their new babies were born. What does this mean to the men? It means that, at a time when they may need to turn inward to their own fantasies or attend to their own tensions and worries or direct energy to resolving their conflicts and concerns or give their spare time to preparation for the newborn, they may be required to give more care to other children.

The increase in time fathers spent with their other children during pregnancy may just reflect the fact that expectant couples spend more time at home than they did prior to the pregnancy.

The other factor, of course, is that pregnant mothers are no longer able to handle many of the routine child-care activities: driving children from place to place, bending over a bathtub, playing softball. So the expectant father fills in. This may feel burdensome for some men who already feel overwhelmed with responsibilities, but many men do not experience it this way. Many now feel glad about the family getting to know one another again. Fathers may now feel more included in the family, and playing with their children offers them the opportunity to relax a little. Many also feel that in "getting back" to their children they are preparing for the new one to come.

If your first child is old enough to formulate a completed sentence, upon learning of the pregnancy she/he will probably ask, in some way, "Where does this baby come from?" Even if you have been through the facts before, the visible reality of pregnancy will raise new questions. If not, you can be sure the child is silently pondering the issue. Even children who have their facts straight are going to be forced to accept the fact that their parents "do it," and this can be difficult. They may work hard at finding other explanations that allow them to deny the way this pregnancy came about. If they share some of these fantasies, you will be impressed with their creativity.

Some parents are more comfortable than others when answering the question "Where do babies come from?" And it is appropriate for a father to fill in the facts for his children—both sons and daughters. Here are a few general points which may be helpful: (1) Keep it simple, (2) be truthful, (3) take one question at a time, and (4) check what the child thinks she/he has just been told. Children often sit and nod and say they understand but then repeat the most fantastic renditions. You may have trouble figuring out where such information came from. But children, like most of us, will take what they hear and interpret it in terms of their own experiences. And children do not have too many experiences that will help them to understand accurately a pregnancy. "Planting a seed" will not conjure up in the child's mind what *you think* you are communicating.

When a child asks about the expanded belly of his/her mother, she/he may be told something about the baby being "in there" and "will soon come out," perhaps "from between mommy's legs." What children know from their own experience is that things get into the belly through the mouth and come out through the anus. And, indeed, many children assume that that is exactly how this baby's journey began and will end. This is not useful information for the child and will not serve him or her well in the future. Some children who have tremendous anxiety about the pregnancy and entertain the fantasy that they are carrying a child, begin to retain their stools.[22] If this does happen with your child, contact your pediatrician and discuss the need for psychological consultation.

Children may be in awe of their mother's pregnancy. Even boys identify to some degree with their mothers and are very impressed with this feat of childbirth she has accomplished or is preparing for. It is not uncommon to hear young children say that they are "going to have a baby the way mommy did." Parents get pleasure in hearing this from a daughter and lovingly assure her that some day she will, but they shudder when they hear it from a son and quickly "set him straight."

Boys should be "set straight,' in the sense that they should be given the facts and taught the role of a man in conception. But a little understanding will go a long way. Boys may well envy their mothers' capacities to bear and nurture children. How they handle this envy and identification and the extent of it are the important issues.

We referred earlier to your other children as "expectant siblings," and you ought to appreciate the fact that they, too, are expecting. Just as you and your wife use the pregnancy period to prepare for the new child, your other children should use these months to prepare themselves emotionally, as well. Tell them early on in the pregnancy and at a time when there is much warmth between you, not when you are angry or have just had a fight or they are being punished. They will think of the new child as a punishment for being "bad" and the threat of rejection will intensify. Encourage them to talk about the baby, don't make judgments about their feelings, and let them know that this is a family event and not something from which they are excluded. Bring it up for discussion regularly, since children often forget things they don't want to hear. Even the child who is truly excited about the prospects of having a brother or sister will have moments of temporary regret. Children have many feelings about a newborn coming home and they may begin during the pregnancy. If your own child seems to be reacting, jump ahead to chapter 8 and read the section on "The Other Children at Home."

Arrangements for child care during labor should be made long before that day approaches. Making a thousand phone calls once labor begins will just raise anxiety at a time when attention should be directed exclusively to your wife and the baby on the way. When the labor does begin, getting the children neatly off to a neighbor's or to grandma's will undoubtedly be your job; so plan all contingencies far in advance. Once your wife gives birth it may be necessary for you to spend more time with your older children than at the hospital, a conflict which is both exhausting and frustrating. *Everyone* will need you then, and there is no way you can get completely around this. Enlist the help of good friends and family and make solid plans in advance. If you can remember that this is a temporary hassle, you will get through.

Some hospitals (very few as of this writing) allow husbands to room-in. If you have children at home who need your attention, it is less likely that you will be able to take this option. The concept of the whole family rooming-in is rarely mentioned, and even if it were feasible, would be enormously expensive, although it certainly is an innovative idea. We look forward to the future to see how it might work if the difficulties of implementation can be overcome.

If your baby is born at home, the family will be together, if not during birth, then shortly after. But most hospital doors, unfortunately, are closed to young children. If your wife goes in one day and is out the next, there is no real problem. But many women spend three days in the hospital, and if there is a complication or a Caesarean birth considerably longer. Children will miss their mother, worry about how she is, and feel anxious about the new baby. If your wife is feeling up to it, it would be very helpful for them to see that she is OK, that she still loves them, and to see, if only through a window, their new brother or sister. If your hospital allows this or closes its eyes to it, bring them in!

Those Other People in Your Life

FRIENDS

Expectant couples often find themselves restructuring some of their friendships. They find they gravitate toward people with young children or those who are also expectant parents. The reason for this is fairly apparent: The couples have one preoccupying interest in common. It is one thing to tell an acquaintance what you are experiencing, another to share feelings together. And you don't have to worry about boring other expectant couples; they never seem to get tired of discussing pregnancy and parenthood. And there is comfort in the support that comes of such talk. It shows you that you are not alone, that together you will all get through it safely and happily. These changing patterns in friendships usually continue after the birth.

It is often hard to anticipate how your old friends will respond to the news that you are going to have a baby. Friends with families usually seem very pleased and will offer their own past experiences. Sometimes you might get the feeling that your news gives them support in their own choices.

Friends without children will also usually express and feel pleasure for you. Often, however, it forces them to think about their own feelings about starting a family. Some may feel envious, wishing they were in a position to have a child. One man told us that an old friend became bitter when he was told about the pregnancy and said, "Everything always comes easy for you. You've really got it made." And many of your no-children friends will be excited about the opportunity to give some of their nurturing urges expression with your baby. They may not be ready for a child of their own but will be perfectly delighted to play with one whom they will be able to hand back to you.

Whatever the state of family relations, a couple often finds itself getting closer to parents and in-laws when it's expecting a child. Parents are notorious for burying the hatchet when they learn they are about to be made grandparents. It indicates to them a continuation of the family line. There are of course many exceptions, but it is not uncommon to find them more accepting now of your marriage and life-style, even if they originally and vehemently disapproved of them. And then, too, their own maternal and paternal feelings will coax them into offering support and assistance at a time they vaguely remember as stressful. It is often a warm time and one for family closeness.

Sometimes, however, the situation backfires. Just as pregnancy often signals to the expectant parents that they are no longer children, it may signal to the expectant grandparents that their children are no longer theirs. A mother may become jealous of her daughter-in-law for making her son a father and taking him out from under her protective mantle. One woman we spoke to said her mother-in-law became extremely hostile and competitive when she learned of the pregnancy. She continually reminded her son what a good mother and cook she was and insulted her daughter-in-law with comments about how unattractive she'd become, referring to her as "the cow." An expectant father might also have to contend with his in-laws' desire to take back their "little girl" and protect her. Her father might look at his son-in-law in a way he never did before and wonder about the man who "knocked up his daughter." One man told us, "My father-in-law was furious. It was as if he had to accept for the first time that I was actually screwing his daughter." The mother, too, may want her daughter back. She may be jealous of the pregnancy and want control of your life, once again trying to make her daughter her own, and by extension, making the unborn child hers too. If these conflicts start to show up, you and your wife are going to have to make some major decisions about how to deal with them and hold a solid front. Parents and in-laws may even have to be turned away if their input becomes too disruptive.

But many parents can also provide needed support during pregnancy. Your wife may turn more to her mother, feeling closer to her as she ponders her own impending motherhood. Many husbands are delighted with this new closeness. They see their wives as happier and feel relieved of the obligation to mother them. Other men feel angry or threatened because they sense (often accurately) their wives turning away from them and feel that the expectant grandmother is taking control of events and decisions that should appropriately be made by the expectant couple. If there was ever a time for couples to redefine their loyalties and work together, it may be now.

It is interesting to note that in our questionnaire, 40 percent of the men reported that their wives had more overall contact with their parents during than before the pregnancy. Eighteen percent said they were actually spending more time with them as compared to 10 percent who said they were spending less time.

Expectant fathers, too, turn to their mothers more during the pregnancy. A man may feel he needs more mothering for himself during this stressful period—a little extra stroking at a time when he may feel pressured to be constantly strong and responsible and "adult." One study found that expectant fathers telephoned and wrote letters to their families more during the pregnancy than before. Men felt more inclined to go home on Mother's Day and reported the reunions pleasurable, usually including the inevitable repertoire of stories about the man when he was a baby.[23]

Twenty-three percent of the men who responded to our questionnaire reported having more general contact with their parents than before the pregnancy. Seventeen percent said they were spending more actual time with them as compared to seven percent who said they saw their parents less frequently.

Just as the woman thinks more about her own mother as she ponders her own future as a mother, the expectant father will do the same kind of thinking about his father and his own paternal role. He may feel closer to him and more understanding or he may feel angry and resentful.

Whatever combination of patterns emerge in your relationship with your parents and in-laws, you and your wife will have to deal with them together. If parents become divisive, it is appropriate to put a stop to their intervention, and this can be difficult since relationships with parents are very complicated. Telling your wife, "You know what you can do with your parents," is not problem solving. Sensitivity and honest communication is more likely to help you to come out on top and united.

Changing Life-styles

As the pregnancy advances, most expectant couples notice that many of their familiar patterns of day-to-day living are changing, and they begin to shape a different life-style. There are many reasons for this. Your wife may lack the energy or even health to keep up her previous pace. In the later months she may find just getting around extremely difficult. Also, if budgeting is an issue, there will be less money available to spend on hobbies, meals out, and entertaining. And preparation for the baby is, in itself, time consuming, usually at the expense of other routine activities.

There are men who insist their life-styles will not change at all and continue at the usual pace, forcing their wives to share every activity with them as though nothing were different. In essence, these men are denying the reality of the pregnancy, and their behavior is just a way of saying "nothing has happened to change things."

It is interesting to note that 34 percent of the expectant fathers answering our questionnaire reported that they and their wives went out less often than before the pregnancy. Only 6 percent reported going out more frequently. These men responded similarly to the question about changes in the frequency they and their wives socialized. And three times as many men reported a decrease in social activities without their wives as those who reported an increase.

What other changes in life-style may occur? Many men report spending more hours at work, an understandable investment of energy considering the pressure about financial issues. More than one out of three men reported spending more time at home, usually doing household chores. Clearly there is less free time, less time for hobbies, and less time for the old ways of "playing."

These changes in life-style are a necessary part of the preparation for parenthood. If couples see them as a prelude to major transitions to come, they can begin the adjustment to becoming parents. Once the child is born, changes in life-style and in the couple's relationship will continue. Some men expect these changes and prepare for them, and as a result, their adjustment to parenthood is easier than those who romanticize the pregnancy and fatherhood and expect no change or only positive change.[24] These romantic expectations leave men unprepared for the realities of having a newborn at home, and their fathering experiences may be off to rocky starts.[25] [26]

In our own survey, 68 percent of the expectant fathers felt that the baby would bring them and their wives closer together while only 47 percent of the recent fathers said this had actually happened. One in three expectant fathers anticipated that the baby would create tension in their marriage. Apparently these men feel that tension need not obstruct closeness. Although only 15 percent of the expectant fathers thought the baby would reduce tension in their marriages, this was almost twice the number of recent fathers who reported that it actually had done so.

The stresses of pregnancy are followed by the demands and tensions of early parenting. The expectant father who can realistically assess what these new issues may be and prepare himself to work with his wife once their child is born will find those early months of fathering much more gratifying and less trying. The romantic expectant father who thinks the stresses of pregnancy will all end with the birth or who thinks nothing will ever be different may feel he has been hit by a lightning bolt in the third-month postpartum.

7
Labor and Birth

It won't be long before your wife will say to you, either on the telephone from somewhere that seems awfully far away or after a gentle nudge at three in the morning, "I think it's happening. Maybe we should call the doctor." Even if you are already a father, the news that a child is actually on its way will make you feel what it means to have sired a child: *your* image, *your* blood, *your* history.

Soon—one short reality moment later—you may be caught up in the phoning, the last minute packing or suitcase checking, or the tying up of loose ends. But before reality intervenes, let yourself experience the sensations. Try not to jump ahead to your planned itinerary for that important day: Instead, replay your wife's words and try to feel what they do to you personally, emotionally. Later, when the day of your child's birth has receded somewhat into the distance, you will want to recall these feelings; so tell yourself now and several times daily between now and the labor day that you will not rush into action for at least two or three minutes, that you will sit down where you are and feel and record those feelings.

A couple aware of the signs of approaching labor will not be so taken by surprise when the first strong contractions begin to happen. Some of the prelabor signals in the following list can precede actual labor by as much as four weeks, while others can come only hours or sometimes minutes before. Remember, these are only *possible* indications and may not even appear.

1. The baby and uterus "drop" as the fetal head positions itself in the pelvic cavity in preparation for delivery. This will be experienced as "lightening" (see chapter 4).
2. The presence of Braxton-Hicks, or practice, contractions which serve to efface and dilate the cervix slightly in late pregnancy. This prelabor process is often referred to as the "ripening" of the cervix. (These contractions can occur much earlier and are not a sign of imminent labor.)
3. There is increased vaginal discharge.
4. The fetus is less active than usual.
5. The mother may experience diarrhea or low backache or even a great spurt of energy.

Onset of Labor

The actual beginning of real labor may be difficult to determine, even for the experienced couple. The following are some of the signals that labor has really begun:

1. *Rupture of membranes or "bag of waters"* (really the amniotic sac). It is not clear what triggers the breaking of the amniotic sac, but it usually happens early in labor. Sometimes the fluid drips gently out through the vagina and may go unnoticed, or it can come with a gush. One woman was in the supermarket when her water broke for her first child, and it caused quite a stir and a lot of embarrassment at the checkout line. When she shopped for groceries late in her *second* pregnancy, she always made sure to put a jar of apple juice in her cart before anything else, so that if her membranes ruptured in the store, she would be able to drop the bottle of juice and say, "I'm so very clumsy. I'm sorry," and nobody would know the difference, she hoped!

Active contractions will usually begin within twenty-four hours following the rupturing of the sac. The only reason for concern is if the fluid is off-color or has a foul smell. This is an indication that the fetus has passed its first stool (*meconium*) in the amniotic fluid and may be under distress. Call the doctor immediately.

2. "*Bloody show*" (a blood-streaked mucousy vaginal discharge which can occur up to a week before actual labor begins). It is not an extremely reliable sign unless accompanied or followed momentarily by fairly strong uterine contractions and often happens after a postpelvic examination in the ninth month.

3. *Contractions of the uterus*. These may first be experienced as very mild menstruallike cramps or like an attack of gas or an intestinal upset. The expectant mother may also feel low back pain or pelvic pressure at this time.

The entire process of labor, you will recall from chapter 4, is divided into three stages. The first stage can be further divided into early, active, and transitional phases, each with its own recognizable characteristics. Remember, the entire first stage of labor is designed to thin out and dilate the cervix, which is the opening to the uterus, so the baby's head and body can be delivered through the vagina, or birth canal. You will need a stopwatch or a digital clock handy so that you can keep an accurate account of the labor's progress.

First Stage

EARLY LABOR

The contractions of the uterus are five to twenty minutes apart and last from forty-five to sixty seconds each. The cervix is dilated from zero to three centimeters or zero to one and one-half fingers. (The examining person uses the width of his/her fingers to estimate the amount of dilatation. Full dilatation is ten centimeters.)

ACTIVE LABOR

Contractions are more intense now; they come every two to five minutes for awhile and each lasts a minute or more. Then the contractions begin arriving at two-minute intervals and last for more than a minute but usually less than ninety seconds. In this portion of the first stage of labor the cervix is dilated three to four fingers, or six to eight centimeters.

TRANSITION

This is the end of the first stage of labor and the most intense period of all. Contractions come two minutes apart, last ninety seconds, and sometimes even ''double peak,'' or come back to back with no rest in between. This stage of labor can last as little as fifteen minutes or as long as ninety minutes. Transition will accomplish full cervical dilatation and force the baby downward. Even though it is the most difficult part of labor, there is comfort in knowing that it won't be long at all before the baby is born and the pain is over.

You will find the Labor Chart on pages 178–179 of great help, since it will allow you, with the aid of a watch or clock, to figure out where your wife is in the labor process.

Getting into Action

But let's get back to the very beginning of labor. When you think it is time to call the doctor, it may be preferable for your wife to speak since she can accurately describe what has been going on, and you don't have to keep saying, ''Wait a minute, doctor, and I'll ask her.'' The doctor will tell you both that it is either time to get to the hospital or that you don't have to rush off yet. Most couples who have had childbirth preparation classes or preparenting classes or home-birth training or who have simply read about labor and delivery will usually not even bother calling their doctors if the contractions are more than twenty minutes apart. They know that the first stage of labor has just begun and will wait for the contractions to be closer together (less than twenty minutes apart) before notifying the doctor that it's about time that he or she start out for the hospital too.

It is unfortunate that more couples don't take the opportunity during this early portion of labor to talk about what they are feeling. Most couples snap into preplanned action. It is not uncommon for the early laboring woman who is not yet experiencing uncomfortable contractions to get a rush of energy and dust and clean and even vacuum the house. Unless the couple has been planning a home birth (we will talk about that later), the time has come to check and recheck the contents of the suitcase which you may have packed days, often weeks, in advance.

Aside from your wife's clothing and personal things, here are a few other items an expectant father will want to include: some sort of lip balm or Chap Stick. During intense labor women breathe very rapidly through their mouths, and the constant rush of air in and out dries the lips. One of the things you may do between contractions in the active stages of labor is to reach over (if you plan to be in the labor room) and coat your wife's lips with this soothing stuff. Also throw a few flat lollipops into your pockets. They are great for dryness of the mouth. Although most hospitals provide ice chips to suck on, nurses and doctors will allow a lollipop, and the candies will probably be welcomed by your wife.

A pair of knee-length socks may also come in handy if stirrups are to be used during a hospital delivery (ask your doctor ahead of time if they will be). Obstetrical stirrups are large, multijointed stainless steel leg supports, and they are often ice-cold. If your wife's legs are uncomfortably chilled by this apparatus, pull out the socks and slip them on for her.

Here is a list of things whose value and use are self-explanatory:

- food for you (sandwich, nuts, fruit, etc.)
- contact-lens case if either of you wear them
- deck of cards
- something to read
- dimes for the telephone
- pen and pad for noting time of contractions

Four A.M. is a heck of a time to worry about an empty gas tank, so fill up the car two weeks before your due date and keep the tank filled until after the birth. If you plan to go to the hospital in a cab, make certain that you have the phone numbers of several taxi companies who will dispatch a car to your door within minutes, at whatever time of day.

One very important responsibility which the expectant father can assume at the onset of labor is to remind his wife that it would be wise for her to have a bowel movement if she can. It is not absolutely vital, but it may make her more comfortable later on. Near the end of labor there will be a great deal of pressure on the mother's rectum as the baby's head moves down the birth canal. An empty bowel will provide more room for the baby's descent and will also reduce the risk of an elimination on the labor bed. Not many women do, but the possibility exists. Your wife can request an enema if she hasn't had a bowel movement and if the hospital staff doesn't suggest or require one. If for one reason or another the doctor has failed to warn her against eating at this stage, the husband should do so, although a few ounces of fruit juice or cup of tea would be permissible. In fact, some herbal teas are believed to have a strengthening effect on the uterus and are recommended by herbalists for the entire prenatal period! Raspberry-leaf tea, available at most natural food stores, is high on the recommended list.

Many adventurous tales have been written about back-seat deliveries by taxi drivers, policemen, and firemen. This rarely happens anymore because of the huge volume of information now available to expectant couples. A couple who times contractions at five minutes will usually not wait at home until they start coming three minutes apart, and as a result there are fewer en-route deliveries.

Some people insist on cutting it close. One couple, expecting their first child early in August, rented a summer cottage in Massachusetts, assuming that when contractions started coming regularly every twenty minutes, they would have plenty of time to make the three-and-one-half-hour car trip to their New York City hospital. With a traffic jam here and a flat tire there, it was questionable as to whether the woman was going to have her child in the hospital elevator or in a delivery room. She was barely prepped and put into stirrups when the baby's head was delivered, followed two pushes later by the rest of its little body.

What might have happened had she said to her husband somewhere along the way, "You'd better stop this car because I think we're going to have the baby in the backseat"? And some babies do come surprisingly fast—there will be no way of your knowing. Remember, whatever your choice, hospital or home delivery, don't take unnecessary chances. Birthing babies is a natural function for human beings, but the process should never be taken lightly. Call your doctor even if you only have the faintest suspicion that labor has begun; let him/her tell you differently.

At the Hospital

All expectant couples, whether they are planning hospital or home deliveries, should fill out preregistration forms for hospital maternity care months in advance of the birth. When you arrive at the hospital your card will be pulled and you'll be a known commodity. Otherwise the delay could be intolerable.

If your wife goes into labor during the day, you will enter the hospital through the main doors and request that the information personnel call up to the maternity floor for an escort. If labor begins after nine or ten o'clock at night, you will normally enter through the emergency room, and make your request there for assistance.

In some hospitals the woman will be wheelchaired to the maternity floor while her husband is directed to the business or credit office to fill out registration forms. This separation will generally last about twenty to thirty minutes, and it is a good idea to bring all your insurance information along so nothing un-necessarily lengthens this time away from your wife.

While you've been filling out forms, your wife will be prep-ped—that is, she will be given a hospital gown, unless she is permitted to wear one of her own (she can request this if it is important to her), perhaps a full or partial (in the area between the vagina and the anus) pubic shave, and an enema, the last two are procedural in some hospitals but not in all. The practice of obstetrical shaving has come under some fire in the last several years. Some women don't seem to mind it, while a growing number feel that it is unnecessary and eventually uncomfortable when the new hair starts growing in, and many doctors agree that during childbirth unshaved women don't get or give infections any more easily than women who are shaved. An outspoken woman at a birthing conference in North Adams, Massachusetts, asked the guest speaker, a male obstetrician, if men with beards had to have their upper lips and chins shaved when they went to a dentist. This issue should be resolved months earlier with your doctor if it is an important concern.

When you arrive on the maternity floor you'll find your wife in her labor room. If labor is not yet intense, it is likely that the doctor will not have arrived. The people you'll see with her are nurses, or nurse-midwives if you are having a midwife-center delivery. These days men are not an uncommon sight on a maternity floor. Most nurses and doctors have not only grown used to having husbands around, many are all for it and have come to accept the positive influence a husband's presence can have upon the course of labor. Still, you may run into a nurse or doctor not yet convinced that the husband's place is alongside his wife, and you may feel their hostility. Try to confront the issues directly, don't get unnecessarily upset or angry, and the chances are good that you can come to some comfortable understanding.

Some obstetricians will reassure you throughout the prenatal period that she/he will accommodate your every wish on the day of the birth. Generally, you can trust your obstetrician, although one expectant father told us that when the team was actually in the delivery room, the doctor pointed a stern finger at him and said, "*You*—sit there!" This domineering attitude stems from certain doctors' beliefs that the delivery room is their territory and that expectant couples who make demands are invading *their* turf.

Obstetrician William H. Hazlett has written eloquently about this problem. The obstetrician, Hazlett says, came into his own when childbirth became more of a hospital than a home phenomenon. "The delivery room became his stamping ground, his arena, his domain—his territory. When on occasion he is faced with the threat of husand-invasion, he defends that territory from his very depths—from his instincts."[1]

This article, of course, was written in 1967, and things have certainly changed for the better since then. But some doctors and some obstetrical personnel, including nurses and anesthesiologists, are slow coming around.

It is not surprising that these doctors and nurses are protective of their roles. One need only glance at the dramatic reduction in maternal and infant mortality rates in this country since 1950 and realize that these medical practitioners have much of which to be proud. The maternal mortality rate is measured in terms of one maternal death for every one hundred thousand live births. So that when the statistics report that the maternal mortality rate of 1935 was 582.1, it means that for every one hundred thousand babies born, more than 582 mothers died as a result of causes directly or indirectly related to childbirth. In 1935, for instance, with that rate of 582.1, there were a total of 8,876 maternal deaths. In 1950, the rate was 83.3, or 2,960 maternal deaths. The rate has continued to decline annually with the exception of 1956/57 and 1962/63. In 1976, the rate was only 12.3. Only 390 women died in more than three million live births.[2] Infant or neonatal mortality in the first month of life is measured in terms of one infant death for every ten thousand live births. In 1950 the rate was 20.5; 1955, 19.1; 1960, 18.7;

1965, 17.7; 1970, 15.1; 1976, 10.9.³ In twenty-six years, then, the infant mortality rate was cut in half.

The procedures introduced into the labor and delivery rooms over these two and a half decades combined with the improved skills of the people using them are undoubtedly responsible for this unparalleled progress in saving lives. The medical profession is justly proud of these extraordinary advances. As Hazlett reminds us, ''We can now understand why so often the obstetrician vigorously opposes and so bitterly resents the woman's desire to give birth on her own. When she expresses her desire to give birth naturally, not only does she dare to invade the obstetrician's territory . . . but she in effect has the gall to shove the factitious hen off the nest.''⁴

The point that we are trying to make is that doctors and nurses are not the parents of the baby about to be born. The awareness and heightened consciousness of laboring parents can actually assist the professionals: Not only is a better-informed couple *not* a hindrance in the delivery room, but in fact their knowledge may have some real bearing on the success rate of modern obstetrics.

Doctors and hospital staff now accept the fact that the more relaxed the couple is, the easier the labor will be. Relaxation comes from many sources, and if a couple sees their preferences getting serious consideration and feels in control of the event they will undoubtedly feel more relaxed.

The following is a list of requests gathered from many couples. Some of them may be important to you, others not; some of them will be granted while others, perhaps many, will be refused. All of these requests should be discussed with your doctor and hospital staff and resolved well in advance of the birth. This list is also appropriate for couples planning a home birth who want to assure themselves of a homier hospital environment if that becomes necessary (only 14 percent of planned home births actually require hospital delivery).⁵

1. Use of the same room for labor, delivery, and recovery.
2. No chemical inducers to start labor.
3. No prep, unless desired. The same for an enema.

4. No routine rupture of amniotic sac.
5. No routine fetal heart monitor.
6. Taped music.
7. Permission for your wife to walk around during labor.
8. Permission for wife to wear her own clothes and to dress newborn with clothes provided by the couple.
9. Permission to use camera in labor room.
10. Permission to have your other children participate in the birth or for them to be able to visit mother during hospital stay.
11. Permission for father to "catch" baby and cut umbilical cord.
12. No sedatives or other drugs unless specifically requested or a medical necessity.
13. Permission for mother to use delivery position of her choice, rather than conventional stirrups and cuffs.
14. No routine episiotomy (incising of perineum).
15. Immediate rooming-in for mother, father, and baby. No separation unless specifically requested by parents.
16. Freedom to nurse the baby immediately.
17. If nursing, no supplemental feedings for baby if it spends time in the nursery—no formula, sugar water, or water.
18. Early discharge from hospital for mother and baby.
19. If the baby requires intensive care for any reason, the couple must be kept constantly informed of their baby's condition.
20. Delay cutting of umbilical cord until it stops pulsating.
21. No pitocin injection to stimulate delivery of placenta, unless medically necessary.
22. Early examination by pediatrician to allow for early discharge from hospital.
23. If Caesarean procedure is required, permission to be "awake" and to have husband in the operating room. Also, no separation from baby if there are no complications.

Some of these requests will be easy to grant, while others might not even be considered by some doctors because they in-

Effects of Agents Used for Pain Relief During Labor[6]

Agent or Technique	Optimal Dose	Therapeutic Effect	Maternal Side Effect	Fetal/Newborn Side Effect	Miscellaneous Information
Sedatives					
secobarbital (Seconal)	100 mg. IM, 50 mg. IV	sedation and sleep	vertigo, decreased perception of sensory stimuli, nausea and vomiting, decreased blood pressure	possible central nervous system (CNS) depression or apnea	may cause restlessness when used alone; may slow labor
pentobarbital (Nembutal)	100 mg. IM, PO, 50 mg. IV				
phenobarbital (Luminal)	100 mg. IV, PO				
Tranquilizers					
diazepam (Valium)	2, 5, or 10 mg. IV, IM, PO	lowered tension and apprehension levels	vertigo, drowsiness, decreased blood pressure	possible CNS depression	enhances analgesic drug action
hydroxyzine (Vistaril)	5–15 mg. IM, PO				
propiomazine (Largon)	20–40 mg. IM, PO				
promethazine (Phenergan)	25–50 mg. IM, PO				
promazine (Sparine)	25 mg. IM, PO				
Analgesics					
meperidine (Demerol)	50–100 mg. IM	increased pain threshhold	nausea and vomiting, mild respiratory and circulatory depression	possible CNS depression	not given when delivery imminent; used in combination with tranquilizers
morphine sulfate	8–15 mg. IM				
alphaprodine (Nisentil)	20–40 mg. IM, I.V.				
General Anesthetics					
trichloroethylene (Trilene)	0.5 percent	analgesia during 1st stage of labor; loss of consciousness in 2nd stage	possible aspiration or cyanosis	possible CNS depression or hypoxia	Trilene volatile; Trilene and Penthrane can be self-administered by hand-held mask
methoxyflurane (Penthrane)	0.3–0.5 percent				
nitrous oxide	40 percent				
cyclopropane	3–5 percent (inhalation)				
diethyl ether	2–5 percent				
halothane	0.5–1 percent				

			effects depend on mode of administration	effects depend on mode of administration
Local Anesthetics Procaine (Novocaine) Dibucaine (Nupercaine) Lidocaine (Xylocaine) Tetracaine (Pontocaine) Mepivacaine (Carbocaine) Chloroprocaine (Nesacaine) Bupivacaine (Marcaine)	concentration varies from 0.5–2 percent solutions	loss of sensation by blocking conduction of nerve impulses		
Types of Local Analgesics epidural block caudal block	5–15 ml. of 1.5, or 2 percent sol.	high degree of pain relief	mild hypotension* is frequent; loss of bearing down reflex in 2nd stage	none unless severe sustained maternal hypotension	may slow labor; epidural blocks pain at each stage of labor; caudal causes mild hypotension
paracervical block	5–10 ml. of 1 percent sol. bilaterally	temporary block of pain during labor	transient depression of contractions	occasional bradycardia	analgesia during labor, but no perineal* anesthesia
pudendal block	5–10 ml. of 1 percent sol. bilaterally	nerve block for 2nd stage of labor	loss of bearing down reflex	rarely any	does not relieve contraction pain, anesthetizes perineum
saddle block	1–1.5 ml., concentration depends on agent used	high degree of pain relief	occasionally, postspinal headache	rarely any	uncomfortable position while block administered; can be used only when delivery is imminent; excellent for delivery

*See Glossary for all starred items.

volve serious medical considerations. It is unlikely that many doctors will allow you to catch your baby as it is being delivered or even cut the cord, although we know of one doctor who turned to the expectant father sitting at the head of the delivery table and said, ''Well, we've got a couple minutes before this baby's going to be born. Why don't you scrub up and catch it on its way out?'' Some men, including this particular expectant father, are thrilled at the chance to be the first to touch their babies, and others are frightened that their incompetent hands might do some damage. But we're getting ahead of ourselves.

Labor and Drugs

Women differ widely in their feelings about the childbirth experience. There are women who would never even consider swallowing an aspirin to take the edge off the discomforts of labor, let alone during the pregnancy itself, and there are those who insist, ''I want to be put out—just put me out!'' Along with the tremendous strides made in obstetrics over the last twenty-five years there has been a concomitant increase in the number of pain-reducing drugs available to the laboring woman. A number of these provide an acceptable middle ground for women who may want some medication to ease discomfort but still want very much to be awake and alert for the occasion. We feel that the expectant couple should be able to exercise options when it comes to drugs in a nonemergency childbirth experience. The preceding chart is a complete list of all the pain-killing or pain-dulling drugs that will be available to you. They are listed by their generic names and their brand names are in parentheses beneath. There are several general categories: sedatives, tranquilizers, and analgesics, which can be given as oral (PO), intramuscular (IM), or intravenous (IV) injections; general anesthetic gases, which are administered with face masks; local anesthetics (injections similar to the shots you get at the dentist); and local analgesics, injected directly in the cervical and pelvic areas in small doses. Ask your doctor about them and their risks and side effects for mother and child.

To Be or Not To Be There

> Mary and Joseph were
> there, indicating this was
> Joseph's rightful place.[7]

Dr. William Hazlett has indicated that an expectant father's feelings of guilt play an influential role for him during his wife's labor.[8] His theory goes something like this: The man associates intercourse with feelings of both love and aggression and associates labor with pain. He is guilty about causing the pain his wife will endure in childbirth; he wants to get out of the situation but calms himself with the thought that he is leaving his wife in the expert hands of the obstetrician. As Hazlett sees it, the doctor helps the man atone for his guilt by assuring him of a safe and uneventful delivery: "The obstetrician fulfills a bizarre trinitarian promise—he atones for the guilt of the husband, becomes the saviour of women, and the giver of birth."[9]

When we discuss with expectant fathers what they expect of their doctors during labor and delivery, they often speak with awe of the powers of these physicians. Just as often, the wives of these same men, when asked what they expect from their obstetricians, answer, "Not much." Whether or not this corroborates Hazlett's theory is uncertain. The fact remains that men often express guilt about the pain their wives will suffer and fear that the experience will be crippling or even fatal. For similar reasons, some men make their decision to be part of the experience with their wives, while others fear that the pain and their own sense of impotence will be too difficult for them and choose the waiting game. Both are OK; neither is necessarily "right" or preferable.

If you're reading this book, there is still time for a change of mind—one way or the other. Many men wait until very late in the pregnancy before deciding for certain whether they will attend the labor and birth. The indecisive man may have passed up his opportunity to enroll in a prepared childbirth class, but that is no longer a prerequisite for attending the birth of his own child. Of course, the more a man knows about what is going on, the less fear and tension he will suffer, but many doctors agree that training is not an absolute necessity. An expectant father can partially make up what he would miss in a series of classes or by reading. And even if he has read little else but this book, he need not be anxious about the birthing day. Birth books are very recent, but men have been attending the births of their children for millions of years. "If both husband and wife are properly motivated, and the great majority are, with a very brief indoctrination the husband can give comfort, assurance and companionship to his wife and allay her fears during the first stage of labor, particularly when the doctor and nurse cannot be present."[10]

Although there is a great deal to be said for a man's presence at the birth of his children, he is just as much a father if he chooses to miss the event. His relationship with his wife and child, his place in the new family configuration, can be established immediately.

Some men stay with their wives during early labor, read with them, play cards, chat, and then leave when active labor approaches. Other men stay right through to the moment their wives are wheeled across the floor or down the hall from the labor room to the delivery room. And some men cannot feel comfortable with any of it. They bring their wives to the hospital, make sure they are safely delivered to the maternity floor, and then say good-bye. The man who chooses to take no part in labor and delivery can still be very much part of the pregnancy, and he can be right on the spot just minutes after the baby has been born to rejoin his family. In our research we have heard of no marriage suffering because the father chose not to participate in the labor and birth. Some women will choose a sister or friend to serve as labor partner when their husbands are not present, and if this is your situation you can be comfortable knowing that your wife has a familiar face to look at.

Expectant fathers in waiting rooms are usually treated with a great deal of consideration by the nurses on the floor who often serve as couriers between the parents-to-be. "She says she's doing just fine and wants to know how *you're* doing" is not an unfamiliar communication on labor day. The time is past when the chain-smoking expectant father was treated like an unwanted child.

If the due date arrives and the expectant father is still undecided about his participation in labor and birth, he might ask himself the following questions to help him make a final, realistic determination:[11]

- How have I reacted in the past when my wife was in stress or pain?
- Have my wife and I worked together well in the past, or do we tend to choose outside help for our problems?
- Do I truly want to be in there with her, or am I just trying to be like other men?
- Does my wife truly want me in there with her, or is she, too, yielding to some pressure?

If you can handle your wife's stress, if you've worked as a team before to solve emotional problems, if both of you have a strong inclination to share this experience, then you will do beautifully. If, on the other hand, it is debilitating for you to see your wife in pain, if the two of you have never really worked together supportively, or if you have both considered husband participation only because it has become fashionable, then the indication would be for you to wait in the wings. Ask to be notified immediately after the baby has been born so you can be with your family.

In the Labor Room

Whether you are in a conventional hospital labor room or one in a midwifery center, there will usually be one nurse attending you and your wife. The doctor generally does not arrive until labor has progressed considerably or unless she/he happens to be in the hospital with another case. If labor begins at night or in the early hours of the morning, the obstetrician will usually keep in touch by telephone to monitor the labor and to prescribe medication if it is requested. When the time approaches, she/he will be there.

The attending nurse, in the meantime, has active charge of the case. One of the things the nurse will do and which the doctor will do later in the labor is a series of pelvic, or internal, examinations to determine how far dilated the cervix is. This can be disconcerting for some couples, but it is necessary. Occasionally, in order to obtain additional information about labor's progress, these examinations are made during a painful contraction and are extremely uncomfortable. If a nurse or doctor seems to be choosing the wrong time to perform an internal, you or your wife should ask if the examination could not be postponed for a minute or two.

Besides performing pelvic exams, the attending nurse will usually be quite supportive, offering encouragement and advice for relaxation during and between contractions. The nurse may even offer to massage the laboring woman. In our survey of recent fathers, most felt that they were treated sensitively by the nurses and doctors during labor and delivery.

The Labor Chart will be extremely helpful to you in monitoring the labor. It will also give you some idea of what your wife may be experiencing and what you and she and the nurse can do to relieve her discomfort.

Labor Chart[12]

Phase of Labor	What Your Wife Might Feel	What You and Your Wife Can Do
Stage I		
A. Early phase 0–1½ fingers dilated or 0–3 cm.	Backache Diarrhea Abdominal cramps "Bloody show"* Ruptured membranes	Time contractions Call doctor Pelvic rock for backache Slow deep breathing Urinate every hour
Contractions: 45–60 seconds long; 5 minutes or more apart	Talkative or "hyper"	Conscious relaxation Get supplies ready

Phase of Labor	What Your Wife Might Feel	What You and Your Wife Can Do
B. Mid-phase 2–4 fingers dilated or 4–8 cm. Contractions: 60 seconds long; 2–5 minutes apart	Stronger, more frequent contractions More serious concentration Preoccupied Dependent on companionship Restlessness Back and/or leg pain	Deep chest breathing Effleurage* Ice chips Vary position of pillows and laboring woman Back rub during and between contractions
C. Transition 4–5 fingers dilated or 8–10 cm. Contractions: 60–90 seconds long; 2–3 minutes apart or back to back and double peak	Leg cramps and shaking Nausea and vomiting Heavy show Hot and perspiring "Sleeping" between contractions Total involvement and detachment Apprehension Increased pressure Desire to push	Breathing: pant, pant-blow, and blow Monitor technique rate and rhythm Use eye-to-eye contact Encourage her to stay in the present Massage thighs between contractions Make sure room is quiet Encourage comfortable positions No pushing until told to
Stage II Expulsion of baby Contractions: 45–90 seconds long; 2–5 minutes apart	Contractions may slow down Pressure on rectum and perineum* Total involvement Stretching sensation Feel head moving down Burning sensation as baby's head is presented (crowning*)	Encouragement for each contraction Relax perineal muscle Push down and forward Don't be afraid to push hard Provide physical support for your wife Stop pushing when head crowns and pant
Stage III Expulsion of placenta	Slight contraction	

*See Glossary for starred items.

Mechanism of Normal Labor

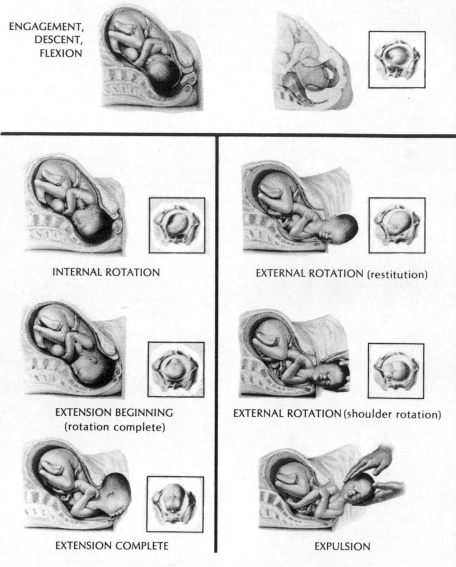

ENGAGEMENT, DESCENT, FLEXION

INTERNAL ROTATION

EXTERNAL ROTATION (restitution)

EXTENSION BEGINNING (rotation complete)

EXTERNAL ROTATION (shoulder rotation)

EXTENSION COMPLETE

EXPULSION

From Clinical Education Aid #13: "Mechanisms of Normal Labor," Ross Laboratories, Columbus, Ohio.

The Physiology of Normal Delivery

The doctor will almost always be on hand before labor reaches the difficult transition phase. The laboring woman will now experience the most intense contractions. They may come hard and fast, with barely a half-minute rest between them. And they will be different from the wavelike contractions of early labor. Early contractions, even difficult ones, are like ocean waves at the shore: They build to a peak, crest, and then subside. Contractions during transition sometimes double peak; that is, they build and build, and just when it appears they will begin to crest they peak again. It is during this phase of labor when a woman most needs support from her partner and from the entire birth team. And it is at this point when she may feel she can no longer carry on, when she may cry out for medication or even seem angry with you for being powerless to help her. She may wish at this time that she had requested a general anesthesia. She may even wish now that she had never carried the child.

It is vital that you assert the strength of your presence now. Don't be afraid to be forceful. She has hard work ahead, and she must keep her mind on it. Tell her, ''I *know* you can do this. You're doing beautifully. You've been in transition for a while now, soon you'll be able to push and then it will be easier.'' No matter how frequently the doctor and nurse may be saying the same sort of thing, *your* words will have special meaning. She will hear *your* voice when the doctor's is only a buzz. Above all, *your* voice, *your* touch will help to keep her relaxed.

Stroke her face gently, get her to relax her jaw, even during a contraction. Get her lower jaw to just hang open, keep her saying yes, yes, yes instead of a clenched-jawed no, no, no. Each yes should be a long, slow drawl: y–e–e–s–s–s.

Transition may last only fifteen minutes, but then again it may take more than an hour. This is your most important time; it will be extremely tough for you to see her in such discomfort, and you will become exhausted after what seems like hundreds of short back rubs, foot rubs, hand rubs, and face stroking and a constant exhorting that she remain brave and courageous. You will have to say and do the same things over and over again. Keep an eye on the clock, both for her morale and your own. Soon you can ask her or you will hear the doctor ask if she feels like "pushing." When she answers yes, you will know that it is *not* the time to push and she will be told not to. It is inadvisable for the woman to push at the first impulse without first being checked for full cervical dilatation. If the cervix is not completely dilated, the pushing will be wasted energy and may even cause swelling in the cervix which will interfere with the baby's descent.

Following a pelvic examination to determine full dilatation, the laboring woman will be wheeled across the floor or down the hall to the delivery room, where she will be transferred to a delivery table. In a midwife center and in some hospitals, the labor bed is also the delivery bed, and the woman is not moved.

In the delivery room, the husband is usually stationed at the head of the table and the doctor at the foot. A large light shines over the center of the table, and attached to it are angled mirrors so the mother and father can see the baby as it is born. When the baby's head is well into the lower birth canal (the vagina) and is ready to be delivered, the mother is told she may push. She will be instructed to bear down hard and push with each contraction. This is now the second or expulsion stage of labor. If you are watching in the mirror, you will see the first signs of the baby's head in the form of a small black coin which will disappear as each contraction ends. The baby is head down now and will emerge looking toward its mother's buttocks.

With each succeeding contraction, more and more of the top of the baby's head becomes visible, and finally there will be a contraction where the baby's head does not draw back. At this point, the head is said to have "crowned". The tissues of the vagina are greatly distended now, and the perineum is under tremendous stress if the woman is in the conventional on-her-back, or *lithotomy,* position, At this point you will probably be at your wife's head, providing comfort and support. Glancing into the mirror at this time will allow you to see the birth of your child. Some men choose not to watch, fearing that they will be uncomfortable at the sight of blood or put off (or turned on) by the bold perspective of their wives' genitals. At this time the doctor will, if she/he deems it necessary, make a simply lengthwise incision in the perineum. This minor procedure, known as an episiotomy (e-peez-ee-*ot*-omy), reduces the tension that the baby's bulging head has placed on the perineal muscles and eliminates the hazard of the uneven tearing of vaginal tissue. Nonlithotomy positions—the woman sitting up with the aid of a back wedge or squatting or even on all fours—allow gravity to assist in the delivery. There is debate as to whether these positions reduce the need for an episiotomy. Still, these are difficult positions to maintain on a conventional and narrow delivery table. Since many woman want to avoid the episiotomy, the expectant couple should take this issue up with their physician well in advance of the birth. In any event, the episiotomy is painless since the pressure created by the baby's head will naturally numb the perineum. When the baby has been born, the perineum will be given a local anesthetic, such as procain or lidocain (it is sometimes injected before the incision to make certain it takes effect before the stitching begins) so the incision can be stitched, or sutured, with minimal discomfort to the mother.

After the baby has crowned, another push or two will deliver its head which rotates from side to side as it is born. This early external rotation is called *restitution* and is followed after another contraction and a push or two by the shoulder rotation which allows for the rest of the baby to be born. This is called *expulsion*. Most men are amazed at how the baby seems to slide right out, almost by itself once the head has been delivered. One man remarked: ''The head took so damned long to make it, I thought 'to myself, for God's sake how long is the rest of him going to be? But I just had time to look up in the mirror and *bloop*, there he came, like a bull out of a rodeo chute.''

Once the baby is born, the first concern of most men is its sex. Although a majority of expectant fathers in our survey (51 percent) claimed they wanted sons (only 12 percent wanted girls and the others claimed no preference), rarely do their faces reveal disappointment in the delivery room. They all delight in the sound of their own baby crying, which happens almost immediately. The doctor then suctions out any mucus or blood from the baby's mouth which might interfere with its breathing. By no means should the doctor pick up the baby by its heels and hang it upside down. Although this has been common practice for many years, some doctors no longer do it since they feel that such an abrupt straightening of the baby's spine may be injurious.[13] And, as for the smack on the bottom to induce a first breath and a good strong cry, we feel that such an act is needlessly violent. As air is sucked into the baby's lungs for the first time, most will give out with a good vigorous cry all by themselves. If the child seems to have respiratory problems, the medical team will quickly get to work.

Once the baby is suctioned and breathing well, two plastic clamps are placed on the umbilicus, one about an inch or so from the navel and another one a couple inches from the first. It is wise—if the baby is not breathing—not to do this until the cord has ceased pulsating. So long as there is a throbbing in the cord, the baby is still receiving oxygen from blood in the umbilicus. The pulsing will last from one to four minutes; there should be no rush to cut, but to avoid confrontations, discuss this issue with your doctor in advance.

There is a lot to notice about a newborn. It is still covered with vernix. It will have streaks of blood and mucus on its body. Its head may be slightly and temporarily misshapen from a difficult passage through the mother's pelvis. When first born, it will be bluish in color, but it will become rosy and pink in a matter of moments. The baby can see but is unable to focus. It can hear, smell, feel. A human being.

Labor is not really completed when the baby is born. The placenta now must be delivered. The uterine contractions required to expel the placenta are still quite uncomfortable, and your wife will still need support. Of course, by this time she will be holding her baby, and the contractions may feel light-years away. The delivery of the placenta may take up to an hour, and unless there are indications of hemorrhage or some other emergency, a drug (pitocin) need not be administered to speed up this placental stage of labor. If the mother plans to nurse the infant immediately on the delivery table (arrangements for this should be made well in advance), the sucking triggers the release of the hormone oxytocin into the blood which in turn will stimulate contractions of sufficient strength to separate the placenta from the uterine wall and stop all bleeding. If a totally drug-free birth is important to you, discuss and resolve this concern with your obstetrician earlier in the pregnancy.

Most new parents, even those who resolved their prebirth fears on the subject, immediately want to know, ''Is my baby healthy?'' Obstetricians and attending nurses perform what is called an Apgar test on the newborn at one minute after birth and then again at five minutes. The test, named for anesthesiologist Virginia Apgar, looks at five vital signs: heart rate, respiratory rate, muscle tone, cry, color. Each is given a point score of zero to two, with two being the best. Here are the guidelines for scoring. The only thing you will not be able to judge yourself is the heartbeat; so *ask*. If the doctor does not offer the Apgar score for you to check against your own, ask for it.

Score	0	1	2
Heart rate	None	Under 100/min.	Over 100
Respiration	None	Slow, irregular	Strong
Muscle tone	None	Slight muscle tone	Vigorous motion
Cry	None	Weak cry	Vigorous cry
Color	Blue all over	Body pink, hands and feet blue	Pink all over

A total score of seven to ten (ten is maximum) is excellent, and the baby is considered to be in great condition. Usually, the five-minute score is higher than the one-minute score, and the entire Apgar will give both: A score of seven, nine, for example, means a one-minute score of seven and a five-minute score of nine.

Possible Complications During Childbirth

CAESAREAN PROCEDURE

There are only a few complications that can occur during childbirth and most are not considered serious. Few require more than some additional work for doctor and mother, while others can create the necessity for a Ceasarean procedure. *Caesarean section* is still the most popular term for this relatively simple surgical procedure, but some people have taken issue with it, saying that grapefruits and oranges have sections, and women have surgery.

It will be reassuring for you to know that it is a simple operation that lasts less than an hour, and the risks are extremely slight. Basically, here is what's done: A six-inch incision is made either vertically or horizontally in the mother's abdominal wall (below the navel), exposing the uterus. A similar incision is made in the uterine wall, and the baby and placenta are delivered simultaneously. The uterine wall is then sewn up and so is the abdominal wall. The incision techniques have become so perfected that the only sign of surgery is what is now called the "bikini-line scar."

If the baby's Apgar score is good and the woman has not been given general anesthesia, there is no reason why mother and child need to be separated at all. Some hospitals have even changed their policy to allow fathers to attend the Caesarean births of their children. Some women know before they enter the hospital that a Caesarean must be performed. For others, the decision is made during labor. In either case, husbands should think about whether they would like to participate. If so, the doctor and his/her hospital should be consulted for permission well in advance.

If the father is allowed to attend, he may be asked to read up on the procedure or take some sort of informal training. Remember, routine though Caesareans may be, they are still surgical procedures, and the last thing the operating-room staff needs is a person who requires more attention than the mother-to-be. Still, the strong desire of the expectant father to share the experience with his wife is almost as much training as he needs. If he is squeamish at the sight of blood (the uterus does bleed rather profusely for a few minutes following the incision), he does not have to look. He can position himself in such a manner that he is looking at his wife's face. The most important thing to the man who decides to attend is that he be a source of comfort for his wife and that he be with his family from the very first moments.

A woman undergoing an unplanned Caesarean and who chooses to be given nongeneral anesthesia will be wide awake and may feel very much abandoned when she enters the operating room and recognizes no one. The nurse who attended her during her earlier labor will not be there. Her husband will not be there. The only face she knows will be her doctor's. You and your wife should explore together your feelings and preferences about this.

Some doctors feel that although it is appropriate for husbands to attend Caesarean births, the operating-room nurses and anesthesiologists are still too uncomfortable to deal with non-medical observers during surgery. Some hospital personnel argue today, as they did twenty years ago, that husbands should not even be allowed to participate in normal vaginal deliveries: They're not trained: they'll get in the way; they'll become hysterical; they'll panic their wives; would we allow him to attend brain surgery we did on his wife? they will increase the likelihood of malpractice suits; what happens if the baby is deformed?

A few of these questions are valid and should be seriously considered by a doctor or hospital allowing a father to participate in a Caesarean birth. Some men would *not* do well. But most men highly motivated to attend will likely do extremely well. Certainly the research about the positive influence of the husband's presence in normal births is equally applicable for Caesarean births. If a woman's fears are calmed when she can keep her eyes on her husband, how could that be bad for the success of the procedure? This controversy will undoubtedly continue just as the demand for the husband's presence in the delivery room did. And if it is sufficiently important to enough expectant couples, the doctors and nurses and hospital administrators will have to listen. Some already have.

One final note about Caesareans. You may have heard the phrase, "Once a Caesarean, always a Caesarean." After a woman has had a Caesarean delivery, the scar tissue on the uterus is considerably weaker than the rest of that muscular organ. During labor, as we have already seen, the uterine muscles are under tremendous stress since the organ contracts continually for many hours. A rupture of the uterus during labor is almost always fatal to the fetus and extremely dangerous for the mother. If this risk is present, most doctors will not chance a vaginal delivery. A few women, however, are able to have normal deliveries after having undergone a Caesarean in a previous pregnancy—if the original indication for the Caesarean is no longer present and if there is no threat of uterine rupture. A prior Caesarean, however, is still a contraindication to home birth.

A woman who undergoes a Caesarean birth will usually be kept in the hospital for seven days. There is some pain associated with the healing of the abdominal incision, but medication is available to provide relief. Still, the mother can nurse her baby if and when she wants, unless the doctor feels that uninterrupted rest for a day or two is essential to her recovery. The stitches are removed in a week, and she is discharged if there are no further complications. Once home she will be required to rest for several weeks.

REASONS FOR CAESAREAN PROCEDURE

Cephalopelvic disproportion. This technical-sounding term, which simply means that the mother's pelvic cavity is too small to accommodate the passage of the baby's head, is the leading cause for Caesarean procedures. Early in the pregnancy, the obstetrician estimates the size of the mother's pelvis, and at term she/he estimates the size of the fetal head. If the disproportion is very large, a Caesarean may be scheduled. If the doctor is not certain that the disproportion would prevent a vaginal delivery, she/he will allow a trial labor to see if the baby's head, under pressure, can mold itself (it actually changes shape temporarily in most births as it passes through the bony pelvis) to the narrow passage and "dip" beneath the pelvic structure into the birth canal. If the baby's progress downward is obstructed, the doctor will order the Caesarean.

Placenta previa. This medical phrase means literally the placenta "going before." Normally, the placenta is attached quite high up on the interior wall of the uterus, but in rare cases it is much lower down and therefore closer to the cervix, which has the opening to the uterus. In these cases, the placenta may be covering all or part of the cervical canal. If the entire canal is blocked (central placenta previa), the baby will simply not be able to be delivered vaginally, and a Caesarean will be ordered.

If the placenta is attached in any way to the cervix, it will be torn a bit at a time from its place as the cervix begins to "ripen" (thin out and open) in the latter months of pregnancy. This can seriously threaten the fetus's supply of oxygen. Any bleeding, however painless, in the third trimester may be an indication of placenta previa, and the doctor will be on the lookout for bleeding during labor. But not all bleeding in late pregnancy is caused by this condition. As long as the obstetrician is aware of the possibilities, she/he will bring the woman successfully through her pregnancy. A Caesarean may be required, but not always.

Breech and other presentations. In more than 95 percent of all births, the baby is born in the head-down, or *vertex*, position. The remaining 5 percent come buttocks (breech) first, face up, or shoulder first. Nature has obviously provided the pear-shaped uterus to accommodate the vertex delivery, which is easiest for both mother and baby.

The breech presentation is somewhat trickier for the fetus, since the chances are greater in this position for the umbilical cord to situate itself beneath the breech. The baby sitting on the cord in this position may jeopardize its own oxygen supply.

There are several techniques for delivering the breech vaginally, and this usually depends on the mother's pelvis being sufficiently large to accommodate the fetal head which will not have the chance to mold itself as in a vertex position.

It is often impossible to tell if a baby is going to be breech. For one thing, the baby is always capable of movement in the final days of pregnancy, particularly among multiparous women. In primiparas, the fetus usually engages it head in the pelvis in the final month of pregnancy, and chances for its turning 180 degrees are slim. Still, this can and does happen. A woman in one of our groups carrying her first child had coincidentally scheduled her last prenatal appointment the day before her due date. After an internal her doctor informed her that the baby was breech. He even took an X ray to be certain. At home that night, he received a call from the maternity floor telling him that his patient had been admitted a few minutes earlier in active labor and that the baby was a vertex. The doctor begged to differ. The nurse stood firm: a vertex baby. "It can't be," said the doctor. But when he arrived at the hospital and performed an internal exam of his own, he found that the baby had indeed turned itself about. Never in all his years of practice had a breech baby righted itself in just twelve short hours!

It is not too uncommon, however, for a breech presentation to require Caesarean birth. This is usually due to the doctor's diagnosis of a possible fetopelvic disproportion.

FORCEPS DELIVERY

When assistance for a speedy delivery is required, forceps are the perfect tool. They consist of two separate steel blades which are inserted separately into the vagina and hinged together only when the baby's head is firmly held in place between them. Most obstetricians agree that a forceps delivery is made only when necessary, since the risk to the infant, although minimal, does increase. The baby so delivered will often have areas of discoloration where the forceps have grasped and sometimes will have dents, but as a rule these disappear soon after birth.

Either fetal or maternal symptoms may indicate the necessity for a forceps delivery. If the fetus is under distress (we will discuss fetal distress in a moment), the doctor will want it born as quickly as possible, and the skillful forceps delivery ensures a speedy birth. If, on the other hand, the mother is having great difficulty laboring (*dystocia*) and progress is extremely slow, a forceps delivery may also be performed. There is considerable controversy within the obstetrical community over the use of forceps, and not all doctors agree that there are certain symptoms that always indicate the need for such a delivery. All you need to be assured of in the delivery room when your doctor asks for the forceps is that they have been judiciously considered. If there are no signs of fetal distress and if in the opinion of you and your wife more time ought to be allowed for an uninterfered-with delivery, by all means make your feelings known. "Can we stall the forceps for a while, doctor?" might be a good way to begin a calm inquiry. If she/he says no, you are entitled to know why.

FETAL DISTRESS

When the baby's blood supply, and therefore its oxygen as well, has been interrupted for one or several reasons, the infant is said to be in distress. This is most usually due to compression of the umbilical cord which may happen in breech presentations (see pp. 189–190). The baby's heart rate is the best indication of how it is faring during labor. Its normal rate has a range from 120 to 160 beats per minute, with girls' heart rates usually at the upper end of the range. During labor your baby's heart rate should not vary more than ten beats up or down from its normal prenatal rate. If you are planning a home birth, you ought to know your baby's prenatal count so that you can monitor the beat during and after the birth.

There are four signs that the fetus is in distress during labor: (1) its heart rate does not return to normal at the end of the contraction; (2) the heart rate falls below 110 beats at any time; (3) the heart rate goes above 160 at any time; (4) or the amniotic fluid has a greenish tint to it or has an unpleasant odor. This last indicates that the fetus has relaxed its sphincters and passed some stool and is not in good shape. A vaginal infection may also cause an unpleasant odor, however. If the child is breech, the passage of meconium is fairly common and not necessarily a sign that the fetus is experiencing distress.[14] You can be certain that the obstetrical staff will be on top of things.

The mother will be given oxygen which almost immediately passes along to the fetus. Simultaneously she will be prepared for a forceps delivery so that the baby can be born as quickly as possible. If the baby's head is not yet visible in the vagina, a Caesarean procedure will be ordered if the doctor feels that any further waiting might be dangerous.

Fetal heart monitor. Since the fetal heart rate is such a prime indicator of distress, most hospitals in this country have begun to use a marvelous new piece of electronic equipment known as the fetal heart monitor. A corkscrew type electrode is inserted through the cervix into the skin of the fetus's scalp in utero or an electronic belt is strapped to the mother's belly, and a pulse tracing is electronically made on a piece of graph paper. The attending nurse or husband who watches these tracings will know when a contraction is coming before the laboring woman feels it, since the fetal heart rate begins to change before the first sensations of the contraction become apparent to the mother. If the fetus is in distress, a nurse trained to read the tracings will discover it immediately.

The fetal heart monitor is an expensive machine. For a while many hospitals would routinely put every laboring woman on the monitor, and then, of course, a controversy arose. Many couples felt this was a needless interference. If you have questions about it, it makes sense to ask if the monitor is an absolute necessity— won't a *fetascope* (an amplified stethescope) do just as well?

Home Birth

The information in the earlier sections of this chapter are as valuable for couples planning a home birth as it is for those having their babies in hospitals or midwife delivery centers. Simply because a child will be born away from the officialdom of hospital greens does not mean the need for understanding hospital procedure is not as great. In fact, most medical home-birth practitioners (doctors and midwives) agree that the couple planning a birth at home should be flexible until the very last minute, since something might arise which would warrant moving the couple from home to hospital. Fourteen percent of those couples planning home births wind up delivering their babies in hospitals, as we indicated earlier. Therefore, the responsible expectant couple will fill out preregistration forms in the event a hospital delivery becomes necessary, no matter how strongly they feel about having their birth at home. Making out official forms in the hospital business office at two in the morning, when either your wife or baby are in distress, will not only be frustrating, it will also prevent you from being with them. So before you make any other preparations, find a hospital whose policies you can tolerate, even file a list of demands if you wish, but fill out those preregistration forms so you will not be just another off-the-street emergency case if you happen to be among the disappointed 14 percent.

When your wife begins prenatal care, the obstetrician will take a detailed personal and family medical history. Questions about previous pregnancies, whether or not she smokes and how much, previous obstetrical or gynecological problems, her approach to nutrition, will all be vital information to help the doctor and midwife decide if your wife is a good risk for a home delivery. (A complete list of contraindications for childbirth at home is provided in Appendix C.)

Home birth is still a controversial topic, and there is a great likelihood that you will meet with resistance from friends and family—among them, surprisingly, people from whom you might have expected support. One expectant father reported that when he told his brother-in-law about his plans to have the baby at home, the man snapped back, ''I'd sooner have my appendix taken out at home.''

Whatever the negative comments you hear, they may be easier for you to accept if you know that most of them are spurred by fear for the well-being of your wife and baby. Once you've reached the decision to have a home birth, make a list of people who would never understand and probably wouldn't even be able to discuss the subject with you rationally. Future grandparents are often the most resistant to the idea of home birth. If you can expect nothing but grief from either your parents or your in-laws, just don't bring up the topic. Some couples choose not to tell their parents at all. On the other hand, if you feel your parents might be worried but could handle the news without becoming obnoxious and intrusive, sharing the decision with them might well enrich the whole experience. Watching people come around during the course of the pregnancy is gratifying. The angry and frightened brother-in-law who quipped about the appendectomy later provided a number of the necessary home-birth supplies from the hospital where he worked.

One of the most satisfying features of preparing for a home delivery is the wonderful sense everyone present has of contributing to the success of the event. The expectant couple not only experiences all the feelings that other couples do around the issue of preparing the baby's room, they have the responsibility to provide all of the supplies and materials necessary for labor and delivery. Of course, the doctor comes with a stethoscope and other vital equipment, but the couple is in charge of setting up the delivery room and preparing for all contingencies.

Here is a list of all supplies needed. Check with your doctor and midwife to see if they have anything to add or remove, and then start gathering the items. The knowledge that everything is in place weeks before the due date will make you feel secure, responsible, and proud.

SUPPLIES FOR CHILDBIRTH AT HOME

Supplies for Mother and Delivery
(Check each box as the item is procured.)

☐ 1. A firm bed, perhaps with a sheet of plywood beneath the mattress

☐ 2. A plastic mattress cover or inexpensive shower curtain to protect mattress

☐ 3. Plastic-lined trash receptacle and a supply of plastic leak-proof bags (eighteen-quart size, for postbirth cleanup)

☐ 4. Accurate clock with a second hand for timing contractions and length of labor

☐ 5. Large metal bowl for placenta

☐ 6. Flashlight and candles in the event of power failure

☐ 7. Two dozen four-by-four-inch gauze pads

☐ 8. One bottle zepharine chloride (dilution 1:750) (an antiseptic for sterilizing instruments)

☐ 9. Fleets enema

☐ 10. Chux bed pads (Sears's or Ward's underpads are less expensive but must be ordered from the catalogs. Allow two weeks for delivery.)

☐ 11. Four-ounce ear syringe for suctioning the baby

☐ 12. Scissors

☐ 13. White shoelaces (preboiled and stored in plastic bag) for tying off umbilical cord

☐ 14. Two maps to your house—one for the doctor, one for the nurse-midwife

☐ 15. A place for the doctor and midwife to sit or lie down for rest

☐ 16. Clean towels and washcloths

☐ 17. Sanitary belt

☐ 18. Four dozen hospital-sized sanitary napkins

☐ 19. Clean gown or pajamas

☐ 20. Bendable straw for sipping drinks

Supplies Needed for the Infant

☐ 1. One or two old receiving blankets

☐ 2. Diapers, diaper pins

☐ 3. Shirt and gown or kimono to dress baby

☐ 4. Clean blankets

☐ 5. Rectal thermometer

☐ 6. Cotton balls

☐ 7. Rubbing alcohol
☐ 8. Scale (bathroom scale will suffice)
☐ 9. Tape measure to measure baby's length
☐ 10. Clean towels and washcloths
☐ 11. Bed or cradle for baby

THE BACKUP PLAN

The great majority of home births go beautifully. But there is still that unquestionable 14 percent. Of these 14 percent only a small number require hospital deliveries due to serious medical emergencies. The rest wind up in the hospital for much less dire reasons. But whether there is a severe emergency (such as maternal and/or fetal distress) or a presentation that the birth team feels could be handled best in the hospital, a backup plan is a must, for only when emergency help is available can a home delivery be considered really safe. One man boastfully reported to us that when his wife went into labor he ran two miles to a pay phone to call the midwife. He had neither phone or car available to him. We don't consider this responsible preparation for home birth. If you find it impossible to arrange for a smooth backup plan, you probably ought to reconsider your decision to have a home birth. (A complete list of medical emergencies and first aid is provided in Appendix D.)

Basically, there are three types of backup plans to transfer the laboring woman to a hospital:[16] (1) the nonemergency situation, when birth is some time off; (2) transfer during active labor; or (3) transfer in a crisis situation. Whatever the conditions under which the transfer is made from home to hospital, here is how to establish your backup:

1. Transportation. If you plan to use your own car in an emergency, make certain you have a full tank of gasoline. Since you will want to be with your wife (she'll be in the back seat), arrange for a friend or the doctor to drive. Have blankets in the car. Make plans for carrying your wife to the car and rehearse the procedure. Do you have a stretcher or a wheelchair in case you're alone? If not, a board covered with a blanket will serve as a stretcher, as will a small table. If carrying becomes necessary, you will need at least two people.

If you do not have a car and an emergency arises before the doctor or midwife arrive on the scene, you will need an ambulance. If there is no ambulance service in your area, perhaps there is a local rescue squad. There will always be a police or fire department, even if you live in a small town. Arrange for their help in advance. Telephone them as soon as labor begins, and if you (in all likelihood) wind up not using their services, notify them later in the day of the successful birth. Make certain beforehand that they will drive you to the hospital of your choice, not just the nearest emergency room—unless, of course, the nearest emergency room is the wisest place to be. Make or secure maps to all hospitals for drivers.

2. Birth teamwork. Some home-birth teams consist of just a doctor, a nurse-midwife, and the parents-to-be. But a great many couples choose a few of their closest friends or family to share the experience with them—either in the birth room or waiting somehere in the house or apartment, looking after the other children, perhaps preparing food, or just being on hand. All things considered (including the loss of some privacy), it is probably a wise practice to have several people around. If an emergency develops, each person becomes a member of the birth team and can carry out previously assigned tasks. The team should be called together in the weeks preceding the due date if at all possible to rehearse emergency procedures. Who will:

- call the doctor, hospital, emergency transport, and be able to provide specific, cool-headed, and accurate information about the emergency?
- carry the laboring woman to the car?
- carry the newborn to the car if it is in distress and needs hospital care?
- drive the car?
- care for the mother on the trip to the hospital?
- attend to the newborn on the trip to the hospital?
- take care of other children or pets at home?

The phone numbers of the following people and services should be posted by the telephone at least two weeks before the due date:

- all birth team members
- your doctor: home phone, office, and hospital numbers
- your doctor's backup: home, office, and hospital numbers
- the hospital of your choice
- the nearest hospital if different from the one of your choice
- police, fire, rescue departments in your area
- two or three cab companies (in case one doesn't respond immediately)
- two or three ambulance services (for the same reason)
- two or three additional friends to back up birth teammates

If we seem to be unduly stressing small details or appear to harp on the possibilities of complications and/or medical emergencies, it is not for the purpose of dissuading anyone from making a choice for childbirth at home. Maternal and infant mortality rates have been drastically reduced because hospitals have been able to plan for just about every medical probability and handle each with speed and efficiency. Couples who choose to have their children born at home do so because they are convinced that a child born in a noninterfering atmosphere is the child born as nature intended it to be. But nature can be cruel, as well as beautiful, so why take unnecessary chances?

Also, couples who opt for home birth do so for the comfort and relaxation they will experience on their own territory, with no "professionals" shoving or ordering them about. But how relaxed or comfortable can a couple be if there are still crucial matters to handle when labor begins? When it comes to preparation for a home delivery, you simply cannot overdo.

And then, it won't be long before your wife will say to you, either over the telephone or after a gentle nudge at three in the morning, "I think it's happening. Let's start making the calls."

8
Early Fathering

> My boy came out like a blue
> onyx Buddha; and as I watched
> him put his peaceful eyes upon
> the world, his wrinkled skin
> turned pink, and for the life
> of me I knew at last why Buddha
> was said to have been born in
> the unfolding of a rose.
>
> Mr. B., a new father

Seeing a child born is a powerful experience; few men take it casually. Some cry unashamedly with joy. Others laugh aloud. Still others find themselves holding their breath in amazement. Some feel the need to touch their babies immediately, while others trust the first contact to their wives or nurses. Men who are normally loud, even boisterous types, find themselves strangely hushed by the baby's arrival, and often soft-spoken men take the opportunity of this wondrous occasion to show their more dramatic and vocal sides.

There is no way to predict how you will respond, nor should you feel that a certain kind of response is superior, more *feeling*, more *appropriate* than another. The reaction you have will be the appropriate one for you. And it is likely that your feelings at the time will be complex, even contradictory. This is perfectly natural. On the one hand you will experience overwhelming joy; on the other, the nagging reminder that life will be different now, that things have changed.

Do not be alarmed at the things you feel which may take you far beyond the ''ordinary'' emotions of pleasure and happiness. One new father held his newborn son in his arms and stared into his eyes for an hour, he told us. He wept quietly for almost the entire time, explaining:

> I loved him right away, as though I'd been waiting for him all my life. But when I held him and looked into his eyes as deeply as he seemed to be looking into mine, I imagined him growing and then he was fully grown, and I was so old and afraid that the time had passed without my having done anything but love my boy. In those minutes, I saw time become an old man in a rowboat, pulling very, very slowly at the oars, receding further and further toward the horizon. And when he reached the horizon, when he was just a little dot far away, then I was so old I died.

Many men mark the beginning of their own history with the birth of their first children, and though to many men a child symbolizes the potential for immortality, the occasion of the birth may also put them in touch with the reality of aging. They have, after all, seen their own parents age.

The possible reactions to childbirth are limitless, and yet some are quite predictable and most new fathers experience them. Whether or not a man attended the birth of his child, once it is born, once he has the news of it, he will be split several ways: He will want to be in the nursery with the baby, in the recovery room with his wife, and on the telephone announcing his fatherhood to the world, all at the same moment. Depending upon hospital procedure, he can probably manage some of each within a short time. If it is hospital procedure (and OK with you) for the baby to be brought to the nursery while the new mother is in the recovery room, you may be able to get to the telephone and make the most pressing calls before you will be allowed to see the baby or even perhaps your wife.

As with almost everything else related to labor and birth, you will be most comfortable if arrangements have been worked out in advance. Some couples insist that they do not need or want a recovery room. Many women wish to nurse their newborns immediately and plan for rooming-in. Other women feel they have just performed a great amount of work and want to be relieved of all additional responsibilities for a while.

As you must have gathered by now, hospital procedure is often hard and fast; if it is to bend to meet the specific needs of a couple, it must have advance notice. Don't wait until the labor day to insist on the things that are important to you.

There is no way we can offer here how the "average" hospital handles the postpartum experience. Each hospital works differently. If you are enrolled in a childbirth preparation class or some other preparenting course, you may be taken on a tour of the hospital where your baby will be born. There, firsthand, you will be told how things are managed. It is an extremely valuable experience, and if it is not part of your course try to arrange a trip for yourself. And even if you choose not to attend all the meetings in a series of classes, you can usually make arrangements with the instructor to join the group on the tour. It may cost you a few dollars, but it will be worth it. Otherwise, everything will come as a complete surprise on the day of your child's birth.

At one hospital in the Berkshire Mountains in Massachusetts, the postpartum procedure (at the time of this writing) is as follows; it may be similar to how *your* hospital does things.

Following the cutting of the cord and the suctioning of the newborn, the mother's episiotomy is sutured while the baby is swaddled and put under a warming light. (Some couples take exception to this practice, claiming that when the baby is laid on its mother's belly, the body heat is more than sufficient to keep the baby's temperature stable.) The father (if he is present) is permitted to hold the baby if he chooses. And the mother may hold and nurse her infant while the episiotomy is being stitched (if that procedure has been performed) or while the birth team is still waiting for the placenta to be delivered. If the placenta is late in coming, the doctor may order an injection of pitocin which causes the uterus to contract forcefully. These contractions serve to expel the placenta and seal off blood vessels which had been attached to it during the pregnancy. (Here again, some couples may take exception if they think the doctor has not allowed enough time for the placenta to be naturally expelled, but this practice should also be discussed prior to the birth.)

Once the placenta has been delivered and the episiotomy has been sutured, the baby is taken to the nursery (unless the mother wants it to remain with her) and the new parents are escorted to a previously assigned room. This room will be the mother's for the duration of her hospital stay (usually three to four days). If the couple has arranged for a private room, the father can remain as long as he wishes. But if the new mother is in a semiprivate room (sometimes this implies three to five other mothers!) or on a small ward and her roommates are sleeping, the nurses will generally ask the father to leave within an hour or so. Your wife's roommates might not care how long you stay; so if there are no complaints about a noisy new father keeping someone awake who wants to sleep, the couple will be allowed to remain together for quite some time. The hospital we are describing is a fairly liberal place. Yours may have stricter regulations.

By and by, though, your wife *will* want to sleep—she has just been through the hardest physical work she will ever do—and you will probably need a few hours of rest yourself. If time permits, this may be the occasion to make the phone calls you couldn't get to earlier. Or you may wish to sit beside your sleeping baby if she/he is in the room with you. Or you might just want to hold the child in your arms and rock or sing or talk quietly. If she/he's in the nursery, you may take the opportunity now to walk down the hall and watch your infant sleep or squawk or whatever it happens to be doing at the time. A sensitive nurse who sees you mooning about may, if you're lucky, wave to you conspiratorially and ask if you want to hold the child ''as long as there seems to be nobody else around.''

The Newborn

Within twenty-four hours postpartum, a pediatrician (one you have selected in advance) will check the baby. Here are some of the things she/he will be looking for. You may use the items listed below as the basis for some intelligent questions. *Always* insist on having *all* available information about your baby; it is your right to know.

1. There should be no difficulty in breathing. Air passage-ways should be free of mucus. The baby will usually be put down on its belly or on its side so that mucus will not drain back into the lungs. If you think the child is having difficulty breathing, call someone immediately.
2. The baby should be alert, and its color should be good; pink for white babies and red or dusky color for darker skinned infants.
3. There should be no redness or apparent irritation around or in the eyes.
4. The baby's head will be checked for excessive molding as a result of the birth process, or for other abnormalities. The *fontanels*, or "soft spots," of the skull will be checked for inflammation or swelling or for concavity.
5. The baby's ears will be checked to make certain the canals are clear and well-formed.
6. Genitalia will be examined: The girl will be checked for clitoris, labia, and opening in the vagina; the boy's testes and penis will be looked at.
7. The doctor will check the baby's anus to see if it is per-forate (if it has the proper opening).
8. The spine will be checked for dimples and creases.
9. The legs will be checked for symmetry: Are the knees in the same place on both legs and are the ankle creases symmetrical?
10. The baby's reflexes will be checked: the palms of the hands and soles of the feet will be stroked and reflexes checked; and the rooting reflex (the reflex which makes the baby turn his/her face in the direction of a touch) is tested by stroking the infant's cheek on the side. If your wife plans to nurse, the breast-feeding routine should be started as

soon after birth as possible, since the baby soon "forgets" how to "root."

11. Toes and fingers will be counted.
12. The roof of the baby's mouth will be checked for a cleft palate.
13. The baby's hips will be rotated to see if they are securely hinged.
14. Hands and feet will be checked for any swelling (edema).

There are several other things to be on the lookout for in the days following the birth. Since these are done procedurally in the hospital, they will be largely the responsibility of parents who are not in the hospital either because they requested an early discharge (often only hours following the birth) or because the child was born at home.

1. The baby must be kept warm for at least two full days. Receiving blankets can be oven warmed and should be changed regularly.
2. The baby will usually urinate within twelve hours following birth. And within twenty-four hours it will pass its first stool, *meconium*. This is a greenish black, extremely sticky substance which collected in the baby's intestine in utero. It consists largely of waste materials (like hair, skin, and other matter) which is normally suspended in the amniotic fluid. Try not to allow meconium to get on anything valuable since it can rarely be washed out. If the meconium is not passed within twenty-four hours (this is of special concern for home births) or if it is streaked with pink or red (a sign of blood in the stool), notify a pediatrician immediately.
3. Anything that does not appear right to you should be reported instantly. Better to be embarrassed over a false alarm than be regretful later over having failed to act quickly enough when time was of the essence.

The First Three Months Postpartum

There is only one fast rule for learning to live with a baby in your house for the first time: *Be prepared to be unprepared*. One of the principal causes for fathers having kept their distance from the day-to-day routines of child care was their sense of ineptitude. This may have derived from a variety of sources which we will discuss shortly, but chief among the reasons was the extremely low tolerance for frustration most new parents experience. They may have practiced how to bathe or diaper or feed a baby for weeks, and then found the baby unappreciative when the time came to put these skills to use. Instead of feeling satisfied that it has been changed into a dry diaper, the child screams, and the father feels that he has done something wrong. He shouldn't; this is the baby's reaction to things—unexpected things in particular—being done.

In the first week at home with baby, life will be in turmoil for almost everyone. It is vital that the new mother rest for at least a week. Over and over again we have heard reports of women who returned home from the hospital claiming they never felt better. They resumed their old routines with astounding vigor, only to find themselves exhausted and depressed a week or two later. However difficult things may become for the new father, the mother should not be obliged or allowed to do physical work for at least a week.

A new father ought to consider taking time off from work: at least a week and perhaps as much as a month or more. Time off can occasionally be negotiated if it is asked for in advance, but for some men it is impossible to get any time away from work. The Swedish government has been experimenting with paid paternity leaves and men appear satisfied with the arrangement. There may be American companies that offer such benefits to their employees, but they are certainly a rare few.

New fathers are almost always put in the somewhat compromising position of having to use some or all of their vacation time when the newborn arrives. The first six months of child rearing are exhausting, and when the working father needs it most, his vacation may still be a year away. This constant contact with the baby and attending to its needs is frustrating to all parents and may be the cause of enormous stress in the marriage relationship, which we will discuss shortly.

GETTING HELP

The mother's need for rest and recovery following the birth of her child is not by any means limited to a single week. She must resume her physical routines gradually until her strength has completely returned to her. And this may take up to a month and often more if there were complications during childbirth. The woman who had a Caesarean birth will require two weeks of complete bed rest and then several additional weeks before she is truly back in shape.

During this time, the duties of running a household fall on the shoulders of the father and/or another relative or a housekeeper, if you have decided to engage one. If there are other children at home, particularly if they are still quite young (under six, say), the constant flurry of activity, while exhilirating at first, will prove exhausting before long. Help is very much needed when a newborn is brought home. The people who come to help should be carefully selected by the couple with the idea that they will indeed make life easier and not more tense. In our culture, it is usually the "womenfolk" in the immediate family who make themselves available to help out. The new father's mother, his mother-in-law, his sister(s) or sister(s)-in-law, or his wife's best friend(s) are almost always on hand. And if none of these women are available—if they live too far away, for example—a couple can always and perhaps would prefer to hire a nurse (who is also likely to be a woman).

The point here, of course, is not to disparage the idea of getting female help (it would be nice to see more men as nurses or housekeepers), but to caution the father about his low threshold for his own frustration. In the presence of women more experienced than he, it is quite likely that he will give up, not only some of his chores, but much of his hands-on involvement as well. Some women will benevolently shoo him aside, while others may feel and act as though he really has no place in the care of his infant. In either case, he may be excluded from the action at just the moment he needs to be invested in it and never even know what is really happening. Experienced child rearers with apparent impunity can chase off even the father who wishes to nurture. Even your wife may have to deal with a preemptive helping hand.

Stay involved. This is your time. Your parents and your in-laws have had theirs already; now they must defer to *you*, particularly in the first days and weeks of the baby's arrival home. You will have to remember that men are often swept aside. If you don't want to be bullied or shooed or patronized, you are going to have to take a stand: Your baby is going to be handled and raised as you and your wife see fit, not according to someone else's rules. If the grandmother of a nursing infant decides the baby needs a bottle of water while the new mother is napping, you will have to object if you feel the bottle is unnecessary: "The baby doesn't really need water, mom. Why don't you sing her that little song you said you sang for me when I was a baby."

The grandmother who has not first asked if it would be all right to supplement the baby's diet is the grandmother who is almost certain to be offended when asked to lay off. Grandparents rarely act out of malice, to be sure, but the birth of a grandchild will often trigger anxiety known as the empty-nest syndrome which forces parents to accept that their children are adults and are doing well on their own. A grandchild may seem a convenient outlet for reasserting parental control. A compassionate way of countering the isolation and loneliness grandparents may be experiencing is to give them a sense of importance when it comes to their new grandchildren. Still, it is vital that you maintain the level of control *desirable for you and your wife*.

Confrontations with grandmothers or nurses or sisters or aunts (you rarely find men intervening in child care) can be handled judiciously and can often produce results that are pleasing to all concerned. Screaming at your mother and then ordering her from your home simply because she has her own method of fastening diaper pins, however much you may feel like doing that from time to time, is not exactly diplomatic or effective communication.

You:	(sitting beside grandmother) That's a very interesting way you have of fastening those safety pins.
Grandma:	It's the best way to do it.
You:	Here's the way Eva and I have learned to do it. (You undo and then redo the pins.)
Grandma:	I would never do it that way. Nowadays everybody thinks they know what's best. If I did such a bad job of diapering, how come you turned out so well?
You:	You did a great job, and I tell everybody that you did. Only I like *this* method.
Grandma:	Do you think my way is going to hurt the baby?
You:	No.
Grandma:	Then why don't you let me do it my way when I'm diapering and you can do it your way when you are?

While you may have sat down with the intention of winning a point, the actual result of this dialogue was a compromise. New fathers can also be quite domineering, particularly if they are leery of preemptive grandparents. When your mother or mother-in-law or nurse or whomever rejects your approach as meaningless and perhaps even ridiculous, you will have to confront the issue. You may discover that you *do have* an impractical approach to certain child-care tasks, and you might in fact stand some instruction from relatives. But nobody likes to be treated as inept or foolish. If a nurse says to you, ''Look, you don't have the sense you were born with when it comes to bathing that baby,'' then a quick, effective corrective step should be taken. "*You* look, nurse. It may be that you know a great deal more about this subject than I do, but I'd appreciate a more thoughtful and helpful attitude.''

When experienced child-care people instruct a new father in child-care skills, they can do so in a way that makes him feel involved or feel like a fool and, therefore, excluded. Even new mothers can be patronizing, making little or no effort to hide their dislike of the way their husbands handle the baby. This may be due to: (1) a high level of competitiveness which has always existed in the relationship, (2) the woman's deep conviction that men are truly clumsy and therefore useless around babies, (3) a belief that children should be a woman's responsibility and men should take other roles, or (4) a neurotic need to have the child to herself.

Men must be given room to experiment and trusted to find unique methods for traditional tasks. If father, for instance, has the chore of bathing the baby, his wife's nervousness that he will bungle the job will only serve to reinforce the man's stereotype as the inept paternal caretaker. Men are generally less skilled at small-motor activities (the kind of work that involves small muscles of the fingers and hands) than women are, probably because of the different training boys and girls are offered in their formative years. As a result, new fathers feel less adept at fastening safety pins, cleaning the creases of baby's neck or anal-genital areas or ears, or cutting baby's fingernails than their wives, who may be just as inexperienced. A woman who stands tensely over her husband as he attempts one of these tasks will only make him more nervous and more convinced that he's simply not cut out to do these chores. The next step may be removing himself, not only from the chore, but from the baby too. "Call me when he's ready for college" is not an uncommon quip new fathers make in frustration, however seriously they mean it.

Some men are very competitive. They are determined to be the better parent, often boasting about their skill and putting down their wives', causing their wives to feel pushed aside. One study found that competitive behavior was most intense in men whose wives were having a lot of difficulty adjusting to parenthood.[1] Some women praised their husbands' skills and felt inadequate in comparison. Other women found the competition irritating.[2] But we are talking about competitive behavior, not sharing. And a man with competent skills who doesn't flaunt them or use them as a point of comparison can be a great comfort to a woman who is struggling to readjust after the birth.

Adapting to the Newborn

Through close contact parent and child become attached to one another, or *bonded*. When a father removes himself from his child, there is a great risk that they will never bond as closely as is possible. A huge quantity of literature is available on the phenomenon of mother-child bonding, but recently the subject of how a father and infant bond together has been given thoughtful treatment. The man who gazed into the eyes of his newborn son for an hour had seriously begun the bonding process. On the other hand, the man who is ready to turn his baby over to the nearest "expert" is forestalling this intimate exchange of feelings and images. Some parents never even adapt to the idea of having children, some simply cannot grow close to them and the results are quite often tragic. The list that follows was established from observation of women with newborns for the purpose of assessing a mother's ability to adapt to her infant.[3] We feel these same criteria can be applied to fathers as well.

SOME SIGNS THAT PARENT-INFANT UNITY IS SATISFACTORY

1. Parents find pleasure in the infant and in tasks for or with him/her.
2. Parents understand baby's moods and can offer comfort, thereby relieving the infant's tension.
3. Parents can read the baby's cues for new experiences; they can also sense the child's fatigue level and do not overstimulate him/her for their own pleasure.

SOME SIGNS THAT PARENTS
ARE NOT ADAPTING TO THEIR INFANTS

1. They see their infants as ugly and unattractive.
2. They are revolted by baby's odors.
3. They become disgusted with infant's drooling and are revolted by the baby's body fluids which touch them or which they happen to touch.
4. They are disgusted by sucking sounds of infant.
5. Parents are distressed by infant's vomiting, but seem fascinated by it.
6. They are annoyed at having to clean up infant's bowel movements and preoccupied by odor, consistency, and number of stools.
7. Parents allow the infant's head to dangle without support or concern.
8. They hold infants away from their own bodies.
9. They pick up the infant without a warning through touch or speech.
10. Parents juggle or play with infant roughly following a feeding, even though the child often vomits as a result.
11. Parents think their infant's natural motor activity is abnormal.
12. They avoid eye contact with infant or stare fixedly into its eyes.
13. Parents do not coo or talk with their child.
14. They think their infants do not love them.
15. They feel their infants expose them as unloving and unlovable parents.
16. They perceive that the infant is judging their efforts as an adult would.
17. They perceive their infant's natural dependent needs as dangerous.
18. They fear their infant will die when signs of a minor cold or diarrhea appear.
19. They are convinced their child has some physical defect, despite examinations which prove their fears goundless.

There are many other signs that would indicate that a parent has not accepted his or her baby. Most of them are rooted deeply in the past emotional history of the parent. If a number of these signs appear and persist, they should be considered serious enough to require professional counseling assistance immediately. The parent who can tolerate neither the baby's natural smells or noises or activities will feel as though she/he is living with an enemy and may begin to behave accordingly. It is enormously important to take corrective action immediately.

Of course, only a small minority of new parents fail to adapt to their new children, however trying the adjustment period may be. And we must point out that life with a newborn is by no means an easy business for the parents who stay directly involved with the day-to-day problems. A newborn is also great fun, and she/he will surely enrich the life of his/her parents. But the work! And the changes!

Many new parents are unprepared for the time they must give up to their babies. And they are equally unprepared for the anger and resentment they feel when their lives are so abruptly taken over and virtually tyrannized by a helpless infant. The problem is not the angry and resentful feelings—those are normal. The problem is denying that the negative emotions exist and insisting that a ''good'' parent should only be a loving parent, or that a parent who loves his/her baby will never be angry with it, will never feel resentful for having to give up the life-style she/he has known. Can you be angry with a baby? If so, how will you choose to express the anger?

Infants obviously cannot understand words, nor can they comprehend disciplinary measures; spanking a crying baby would have no positive effect, rather it would be extremely detrimental to the child. Telling a two-week-old infant that you are angry for having to get up for the fourth time in one night is not going to make the child respect your feelings and be a ''good'' baby. It will however, do you worlds of good as you go about changing the diaper or warming the bottle to mutter: ''You little monster, you; don't think I'm just a little ticked off that you've gotten me up four times since ten o'clock last night and that I'm going to have to get up for work exhausted in an hour.'' Respect the fact that you have feelings.

Of course it will be much more rewarding to discuss your feelings with your wife as you return to bed or over breakfast later in the morning. Being roused even once in the middle of your sleep can be disturbing and even infuriating. So acknowledge the feelings; there is no need to be ''Super-Parent.'' To be unfeeling is not a virtue. On the other hand, it will not be productive to go around furious *all* the time. One of the realities of living with a newborn is that you will have to get up for the baby at night. Growling and snapping because you have to get up won't do much for the household and usually displaces some feelings you may be guilty about. But *knowing* that you are angry and admitting that it is OK is more than half the battle.

Allowing uncomfortable feelings to build now will almost guarantee their unpredictable and far more damaging appearance when you least expect them. One recent father in our support group for new parents said, ''If only someone had told me how angry I would get, I would have been more prepared.'' The other men in the group were not as forthcoming about their negative feelings. One of them revealed privately, however, that when his baby was about ten weeks he was taken with a twenty-four-hour intestinal virus which kept him nauseated and vomiting much of the time. For several nights he awoke at two in the morning with an attack of anxious feelings concerning the resumption of his stomach virus. For weeks thereafter he was extremely cautious about what he ate, dreadfully afraid that he would be sick again and forced into the uncomfortable experience of throwing up.

Certainly vomiting is unpleasant. Only this man, Mr. B., was more than normally upset about it happening to him. We asked if he might conceivably be substituting vomiting for anger. Mr. B.'s baby had colic, was nursing several times during the night, and cried a great deal when his father had charge of him. Mr. B. had obviously experienced enormous frustration and anger without ever having been able to either express or share it—and then the phobia about vomiting. We could easily postulate that his fear of throwing up was associated with his fear of expressing anger.

Anger is not a feeling easily shared. We are taught at an early age that anger is a sign that we are out of control and therefore potentially destructive. In response to our questionnaire inquiry "Which of the following feelings does your baby arouse in you?" 32.4 percent said "frustration"; 23.5 percent reported "anxiety"; 14.7 percent felt "trapped"; and yet only 5.9 percent experienced "resentment," and only 8.8 percent reported "anger." How is it possible for someone to make you feel anxious, frustrated, and trapped, *and for you not to be angry and resentful in response?* Perhaps the more positive feelings aroused in fathers by their babies short-circuited the anger. The following is the entire response of thirty-four fathers. They were told to check as many feelings as applied.

Which of the Following Feelings Does Your Baby Arouse in You?

Pride	91.2%
Love	94.1%
Anxiety	23.5%
Inadequacy	8.8%
Strength	58.8%
Resentment	5.9%
Trapped	14.7%
Immortal	2.9%
Anger	8.8%
Frustration	32.4%
Jealousy	0%
Masculinity	26.5%

POSTPARTUM DEPRESSION

Much has been written about postpartum depression in women. (Some women become depressed after the birth of their child. This lasts from a couple of weeks to several months and can be intense or mild.) Debate persists about whether this is a psychological reaction to parenthood or the result of chemical changes in the body. Clearly there are hormonal adjustments going on in the postpartum woman and they contribute to her moods. But we are complex beings and things going on around us will always be part of our reactions. You may find yourself living with a woman who feels sad and irritable for a while.

Postpartum depression occurs in men as well. This connection between the man's emotional state and the recent birth often goes unnoticed. Mental-health workers have recently started giving increased attention to fatherhood as a precipitant of emotional difficulties. Sometimes it is just a mild depression and it passes. Sometimes men deal with these feelings by acting out—drinking, running around, taking risks. If you are feeling out of control, like you can't really cope, seek some counseling for help.

BREAST-FEEDING

Men are often fascinated by their wives breast-feeding. The man sitting and watching his wife nursing their child may have many feelings. Most men feel good about it—warm and loving. On the other hand, a man may feel excluded from this symbiotic act he can't participate in. He may identify with or envy his wife or his child. Some men envy their wives' ability to nurse—just as they envied their ability to gestate and give birth. An example is seen with men who encourage their wives to nurse ''because it would feel so good,'' as though they themselves are experiencing it.[4] Some men identify with their babies. One man we spoke to said he experienced unexplained sadness when his baby was weaned, as though he himself had lost something. Over half of the recent fathers responding to our questionnaire whose wives were nursing tasted their wives' milk—most by sucking the breast. The reactions ranged from pleasant to indifferent to inappropriate to repulsed.

The changes that occurred in your wife's breasts during pregnancy and the effects it can or did have on breast play during lovemaking will, of course, continue if your wife is nursing. Turn back to chapter 5 and read this section if a review will be helpful.

For first-time parents, the family has now grown from two partners to a family triad. Many of the reactions that we discussed in chapter 6 about the father's feelings for his wife and fetus during pregnancy may surface once the child is actually in the home. A man may feel jealous of his child's relationship with his wife, feeling he is being excluded, that someone has taken away his woman. Old childhood conflicts may ignite, and a man may intensely reexperience his needs for "mothering."

Mild reactions can almost always be expected and can offer personal insight without interfering with the things that need to be done, the new life that has to be adjusted to. Many men react to these feelings of envy or identification with the child and wife by becoming more involved in child care. They use this opportunity to get some gratification for themselves and become partners in child rearing. Sometimes the feelings are frightening and the man rejects any nurturing role as a result. If the feelings are intense and interfere with the marriage relationship, talk to someone who can be more objective than you about the situation.

Reestablishing the Marriage Relationship

For weeks after the birth couples are busily occupied with new tasks. Husband and wife rarely have the chance for quiet hours together. If the baby did nothing else but disrupt this highly important activity for its parents, it would have done a great deal. The amount of time a couple will now have for one another separate from the baby is of necessity drastically reduced.

This time factor will have an impact on the way in which the couple resumes its sexual relationship. For, if anything, the couple requires *more* time together to become sexually reacquainted. Many women experience vaginal soreness for weeks after birth, whether or not an episiotomy had been performed, and are extremely fearful of the pain that would result from intercourse. Normal sexual relations will have to be eased into, with great gentleness, and this requires time.

One woman told us that reestablishing an intimate physical relationship with her husband after the birth of her first child reminded her of being out on a date. He was very solicitious of her and did many subtle things to arouse her. His gentle sexual nuances led the way to their first ''serious'' genital contact since the eighth month of the pregnancy—almost four months earlier. She told us:

> When we at last had intercourse, it was on a sunny afternoon in autumn. The baby was with its grandmother for the day, and my husband took the day off from work. He seduced me so nicely that any fear I had about feeling pain from the stitches flew right out the window. I'll always remember that day, and often I say to my husband, ''Do you remember how we made love in the orange room?''

But, when the couple is ready to resume a sexual relationship, events may conspire against them. Here is one possible scenario:

Father is home for supper at six and finds baby still awake (which he is glad of, by and large). He plays with baby and then rocks it to sleep. Mother and father prepare dinner and just as they are about to eat the phone rings. The baby wakes up screaming. The voice at the other end of the phone (grandma) is saying something about wanting to see the baby—it's been four days. You tell her, ''Hold on, here's Julie,'' and you whisper fiercely to your wife as she is about to take the phone, ''Tell her not tonight. Tell her tomorrow night. This is *our* night.'' And you trudge off to get the screaming baby while Julie puts your mother off.

The baby is held at the table and screams while you try to eat. You get up and walk around the room with her. She stops crying. You sit down and she starts again, so Julie gets up to walk the floors. Your food is cold. But the heck with the food, let's get the baby to sleep. The baby is down, quiet for the moment, and two quick showers later you're up in bed. The phone is off the hook, the aggravation of dinner forgotten, and only the sensuous pleasure of now counts. And then . . . then the baby starts crying again. You wait in tense and cautious silence for two, three, four, five minutes for the screaming to stop. It only intensifies. So you rise from bed and get the baby from the next room and hand her to Julie. She puts the baby to her breast, and you watch—annoyed because your own needs take second place, ashamed for feeling so angry, ashamed of envying the sucking infant, jealous of Julie for her ability to have the baby and have a natural means of making contact. You feign great tenderness for madonna and child in their classic love pose. Ten minutes pass. Fifteen. Thirty. So does Julie's passion. And yours. You return the cooing baby to its crib and slink back to bed. If only she will sleep for three hours straight, you plead to the ceiling. Body stiff with tension, you pray for sleep.

Blackout.

That is the worst of it. Sometimes it all comes in a single evening; sometimes it spreads itself over several days. But there is no getting around ringing phones and a baby that cries, other children struggling for your attention, or just being too tired or frustrated to make love. These are the dynamics of early parenthood. The couple who insists that nothing will change after the pregnancy are fooling themselves. Wishful thinking will not make a crying baby stop or vanish at one-thirty in the morning. Nor will wishful thinking eliminate the strain that has been placed on you and your wife. Nor will it fulfill the needs of your other children.

Some people have the ability to turn off, to make themselves oblivious to realities. But we already know that such behavior is like sweeping the dirt under the rug.

Partnership is still the key to getting over the strained times. And we're not discussing partnerships that are simply mutual admiration societies, but working partnerships with attainable goals:

- Give baby the best possible care.
- Give ourselves the best possible care.
- Make sure the other children are getting the best we can give.

Each objective has problems all its own. And in time most problems can find resolution, if the partners are willing to put forth the necessary energy. Some couples never do manage to resolve the vexing strain and the marriage falls apart. As one researcher put it, "A facetious restating of marriage vows might include 'till birth do us part' " as an appropriate addendum for a growing number of young parents.'

The Other Children at Home

We have been repeating, ad infinitum, that pregnancy is a stressful time for the expectant couple. We have mentioned that it is also a stressful time for expectant siblings. Expecting and then having a baby in the house may not be the easiest thing for your other children.

Since children already at home are part of the stress with which new parents will be dealing, it seems wise to list here some of the things you can expect from them after the baby is born. Of course, a ten-year-old will react differently from a three- or four-year-old, or even a five-year-old; but there are some general issues that are common for almost all children, regardless of age. Since entire volumes have been written on just this subject, we feel it's only necessary to cover it briefly.

When a newborn enters the household, children often fear the possibility of being forced to relinquish their place in the family to the intruder. If a child is old enough to understand that "expecting a baby'' means that a baby will actually be moving in, these very real fears will begin during the pregnancy. Inevitably, children will resent the newcomer, will undoubtedly have fantasies of getting rid of the child, and will be furious with their parents for letting this happen.

These fears, it turns out, are not unfounded. The newborn will indeed take up a considerable amount of its parents' time, and children who were formerly the center of attention will have to give up that status in the early weeks and months following the newborn's arrival. The jolt for some children can be crushing, and its lingering effects relived when that child is an expectant parent and fears, once more, that a baby will usurp his or her place in an established family.

Many parents unknowingly turn away from their other children when a new baby enters the home. The newborn is helpless and requires time and attention, after all. Often an older child will begin acting like a baby, seeing this behavior as the most effective and reasonable means for resecuring his/her parents' attention. This regressive behavior is quite common, and you might see some of it in your children, even if the woman next door, and not your wife, has just brought home a new baby. Regression is spurred by more than a child's fears of having his/her role usurped by an infant. Everyone uses it as a means of dealing with the separation from their own infancy and childhood. You may find it obnoxious and insist that they grow up. ''We only have *one* baby in this house, so you better start acting your own age'' is a common admonition, but it only exacerbates a child's fears. Sometimes parents start to make unreasonable demands for adult maturity from their children.

Of course, it can be quite disagreeable for parents to see their five-year-old start up with the old baby talk or hop into the baby's crib or want to drink from his ''ba-ba.'' With such behavior, the child may just be asking, ''Will you love me whatever I do?'' She/he wants from you what the baby has. She/he might be testing your love. A child launched on a regressive tack may find it comforting and even disarming if she/he is *permitted* by his parents into the crib, *allowed* a sip from the baby's bottle or even a bottle of his/her own, and cooed at the way you talk to your baby. Such support will help the child work it through alone. Provide the child with special loving attention and you will find the behavior slowly coming around to something more appropriate for the age. The child, after all, needs the same love and care as before the birth of his/her brother or sister.

Keep your children involved in the new family group through specially assigned responsibilities which will make them feel important in the daily operation of things and extremely supportive of you. Give them every opportunity to do as much as possible. Picking a sweater for the baby is something even a four-year-old can attempt, and you would be surprised at the number of tasks a five-year-old can perform.

Young children who want to help out and be like "mommy" or "daddy" can, of course, slow you down. It is easy to get angry with their poor skills and judgment, which may only cause you more work. But allowing him/her to participate gets the child working with you, not against you, and helping children to define and refine their own roles in the family will ultimately contribute to the stability of the household, although it may not seem that way when the baby's food is on the floor instead of in the bowl where it belongs. You can always expect fluctuations in the child's adapting to the newborn.

Set aside special times to talk with your children, even if it requires a friend baby-sitting the newborn. Let the older children know how you've been feeling, that you've been cranky because of losing so much sleep, that your moods are not their fault. Repeat that information whenever you think of it. And find out what's going on in *their* heads. If you are gentle, such discussions will be seen as love forums to be looked forward to, even if the agenda always seems to include why "we are all having such a difficult time." If you are free to say what you wish, don't deny your children the same right, however distasteful the subject matter. Continual censoring of a child's agenda will keep him/her from venturing into open discussion with you again. And once the child forms a pattern of keeping things to himself/herself, for fear of displeasing his/her parents, the groundwork for nonproductive communication behavior will have been laid. Your child may not only feel that you are unapproachable for certain things but that those topics are generally taboo. And so another consipirator of silence will have been pushed into the world.

When a parent hears himself/herself setting out rules for what a child may or may not do, may or may not say, it would be good to stand back and think, "Who put that notion into my head? Was it my father? My mother? Do I really agree with it or did I just swallow it? And am I asking my child to swallow what I'm saying the same way?" These are important questions for every parent at any time, but they are especially so when the family is in flux. And when a baby enters a home with other children, *the family is in flux*. Every family. Not nine out of ten families (with yours as the possible exception), but ten out of every ten families go through change after the birth of a child.

Epilogue

Last winter, we invited a woman from a local outreach program to talk about her agency's services to one of our support groups for new parents. Following the short presentation she stayed on to participate in a group discussion about how life had changed with a new baby at home. A number of men in the group spoke quite frankly about some of the great difficulties they were experiencing as new parents. Feelings were passed heatedly around the room—one couple exchanged angry quips, another became furious and then morose when speaking of the maternal grandparents' disruptive intrusions into the new family.

Apparently unable to listen to any more of these disturbing feelings, the guest speaker blurted out, "Well, all this may be so, but in two years, when your baby greets you at the door with a 'daddy, daddy!' all this will be forgotten."

The comment was undoubtedly well-intentioned, but it was obviously designed to mean, "Why don't you people shut up!" And in fact everyone did. Each attempt to resurrect the discussion failed miserably.

It is true that there is great joy and pleasure to be had from raising children. It is also true that the project is a difficult one which requires a tremendous commitment in time and energy. We are concerned that our readers may feel we have dealt more heavily with the problems than the rewards of expectant and actual parenting. We certainly do not wish to leave you with a sense that becoming a parent is more frustrating than rewarding.

The process of parenting a newborn is essential to the formation of a relationship with your child and to your child's own rudimentary understanding of how relationships are made. The guest speaker who pressed for looking ahead instead of examining *the here and now* was patently wrong. So don't shut up. Keep talking. And keep feeling. Try not to worry if some of the feelings are contradictory: Recognizing that some strong feelings get mixed up with others that seem totally opposite need not panic you. Nor should it force you to reconcile them. Your baby cries in the night and wakes you. You are frustrated, hurt, and even furious. Two minutes later you are holding that same baby, giving it a bottle or just the warmth of your hands and chest, and you feel the tenderest love a parent can feel for a child. Must you now feel guilty about the anger, the frustration? What purpose would it serve? What counts is that *in spite of the anger*, along with the anger, you can still love your child deeply.

Things get easier as babies develop, and your child's increasing independence brings with it a different set of choices for you. Still, it is unnecessary to look ahead for pleasure and pride and love; your baby will get you to smile and coo and laugh and cry with love ten times before lunch. Enjoy yourself: This is going to be an experience unlike anything you've ever known.

Appendix A:
Selected Questionnaire Findings

The following are selected findings from the questionnaire. The findings are presented as the percentage of men who selected each of the available choices for a particular question.

Expectant and recent fathers' responses are combined unless otherwise indicated. When the two groups of men answered differently, it is indicated by a footnote, and more specific information is provided in the notes at the end of this section.

Recollections from Childhood

Check the phrase that best describes the *quality* of time spent with your father: Very fulfilling—36.0%; Moderately fulfilling—45.6%; Not fulfilling—18.4%

Check the word that best describes how *much* time you feel your father spent with you as a child: Abundant—16.7%; Moderate—59.6%; Little—23.7%

Do you ever remember wishing you could have a baby? Yes responses: Expectant fathers—9.9%; Recent fathers—20.6%; Total—13.0%

The Pregnancy

Did/do you want a boy or a girl? Boy—45.2%; Girl—13.0%; No preference—41.7%

Did/does your wife want a boy or a girl? Boy—23.5%; Girl—38.3%; No preference—38.3%

Did/does your wife make new demands on you (during the pregnancy)? Yes—28.9%; No—71.1%

Were/are the demands stressful for you? Yes—34.1%; No—65.9%

During the pregnancy, were/are you under additional stresses? Yes—52.6%; No—47.4%

Did/do you talk to someone about the concerns of pregnancy and fatherhood? Yes—45.1%; No—54.9%

Did/do you feel neglected in light of the attention your wife is/was receiving (during the pregnancy)? Yes responses: Expectant fathers—3.8%; Recent fathers—14.7%; Total—7.1%

What could your wife have done/do to have made/make the pregnancy go smoother for you? Responses indicating nothing—69.6%; Responses indicating something—30.4%

Did you meet the person who delivered/will deliver your baby prior to the birth? Yes—70.4%; No—29.6%

Did/do you feel this is more your baby or your wife's? Wife's—14.8%; Both equally—83.5%; Yours—1.7%

Feelings and Behaviors
Changes in feelings and behaviors *during* the pregnancy.

	% of men responding to each alternative		
	Increased	Unchanged	Decreased
Need to be taken care of	10.3	79.4	10.3
Need for affection	18.3	76.1	5.5
Feelings of inadequacy	11.2	74.5	14.3
Need for support	18.3	75.0	6.7
Feelings of pride	80.4	18.8	.9
Jealousy[1]	5.3	79.8	14.9
Strength	34.9	63.2	1.9
Sexual potency[2]	18.5	72.2	9.3
Depression/sadness	8.1	74.7	17.2
Quick-temperedness	21.6	57.8	20.6
Nervousness[3]	31.7	61.5	6.7
Restlessness[4]	28.0	65.0	7.0
Sleeplessness	25.5	67.6	6.9
Food consumption	30.9	64.5	4.5
Energy level[5]	18.0	74.8	7.2

	Increased	Unchanged	Decreased
Alcohol consumption[6]	8.5	80.2	11.3
Use of medication	2.1	93.7	4.2
Use of marijuana	5.3	81.6	13.2
Use of other illegal drugs	1.8	91.1	7.1
Smoking	17.3	76.0	6.7
Hours at work[7]	21.2	62.5	16.3
Energy on the job[8]	15.4	67.3	17.3
Social activities (without your wife)	7.0	73.0	20.0
Dreaming	19.4	79.6	1.0
Daydreaming	29.7	67.3	3.0
Time at home[9]	33.0	57.8	9.2
Hours sleeping[10]	11.8	60.9	27.3
Time with your other children (if applicable)	34.6	63.5	1.9
Spending money	36.4	53.3	10.3
Gambling	3.0	95.5	1.5
Reading	17.8	69.3	12.9
Television watching	19.8	66.0	14.2
Time spent with hobbies	8.8	78.4	12.7
Time spent on house chores	51.9	45.4	2.8
Attention to personal appearance	10.1	84.4	5.5

Changes in feelings and behaviors *after* the child was born (recent fathers only).

	% of men responding to each alternative		
	Increased	Unchanged	Decreased
Need to be taken care of	13.3	76.7	10.0
Need for affection	16.7	76.7	6.7
Feelings of inadequacy	3.7	77.8	18.5
Need for support	14.3	78.6	7.1
Feelings of pride	87.5	12.5	0

	Increased	Unchanged	Decreased
Jealousy	7.4	77.8	14.8
Strength	36.7	60.0	3.3
Sexual potency	24.1	69.0	6.9
Depression/sadness	10.3	75.9	13.8
Quick-temperedness	6.9	69.0	24.1
Nervousness	10.3	79.3	10.3
Restlessness	24.1	62.1	13.8
Sleeplessness	24.1	69.0	6.9
Food consumption	12.9	83.9	3.2
Energy level	12.9	71.0	16.1
Alcohol consumption	0	100.0	0
Use of medication	3.8	96.2	0
Use of marijuana	0	85.7	14.3
Use of other illegal drugs	0	94.7	5.3
Smoking	4.5	81.8	13.6
Hours at work	21.4	53.6	25.0
Energy on the job	17.9	60.7	21.4
Social activities (without your wife)	20.7	55.2	24.1
Dreaming	17.2	82.8	0
Daydreaming	6.9	89.7	3.4
Time at home	32.3	64.5	3.2
Hours sleeping	6.5	45.2	48.4
Time with your other children (if applicable)	33.3	61.1	5.6
Spending money	41.9	51.6	6.5
Gambling	0	100.0	0
Reading	10.7	78.6	10.7
Television watching	10.0	56.7	33.3
Time spent with hobbies	0	69.0	31.0
Time spent on house chores	38.7	48.4	12.9
Attention to personal appearance	9.7	87.1	3.2

Health

Most of our respondents did not report changes in their own physical symptoms (i.e., headaches, allergies, etc.) during the pregnancy. The one notable exception was:

Weight Gain

Not applicable	59.8%
Greater than before the pregnancy	23.2%
Gaining but at the same rate as before	11.6%
Decrease in weight gain	5.4%

Marital Relationship

Regarding your relationship with your wife, the baby has/will:

	Expectant	Recent	Total
Brought/bring you and your wife closer together	67.9%	47.1%	61.7%
Not change(d) things	29.6%	47.1%	34.8%
Create(d) distance between you and your wife	2.5%	5.9%	3.5%

In your marriage the baby has/will:

	Expectant	Recent	Total
Reduce(d) tension	15.2%	8.8%	13.3%
Not made/make a difference in level of tension	51.9%	73.5%	58.4%
Create(d) tension	32.9%	17.6%	28.3%

How much time did/do the two of you spend with your wife's parents (during the pregnancy)? More time than before

—18.4%; About same as before—71.1%; Less time than before
—10.5%

In general did/does your wife have more contact with her parents (during the pregnancy)? Yes—39.5%; No—60.5%

How much time did/do you spend with your parents (during the pregnancy)? More time than before—16.7%; About same as before—76.3%; Less time than before—7.0%

In general, did/do you have more contact with your parents (during the pregnancy)? Yes—23.0%; No—77.0%

Since your wife gave birth, how much time have the two of you been spending with her parents (recent fathers only)? More time than before the birth—30.3%; About the same as before the birth—60.6%; Less time than before the birth—9.1%

In general, has your wife had more contact with her parents *since* the birth (recent fathers only)? Yes—48.5%; No—51.5%

Since the birth, how much time have the two of you been spending with *your* parents (recent fathers only)? More time than before the birth—21.2%; About the same as before the birth—72.7%; Less time than before the birth—6.1%

In general, have you had more contact with *your* parents since the birth (recent fathers only)? Yes—21.2%; No—78.8%

During the pregnancy, you and your wife went/go out:

	Expectant	Recent	Total
More often than before	6.3%	11.8%	7.9%
Same as before	60.0%	76.5%	64.9%
Less than before	33.8%	11.8%	27.2%

During the pregnancy, you and your wife socialize(d):

	Expectant	Recent	Total
More often than before	8.6%	0 %	6.1%
Same as before	61.7%	88.2%	69.6%
Less than before	29.6%	11.8%	24.3%

Since the *birth* you and your wife go out (recent fathers only): More often than before—8.8%; Same as before—23.5%; Less often than before—67.6%

Since the *birth,* you and your wife socialize (recent fathers only): More often than before—14.7%; Same as before—44.1%; Less often than before—41.2%

Since the birth, do you discuss the feelings and concerns of fatherhood with your wife (recent fathers only)? Yes—73.5%; No—26.5%

Did/do you and your wife tell pregnancy and/or expectant parent jokes? Yes—33.9%; No—66.1%

How involved were/are you in preparing for the baby's arrival (e.g., clothing, furniture, etc.)? Very—48.2%; Moderately —30.4%; Minimally—16.1%; Not at all—5.4%

How would you rate your overall involvement in the pregnancy?

Very intensely involved—32.7%

Intensely involved— 31.0%

Moderately involved— 31.9%

Marginally involved—4.4%

Almost not at all involved—0%

Child Care

Are you/do you intend to be involved in the following child-care activities?

	Yes responses		Yes responses
Diapering[11]	94.6%	Talking to	100.0%
Feeding	63.4%	Night wakes[14]	78.7%
(35% are using, or intend to		Playing	100.0%
use, breast-feeding)		Doctor visits	70.0%
Dressing	92.8%	Baby's laundry	47.3%
Bathing[12]	80.2%	Food preparation	50.9%
Holding	100.0%	(35% are using, or intend to	
Cutting nails[13]	53.6%	use, breast-feeding)	

Note: It is interesting that a greater percentage of expectant fathers reported that they intend to be involved in diapering, bathing, cutting nails, and night wakes than recent fathers actually report they are. See notes section at end of this appendix.

Do you help make the decisions regarding (recent fathers only):

	Yes responses
The baby's diet	65.6%
The baby's clothing	54.5%
The baby's medical attention	97.0%

Do you wish you could be more involved with child care (recent fathers only)? Yes—19.4%; No—80.6%

Does your wife wish you could be more involved with child care (recent fathers only)? Yes—44.8%; No—55.2%

Have you and your wife talked about what roles you should both take in child rearing? Yes—60.2%; No—39.8%

If no in the response to the preceding question, is there an unspoken understanding about it?

	Yes responses
Expectant	65.6%
Recent	94.4%
Total	76.0%

Which of the following describe the feelings your baby arouses in you (recent fathers only)?

	Yes responses
Pride	91.2%
Love	94.1%
Anxiety	23.5%
Inadequacy	8.8%
Strength	58.8%
Resentment	5.9%
Trapped	14.7%

	Yes responses
Immortality	2.9%
Anger	8.8%
Frustration	32.4%
Jealousy	0 %
Masculinity	26.5%

Do you think you will be a father just like your own father?
Yes—25.5%; No—74.5%

Notes for Appendix A

1. Expectant and recent fathers' responses differed on:

Jealousy	Increase	Decrease
Expectant fathers	1.5%	16.2%
Recent fathers	15.4%	11.5%

2. Expectant and recent fathers' responses differed on:

Sexual Potency	Increase	Decrease
Expectant fathers	16.9%	13.0%
Recent fathers	22.6%	0 %

3. Expectant and recent fathers' responses differed on:

Nervousness	Increase	Decrease
Expectant fathers	35.1%	9.5%
Recent fathers	23.3%	0 %

4. Expectant and recent fathers' responses differed on:

Restlessness	Increase	Decrease
Expectant fathers	31.9%	9.7%
Recent fathers	17.9%	0 %

5. Expectant and recent fathers' responses differed on:

Energy level	Increase	Decrease
Expectant fathers	12.7%	8.9%
Recent fathers	31.3%	3.1%

6. Expectant and recent fathers' responses differed on:

Alcohol consumption	Increase	Decrease
Expectant fathers	10.7%	14.7%
Recent fathers	3.2%	3.2%

7. Expectant and recent fathers' responses differed on:

Hours at work	Increase	Decrease
Expectant fathers	26.7%	17.3%
Recent fathers	6.9%	13.8%

8. Expectant and recent fathers' responses differed on:

Energy on the job	Increase	Decrease
Expectant fathers	18.7%	20.0%
Recent fathers	6.9%	10.3%

9. Expectant and recent fathers' responses differed on:

Time at home	Increase	Decrease
Expectant fathers	37.2%	12.8%
Recent fathers	22.6%	0 %

10. Expectant and recent fathers' responses differed on:

Hours sleeping	Increase	Decrease
Expectant fathers	15.4%	30.8%
Recent fathers	3.1%	18.8%

11. Expectant and recent fathers' responses differed on: *Diapering:* Expectant—97.5%; Recent—87.9%

12. Expectant and recent fathers' responses differed on: *Bathing:* Expectant—88.5%; Recent—60.6%

13. Expectant and recent fathers' responses differed on: *Cutting nails:* Expectant—59.7%; Recent—39.4%

14. Expectant and recent fathers' responses differed on: *Night wakes:*Expectant—88.%;Recent—57.6%

Appendix B:
Home-Birth Agencies

The agencies listed in the following resource list can give you information about the availability of home deliveries in your area.

Association for Childbirth
  at Home (A.C.H.)
16705 Monte Christo
Cerritos, Cal. 90701

American College of Home
  Obstetrics
2821 Rose St.
Franklin Park, Ill. 60601

Birth Day
Box 388
Cambridge, Mass. 02138

Birthwork
55 Loomis St.
Burlington, Vt. 05401

Note: The material included in Appendix B was reprinted with the permission of Maternity Center Association, New York, N.Y.

Homebirth, Inc.
89 Franklin, Suite 200
Boston, Mass. 02110

Home Oriented Maternity
    Experience (H.O.M.E.)
511 New York Ave.
Takoma Park, Md. 20012

Maternity Center
    Associates, Ltd.
5411 Cedar La., Suite
    208–A
Bethesda, Md. 20014

National Association of
    Parents and Profes-
    sionals for Safe Alter-
    natives in Childbirth
    (N.S.P.P.S.A.C.)
P.O. Box 1307
Chapel Hill, N.C. 27514

Appendix C:
Contraindications for Home Birth

The mother who chooses to give birth at home will not have access to the sophisticated technology of the hospital, technology that in the case of a high-risk mother and/or baby could mean the difference between life and death. The vast majority of situations that require resources available only in a hospital can be predicted in advance. The purpose of this appendix is to acquaint you with just those situations—situations that would cause a mother and/or baby to be classified as high risk and hence make birth at a hospital imperative. This list should not be taken literally: Very often it is the degree rather than the presence of a certain high-risk factor that would preclude home birth. Also, in many cases it would take a combination of these factors to put one in the high-risk category. If you feel that any of these contraindications are present in your case history, talk the matter over with your doctor and/or midwife. The final decision as to risk or any aspect of the birth experience must, however, rest with the couple itself.

I. *Preconception.* In some cases medical contraindications to home birth can be predicted in advance of conception; these contraindications might even influence the decision to procreate.

Note: The material included in Appendix C was reprinted with the permission of Homebirth, Inc., Boston, MA (Reprint 102, November 1975).

A. *Family History.* The risk in childbirth could be increased if among your near relatives (grandparents, uncles and aunts, parents, siblings) any one of these diseases were present:

   1. *Serious hereditary and familial abnormalities*—cystic fibrosis, osteogenesis imperfecta, Down's syndrome

   2. *Significant congenital anomalies* involving the central nervous system, heart, or skeletal system

   3. *Sickle-cell disease*

   4. *Poor nutrition, medical indigency*

B. *Maternal History.* The mother's medical history previous to this pregnancy must also be considered in evaluating her risk in childbirth.

   1. *Metabolic disease in the mother*—thyroid disease and diabetes

   2. *History of reproductive failure*—as evidenced by miscarriages, toxemia, prolonged periods of infertility, and premature or small-for-dates size infants

   3. *Anemia*—hematocrit below 32 percent

   4. *Height and weight*—a mother might be high risk if she is under sixty inches tall and had a prepregnant weight of less than 20 percent under or over the standards for weight and height

   5. *Smoking*—heavy smoking can contribute to prematurity or miscarriage

C. *Obstetrical Factors.* There are conditions related to pregnancy itself that might put a mother into the high-risk category.

   1. *Maternal age*—if a mother is on the fringes of the childbearing years, that is over forty (thirty-five if it is a first baby) or under sixteen, her chances of having difficult labors and/or babies born with birth defects are significantly higher

   2. *Excessive multiparity*—after five or more pregnancies the chances of risk are greater

   3. *Obstetric complications, past or present*—if any of the following medical conditions are present in this pregnancy or in previous pregnancies, the chances of risk are higher

     a. *Blood-group incompatibility*—RH incompatibility is not in itself a contraindication for home delivery, unless the mother has been pregnant before and has built up antibodies that would harm her next baby. These antibodies could be built up even if the previous pregnancy was terminated in the first trimester. This build up of antibodies can be stopped by giving the mother an injection of Rhogan shortly after delivery.

     b. *Toxemia of pregnancy*

     c. *Placental separation*—if the placenta detaches in late pregnancy or early labor

d. *Hydramnious*—too much amniotic fluid, commonly associated with twins and babies with birth defects

4. *Previous Caesarean section*

II. *Prenatal.* A number of factors during pregnancy will alert one to the possibility of complications in the fetus, or ultimately in the newborn infant as well as in the mother.

A. *Medical Factors:*

1. *Infection* in the mother during pregnancy

2. *Maternal drug addiction*—narcotics, barbiturates, amphetamines, LSD

3. *Poor nutrition*

4. *Lack of prenatal care*—long delayed or absent

5. *Severe emotional tension*

6. *Operations for surgical problems during pregnancy,* especially under general anesthesia

7. *Radiation*—use of radiation treatments during pregnancy or previous to it

8. *Cardiovascular disease*—congenital heart disease or hypertension

9. *Renal disease*

10. *Diabetes*

11. *Intercurrent chronic disease*—especially malignancy

B. *Obstetrical Factors:*

1. *Abnormal presentation*—if just prior to the onset of labor the baby is not in the normal head-down position but rather breech or transverse

2. Fetus that fails to gain normally or is *disparate in size* from that expected

3. *Postdue baby*—fetus over forty-two and one-half weeks gestation (two and one-half weeks after the expected due date)

4. *Premature baby*—fetus that is born more than two and one-half weeks before the expected due date

5. *Multiple birth*—twins or triplets

6. *Toxemia of pregnancy*—(eclampsia and preeclampsia)

7. *Fetal-heart aberrations*—the heartbeat of the fetus should be strong and steady and between 120 to 160 beats per minute

III. *Natal.* There are some contraindications to birth at home that will occur only during labor or even following delivery, hence the importance of constant observation and monitoring during labor and delivery and postnatally

A. *Maternal or Fetal Conditions During Labor.* If these conditions develop during labor, it is best to go to the hospital if time permits

1. *Fever* in the mother which might be a sign of infection

2. *Premature rupture of membranes*— if the bag of waters has broken more than twenty-four hours before the onset of labor

3. Fetal distress as evidenced by *abnormal fetal heartbeat,* either too fast or too slow, 120 to 160 beats per minute being normal

4. Fetal distress as evidenced by the presence of *meconium in the amniotic fluid.* Normal amniotic fluid is clear, odorless, and tastes salty. The meconium will stain the fluid yellow, green, or dark brown and gives it a foul smell.

5. *Prolonged labor*—especially a second stage longer than two hours and an active first stage longer than twenty-four hours

6. *Precipitous delivery*—a very fast labor and delivery, shorter than two to three hours

7. *Tight nuchal cord*—the cord is wrapped very tightly around the neck of the fetus (in most cases there would not be enough time to get to the hospital in this case and emergency procedures must be done in the home)

8. *Heavy bleeding in the mother*—hemorrhage

   a. Before birth it usually means that the *placenta has detached* and an immediate Caesarean section is necessary

   b. After birth it is usually caused by a *uterus that will not contract,* sometimes due to the retention of part of the membranes or placenta

9. *Cord prolapse*—the umbilical cord is being born first. (The mother should be put on her hands and knees with hips in the air and rushed to a hospital because her baby must be delivered by Caesarean section.)

10. *Presentation of any fetal part except the head*—a foot or hand is born before the head

11. Fatigue and dehydration causing *maternal distress* as evidenced in part by pulse and blood-pressure readings

B. *Infant at Birth.* Although the baby will have been born at home, the presence of any of these factors at birth or after will necessitate hospital care:

   1. *Congenital anomalies*—that is, the baby is born with an obvious abnormality such as cleft palate, diaphragmatic hernia, tracheoesophageal fistula, cardiovascular anomalies, imperforate anus

   2. *Single umbilical artery*

   3. *Low Apgar score,* especially at five minutes

   4. *Placental abnormality*—a placenta that is not normal could indicate a problem with the baby

   5. *Prematurity*—low birth weight

   6. *Disproportion* between weight or length and gestational age

   7. *Depression*

   8. *Birth trauma*

   9. *Abnormal respiration*

   10. *Severe blood loss*

Appendix D:
Medical Emergencies
in Home Births

This section should not be construed as a training program to teach lay persons how to deal with medical emergencies. It is merely to inform parents of the possible emergencies that can occur in childbirth at home and the steps that should be taken if emergencies do occur. This information is necessary for parents to make rational decisions and hence be responsible for their birth experiences.

The subjects covered in this section are: I hemorrhage, II prolapsed umbilical cord, III arm or leg presentation, IV fetal distress, and V respiratory distress in the newborn. If any one of these complications occurs, institute first-aid measures and alert your medical backup team in order to get mother and/or baby to a hospital as soon as possible.

In addition to the medical emergencies listed here, there are other situations that would cause the birth to deviate from the normal. These situations, which include tight nuchal cord, shoulder dystocia, and previously undiagnosed breech presentation, are not considered medical emergencies as such since the ability to deal with them should be well within the realm of the medical professional in attendance.

For further information concerning management of the actual birth, we highly recommend Gregory White's *Emergency Childbirth* manual, available through Homebirth, Inc.

Note: The material included in Appendix D was reprinted with the permission of Homebirth, Inc., Boston, Mass. (Reprint 107, April 1976).

I. *Hemorrhage.* In a normal birth the amount of blood lost is one-half to one cup. Also a few spoonfuls of blood mixed with mucus (like red currant jelly) lost before or during labor is normal. A blood loss of over two cups is not normal.

   A. *Signs* of Hemorrhage:

      1. Blood loss:

         a. *Before or during labor:* Loss of more than a few spoonfuls of blood

         b. *During and after delivery:* Loss of more than two cups of blood (total)

      2. Shock as indicated by:

         a. Pallor, cold sweat

         b. Feeling faint, dizzy, confused, apprehensive

         c. Falling blood pressure, rising pulse

      3. Abdominal pain (not present in all cases)

   B. *Treatment* of Hemorrhage:

      1. In all cases of hemorrhage:

         a. Take mother to hospital quickly

         b. Alert emergency back-up team

         c. Have mother lie down with lower half of body elevated

         d. Keep mother warm with a blanket

         e. Have mother drink water (salt water, if possible), one-half cup every twenty to thirty minutes

      2. If hemorrhage occurs after birth, in addition to the above, also:

         a. Have baby (or anybody) nurse to stimulate uterine contractions

         b. Massage uterus gently, do not pull on cord

         c. If placenta has been delivered and uterus does not contract with massaging, begin bimanual compression

II. *Prolapsed Umbilical Cord.* This means that the cord comes out of the cervix or vagina before or alongside the baby's head. Since the cord carries the baby's oxygen supply, compression of the cord by the after-coming head would cause distress in the baby.

   A. *If head Is Crowning:*

      1. The woman must bear down and birth the baby as quickly as possible

      2. Alert emergency back-up team

   B. *If the Head is Not Visible in the Vagina:*

      1. Transport mother to *closest* hospital emergency room as quickly as possible in the *knee-chest position*

      2. Alert emergency back-up team, especially alerting hospital emergency room to the exact situation

3. The cord:

    a. Do not compress or pull on the cord. As long as it is still pulsating, the baby is receiving oxygen.

    b. If possible, while mother is in knee-chest position, gently hold cord up in vagina

    c. If unable to put cord back into vagina, wrap it in a clean, warm, moist cloth and hold close to vagina

4. Using sterile gloves, the presenting part may be gently elevated in the vagina

III. *Arm or Leg Presentation.* This is when an arm or leg appears at the cervical or vaginal opening before the head. Unless baby is very tiny, labor is mechanically impossible since baby is wedged crosswise in the birth canal.

A. Transport mother to the hospital as quickly as possible

B. Keep mother in knee-chest position

IV. *Fetal Distress.* This means that the baby's blood supply (and therefore its oxygen supply) has been interrupted. This is usually due to cord compression. The fetal heart rate is the best guide to how the fetus is faring. The normal fetal heart rate varies from 120–160 beats/minute. Each baby's heart rate should not vary more than 10 beats/minute in either direction from its prenatal rate. Be familiar with your baby's normal rate.

A. *Signs of Fetal Distress:*

    1. It is not unusual for the fetal heart rate to fluctuate during a contraction, but if it *does not return to normal after the contraction,* the baby is in distress.

    2. If the fetal heart rate goes *below 110 beats/minute* at any time, the baby is in distress.

    3. If the fetal heart rate goes *above 160 beats/minute* at any time, the baby is in distress.

    4. If the *amniotic fluid is not clear,* that is, colored yellow, green, or brown and/or is foul smelling, this indicates that the baby has passed some meconium which is a sign of fetal distress.

B. *First Aid for Fetal Distress:*

    1. *If the baby's head is crowning:* Birth the baby as quickly as possible

    2. *If the baby's head is not visible in the vagina:*

        a. Transport the mother to the closest hospital emergency room quickly

        b. Mother should be in the position that brings the fetal heart rate closer to normal, such as knee-chest or side positions

        c. If oxygen is available, mother should breathe it deeply

C. *Precautions:*

    1. Always check the fetal heart rate after the membranes rupture

    2. Check the fetal heart periodically during labor and more frequently as labor progresses

V. *Respiratory Distress in the Newborn.* A normal newborn will initiate respirations as soon as the cord stops pulsating (usually within two minutes) if not sooner.

  A. *Signs* of respiratory distress:

    1. Baby's body (other than hands, feet, and presenting part) does not get pink after respirations have begun

    2. Difficulty breathing: Nasal flaring, retracting (with each inspiration the outline of the ribs is visible), groaning or grunting with each respiration

    3. Normal respiratory rate in the newborn is 40–60 respirations/minute. If respirations are quite slow and gasping, the baby is in distress.

    4. No spontaneous respirations

  B. *First Aid.* To be instituted immediately and on the way to the hospital where baby should be transported as soon as possible:

    1. Place baby in horizontal position with head turned on side on flat, hard surface.

    2. Using bulb syringe, suction mucus first from the mouth and secondly from the nostrils, if necessary. (Always squeeze the bulb before placing tip in mouth or nostril.) If no bulb syringe is available, wipe out the mouth with a clean cloth.

    3. Dry off baby and *keep warm*

    4. If the baby is breathing on its own and oxygen is available, hold the oxygen mask near the baby's face.

    5. If the baby is having, slow, gasping respirations and is limp, or if there are no spontaneous respirations, begin mouth-to-mouth resuscitation

      a. The technique of mouth-to-mouth resuscitation is not difficult in itself, but should be studied by attendants *before* labor begins as part of one's prenatal preparation. An excellent source is the *American Red Cross First Aid Textbook.*

      b. *Steps* in mouth-to-mouth resuscitation:

        i. Clear any mucus from mouth

        ii. Extend head slightly back—football hold is excellent way to hold baby

        iii. Placing mouth over baby's mouth and nose, gently puff a small amount of air into the newborn (not more than a mouthful of air)

        iv. The chest should rise and fall with each respiration

        v. Breathe into the baby about twenty times per minute

vi. Keep a hand gently placed on the infant's stomach to prevent it from becoming bloated with air

vii. If the baby begins to breathe spontaneously at a normal rate, resuscitation may be stopped; if not, continue resuscitation en route to the hospital

c. Any baby who requires resuscitation at birth should be taken to a hospital as soon as possible even if the crisis is apparently passed.

Notes

1

1. W. H. Trethowan, "The Couvade Syndrome," *Modern Perspectives in Psycho-Obstetrics*, John G. Howells, ed. (New York: Brunner/Mazel, 1972), pp. 68–93.
2. Ibid.
3. Ibid.
4. Ibid.
5. Ibid.
6. Ibid.
7. Ibid.

2

1. Information was obtained by the authors from the first two expectant parents groups at the Williamstown Visiting Nurses Association: September 1977, February 1978.
2. D. B. Lynn, *The Father: His Role in Child Development* (Monterey: Brooks Cole Publishing Company, 1974), p. 14.
3. A. Colman and L. Colman, *Pregnancy: The Psychological Experience* (New York: Bantam Books, 1977), pp. 101–102.
4. W. F. Windle, *Fetal Physiology* (Springfield: Thomas Publishing Company, 1971), p. 73.
5. A. S. Wente and S. B. Crockenberg, "Transition to Fatherhood: Lamaze Preparation, Adjustment Difficulty, and the Husband-Wife Relationship," *Family Coordinator* 25 (4) (October 1976): 351–357.
6. R. A. Fein, "Men's Entrance to Parenthood," *Family Coordinator* 25 (4) (October 1976): 341–348.
7. Colman and Colman, *Pregnancy: The Psychological Experience*, p. 12.
8. Ibid, p. 13.
9. Ibid, p. 14.
10. Ibid, p. 122.

3

1. F. Leboyer, *Birth Without Violence* (New York: Knopf, 1975), p. 17.

2. A. Colman and L. Colman, *Pregnancy: The Psychological Experience* (New York: Bantam Books, 1977), p. 45.

3. This information was gathered from separate discussions with expectant mothers and expectant fathers in the second Williamstown VNA group: February 1978.

4. G. Dick-Read, *Childbirth Without Fear* (New York: Harper & Row, 1970).

5. F. Lamaze, *Painless Childbirth: The Lamaze Method* (New York: Pocket Books, 1972).

6. Leboyer, *Birth Without Violence*.

7. R. K. Marquart, "Expectant Fathers: What Are Their Needs?" *American Journal of Maternal Child Nursing* (January/February 1976): 32–36.

8. Ibid.

9. Ibid.

4

1. Film: "Are You Ready for the Postpartum Experience?" (New Jersey: Parenting Pictures, 1974).

5

1. For examples see:

Masters and Johnson, *Human Sexual Response*.

B. Liebenberg, "Expectant Fathers," *Child and Family* 8 (1969): 265–278.

2. For examples see:

Masters and Johnson, *Human Sexual Response*.

J. A. Kenny, "Pregnancy, Childbirth and Breastfeeding as They Relate to the Sexuality of Women." *Human Sexuality*, May 1971.

3. D. A. Solberg, J. Butler, and N. Wagner, "Sexual Behavior in Pregnancy," *New England Journal of Medicine* 288 (1973): 1098–1103.

4. N. N. Wagner and D. A. Solberg, "Pregnancy and Sexuality," *Medical Aspects of Human Sexuality* 8 (1974): 44–66.

5. G. Brewer, *What Every Woman Should Know About Pregnancy* (New York: Random House, 1977), p. 18.

6. A. Comfort, *The Joy of Sex* (New York: Simon and Schuster, 1972), p. 241.

7. Wagner and Solberg, *Medical Aspects of Human Sexuality*, pp. 44–66.

8. R. L. Naeye, "Coitus and Associated Amniotic-Fluid Infections," *New England Journal of Medicine* 301 (1979): 1198–1200.

9. E. Bing and L. Colman, *Making Love During Pregnancy* (New York: Bantam Books, 1977), p. 22.

10. Ibid, p. 28.

11. Boston Women's Health Book Collective, *Our Bodies Ourselves,* 2nd ed. (New York: Simon and Schuster, 1976), p. 225.

12. Bing and Colman, *Making Love During Pregnancy*, p. 124.

Note: The Bing and Colman book is an informative book presenting the lovemaking experiences of expectant couples. It is highly recommended.

6

1. R. D. Towne and J. Afterman, "Psychosis in Males Related to Parenthood," *Bulletin of the Menninger Clinic* 19 (1955): 19–26.

2. G. Zilboorg, "Depressive Reactions Related to Parenthood," *American Journal of Psychiatry* 10 (1931): 927–962.

3. Colman and Colman, *Pregnancy: The Psychological Experience*, p. 114.

4. J. Curtis, "A Psychiatric Study of 55 Expectant Fathers," *United States Armed Forces Medical Journal* 6 (1955): 937–950.

5. E. Jacobson, "Development of the Wish for a Child in Boys," *Psychoanalytic Study of the Child* 5 (1960): 139–159.

6. S. Coley and B. James, "Delivery: A Trauma for Fathers?" *Family Coordinator* (October 1976): 359–363.

7. B. Liebenberg, "Expectant Fathers," *Child and Family* 8 (1969): 265–278.

8. R. Munroe and R. Munroe, "Male Pregnancy Symptoms and Cross-Sex Identity in Three Societies," *Journal of Social Psychology* 84 (1971): 11–25.

9. W. H. Trethowan and M. F. Conlon, "The Couvade Syndrome," *British Journal of Psychiatry* 111 (1965): 57–66.

10. K. van Leeuwen, "Pregnancy Envy in the Male," *International Journal of Psychoanalysis* 47 (1966): 319–324.

11. Colman and Colman, *Pregnancy: The Psychological Experience*, p. 99, p. 109.

12. A. A. Hartman and R. C. Nicolay, "Sexually Deviant Behavior in Expectant Fathers," *Journal of Abnormal Psychology* 71 (1966): 232–234.

13. T. Reik, *Ritual* (New York: Farrar, Straus, 1946), pp. 27–89.

14. Trethowan and Conlon, "The Couvade Syndrome," pp. 57–66.

15. R. J. Gelles, "Violence and Pregnancy: A Note on the Extent of the Problem and Needed Services," *Family Coordinator* (January 1975): 81–86.

16. R. B. Lacoursiere, "Fatherhood and Mental Illness: A Review and New Material," *Psychiatric Quarterly* 46 (1972): 109–124.

17. Ibid.

18. L. Obrzut, "Expectant Fathers' Perception of Fathering," *American Journal of Nursing* 96 (1976): 1440–1443.

19. R. A. Fein, "Men's Entrance to Parenthood," *Family Coordinator* (October 1976): 341–348.

20. Colman and Colman, *Pregnancy: The Psychological Experience*, p. 132.

21. Obrzut, "Expectant Fathers' Perception," pp. 1440–1443.

22. E. Erikson, *Childhood and Society* (New York: W. W. Norton, 1950), pp. 53–58.

23. Liebenberg, "Expectant Fathers," pp. 265–278.

24. Obrzut, "Expectant Fathers' Perception," pp. 1440–1443.

25. E. E. LeMasters, "Parenthood as Crisis," *Marriage and Family Living* 19 (1957): 352–355.

26. E. Dyer, "Parenthood as Crisis: A Re-study," *Marriage and Family Living* 25 (1963): 196–201.

7

1. W. H. Hazlett, "The Male Factor in Obstetrics," *Child and Family* (Fall 1967): 3–11.

2. National Center for Health Statistics, Mortality Statistics Division, Columbia, Md.

3. Ibid.

4. Hazlett, "The Male Factor," pp. 3–11.

5. Homebirth, Inc., from Reprint 103 (Boston, 1976).

6. R. K. Grad and J. Woodside, "Obstetrical Analgesics and Anesthesia: Methods of Relief for the Patient in Labor," *American Journal of Nursing* (February 1977): 242–245.

7. Vice-Chancellor of the Catholic Diocese of Evansville, Indiana, cited by John S. Miller, "Fathers in the Delivery Room," *Child and Family* (June 1964): 1–9.

8. Hazlett, "The Male Factor," pp. 3–11.

9. Ibid.

10. G. Schaeffer, "The Expectant Father: His Care and Management," *Postgraduate Medicine* (December 1965): 658–663.

11. Ibid.

12. Homebirth, Inc., from Reprint 113 (Boston, 1975).

13. Leboyer, *Birth Without Violence*, p. 28.

14. A. F. Guttmacher, *Pregnancy, Birth and Family Planning* (New York: New American Library, 1973), p. 245.

15. Homebirth, Inc., "Planning for Problems in a Home Birth," *Homebirth Newsletter* (Spring 1978): 3–4.

8

1. Liebenberg, "Expectant Fathers," pp. 265–278.

2. G. Caplan, *An Approach to Community Mental Health* (New York: Grune and Stratton, 1961), p. 155.

3. B. Bishop, "A Guide to Assessing Parenting Capabilities," *American Journal of Nursing* 11 (1976): 17.

4. Liebenberg, "Expectant Fathers," pp. 265–278.

5. J. R. Hott, "The Crisis of Expectant Fatherhood," *American Journal of Nursing* 96 (1976): 1436–1440.

Glossary

Acting Out. Taking action on ideas, fantasies, or anxieties rather than talking about them.

Active Labor. The second part of the first stage of labor; contractions are from two to five minutes apart and last sixty seconds or more; the cervix dilates to three to four fingers (six to eight centimeters).

Adrenal Glands. Two small glands located on the upper part of the kidneys which secrete hormones, stimulate the metabolic rate, raise the blood pressure, increase the rate of respiration and heartbeat, and generally prepare the body for a ''fight or flight'' response.

Afterbirth. The placenta and other membranes that are expelled (or delivered) during the third stage of labor, after the baby is born.

After Pains. Contractions of the uterus after the birth of a baby which are felt as cramping discomfort by some women. These contractions help the uterus return to its normal size. *See* involution.

Amniocentesis. A procedure in which some of the amniotic fluid surrounding the fetus is removed by passing a needle through the abdominal wall of the mother. Often done in order to perform tests which give some information about the fetus.

Amnion. The innermost membranes of the placenta enveloping the embryo and amniotic fluid.

Amniotic Fluid. The three or four pints of liquid surrounded by the amnion, in which the fetus floats while in utero. It serves to protect the fetus from outside shocks, as insulation from heat and cold, and allows the fetus to move unhampered. This is the fluid which escapes when the ''bag of waters'' breaks at the outset of labor.

Amniotic Sac. The membranes surrounding the amnion and fetus. *See* amnion, placenta.

Analgesic. A drug, gas, or other agent that relieves or reduces pain without causing unconsciousness.

Anemia. A condition of the blood in which there is a reduction of red blood cells or of hemoglobin, or of both.

Anesthetic. A drug, gas, or other agent that deadens, numbs, or otherwise prevents pain. General anesthetics induce sleep while local anesthetics desensitize specific areas of the body through an injection into muscle or other tissue or into the spinal canal. *See* block.

Apgar Test. A test given to the newborn at one minute and five minutes after birth to check the infant's physical condition. It includes: heart rate, respiratory rate, muscle tone, cry, and color.

Areola. The colored or pigmented area surrounding the nipple of the breast.

Bag of Waters. The sac or bag surrounding the amniotic fluid and fetus. The common name for the amniotic sac and amniotic fluid. *See* amniotic sac, amniotic fluid.

Birth Canal. The passageway from the uterus through which the baby is born (i.e., the cervix, the vagina, and the vulva).

Blastocyte or Blastula. An early stage in the development of the embryo, when it consists of a hollow sphere made of one or several layers of cells.

Block. A type of local analgesia in which the passage of a nervous impulse is stopped. Most often used to stop pain when it is necessary for the patient to remain awake and alert. A *caudal* block is an injection into the lowest region of the spine near the coccyx, numbing the pelvic region. An *epidural* block is injected into the lumbar region of the spine, numbing the abdomen and feet.

"Bloody Show." A mucous discharge streaked with blood which can occur as much as a week before labor actually begins and may signal impending labor.

Bond (bonded, bonding). The feelings of attachment between parent and child.

Bradycardia. Unusually slow heartbeat.

Braxton-Hicks. Practice contractions of the uterus occurring late in pregnancy, which prepare the cervix for delivery by effacing and dilating the cervix. Also called ripening of cervix.

Breech (delivery). Position of the baby during delivery in which the buttocks are presented first instead of the head.

Caesarean Procedure. A surgical procedure in which the baby is delivered by cutting through the mother's abdominal and uterine walls.

Castration Fears. A male fantasy in which his penis and testicles are cut off; fear of being emasculated; more generally a fear of being powerless, losing strength or control.

Catheterization. The insertion of a small pliable tube into the bladder through the urethra, to draw off urine.

Cephalopelvic Disproportion. A condition in which the opening through the bones of the mother's pelvis is too small to allow for the passage of the baby's head; usually indicating that a Caesarean procedure is necessary.

Cervix. A thick disclike apparatus that is the mouth of the uterus and opens into the vagina.

Circumcision. The surgical removal of the foreskin of the penis.

Clitoris. In the woman, a highly sensitive piece of erectile tissue located in front of the urethra opening and covered by the labia minora.

Coccyx. The last two or four fused vertebra at the end of the spine; "tail bone."

Coitus. Sexual intercourse. *See* copulate.

Colostrum. The watery fluid secreted by the breasts immediately preceding and shortly after childbirth before milk is produced.

Compulsive Behavior (also called compulsion). The irrational and repetitive performance of an act.

Conception. The fertilization of the egg; the beginning of a new life.

Contraceptive. Any device used to prevent pregnancy, i.e., diaphragm, condom, foam, pill, intrauterine device.

Contraction. The tightening and shortening of the uterine muscles during labor which force the baby downward and outward. The pressure against the cervix from the baby's head is what causes the cervix to efface and dilate until the baby can pass through.

Copulate. To engage in sexual intercourse.

Couvade Ritual. A primitive ritual of sympathetic magic during which an expectant father simulates labor and birth, ostensively to decoy evil spirits from the mother and new child. Sometimes the ritual involves the postpartum period as well.

Couvade Syndrome. A set of physical symptoms experienced by an expectant father which disappear almost immediately after his wife has given birth.

"Crowning." The appearance at the vaginal opening of the presenting part of the baby, usually the top of the head, during the second stage of labor.

Defense Mechanism. A generally unconscious and reality-distorting psychological strategy intended to maintain an individual's feelings of adequacy, self-worth, and self-image, by avoiding awareness of an impulse or reality, rather than coping directly with the anxiety-producing situation or thought.

Delivery. Giving birth; the child's passage from the uterus into the external world through the birth canal.

Demerol. A synthetic narcotic used as an analgesic agent for labor. It acts as a depressant to the central nervous system (CNS).

Denial. A psychological defense in which some aspect of external reality is ignored or put out of mind (forgotten) in order to avoid the anxiety that would result from facing it.

Dilatation (dilation). The gradual opening up of the cervix to allow the baby to pass through. It is one of the indicators of the progress of the labor, and when "complete" the diameter of the cervical opening is ten centimeters, or five fingers.

Displaced Anxiety. A psychological defense in which an emotional attitude is transferred from one object, for which the attitude would be anxiety provoking, to another, which is safer and does not arouse anxiety. Also called displacement.

Double Bind. Being in a no-win position—one will suffer for doing an action but also for not doing it. What is meant by the expression "damned if you do and damned if you don't."

Early Labor. The first part of the first stage of labor. Contractions range from five to twenty-five minutes apart and last forty-five to sixty seconds. The dilation of the cervix goes from zero to three centimeters, or zero to one and a half fingers.

Edema. Abnormal retention of water by body tissues causing weight gain and swelling.

Efface. The process of stretching and thinning that occurs to the cervix during labor to allow it to dilate so that the baby can pass through. *See* cervix.

Effleurage. A type of massage that is effective in relieving some of the pain of contractions during labor.

Ego. The self; a person's awareness and image of himself/herself; concept of self. The psychological process that deals with reality.

Ejaculation. The release of semen that takes place during most orgasms in the male.

Embolism. A bubble of air in the blood stream.

Embryo. Term for the baby during the first two months of life in the uterus.

Empty-Nest Syndrome. Anxiety, along with feelings of loneliness and isolation, encountered with the realization that one's own children have grown up and left the parents' home.

Endometrium. The lining of the uterus containing many blood vessels. It is shed during menstruation but remains during pregnancy to support the development of the placenta.

Engagement. The positioning of the fetus into the upper opening of the pelvic canal, readying itself for passage through this structure. *See* "lightening."

Engorgement. Congested with blood or other fluid; refers to the excessive fullness of the breasts during pregnancy and lactation, and to the breasts and genitals (male and female) during sexual arousal, when they become filled with blood.

Episiotomy. A lengthwise incision of the perineum to relieve the pressure of the baby's head and reduce the hazard of uneven tearing of vaginal tissue.

Estrogen. A female hormone produced in the ovaries and adrenal glands. It affects the functioning of the reproductive cycle and the development of secondary sexual characteristics.

Fallopian Tubes. In the female, the tubes extending from the uterus to the ovaries. The mature egg, which travels from the ovary down the fallopian tubes to the uterus, is fertilized in the fallopian tubes.

Fertilized. The joining of egg and sperm to form a complete set of chromosomes, constituting the beginning of an organism. *See* conception.

Fetal Distress. A term that describes a condition where the blood supply and oxygen of the fetus are threatened.

Fetal Heart Tones. The infant's heartbeat as monitored through the mother's abdomen.

Fetus. The unborn child, still in the uterus, from three months prenatal until birth.

"Fingers." Unit of measure used to describe the progress of dilation. One finger equals two centimeters. Full dilation is five fingers. *See* dilatation.

First Stage of Labor. The longest part of labor during which the cervix dilates to let the baby pass through. It ends when the cervix is dilated ten centimeters.

Fontanel. The soft spot on the top of the baby's head where the cranial bones have not grown together. This allows the head to be flexible enough to change shape during birth and allows the skull to grow after birth. The bones fuse between nine months and two years of age.

Forceps. An obstetrical instrument sometimes used by the doctor to assist the delivery and help lift the baby's head out of the birth canal.

Fundus (of the uterus). The top, or bulged portion, of the uterus.

Free-Floating Anxiety. A general condition of emotional tension with no apparent direct focus or cause.

Genes. The fundamental units of heredity, each consisting of a unique configuration of DNA. Their configuration on the chromosomes determines physical characteristics (hair color, height, etc.).

Genitalia. The sexual or reproductive organs, either male or female.

Gestation. The length of time necessary for the development of the egg into an individual capable of surviving outside the mother's body; pregnancy.

Gravida. A pregnant woman. A woman who is pregnant for the first time is called a primigravida, and one who has had previous children is a multigravida.

Hemorrhoids. A swelling (or varicosity) of veins in the anus, sometimes causing discomfort and bleeding. Also called "piles."

High-Risk Baby. An infant whose mother has been exposed to one or more of the complications of pregnancy.

High-Risk Pregnancy. One which is complicated by one or more various conditions that may cause the loss of the pregnancy or be injurious to the health of the mother and/or infant. For example, conditions of toxemia, diabetes, and previous poor obstetrical history.

"Husband-Coached" Birth. A childbirth in which the husband participates by offering support in the form of reminding his wife to breathe, monitoring contractions, etc. *See* natural childbirth, Lamaze classes/course.

Hyperventilation. Overbreathing, causing an imbalance in the oxygen–carbon dioxide levels in the system leading to giddiness, dizziness, or numbness.

Hypotension. Blood pressure that is below normal; can be caused by blood loss or drugs.

Identification. The tendency to imitate or become like another person by adopting some aspect of their thought or behavior.

Implantation of Egg. The attaching of the fertilized egg to the wall of the uterus occurring six to seven days after fertilization.

Impotency. In the male, the inability to achieve an erection.

Incest. Sexual relations between closely related individuals, e.g., parent and child or brother and sister.

Induction. Artificial initiation of labor either through the administration of medications or surgical rupture of the membranes surrounding the fetus.

Infertility. Not capable of producing ova (female) or sufficient sperm (male) for conception to take place; inability to conceive.

Intrauterine Life. Life within the uterus, i.e., the fetus.

Intravenous. Medication that is delivered directly to the bloodstream via a needle inserted into a vein or artery.

In Utero. Literally within the uterus.

Involution. The return to normal size of the uterus after the birth of a baby. The process generally takes five or six weeks but will occur sooner if the mother nurses. *See* after pains.

Labia. Literally meaning lips. The folds of skin surrounding the genital and urinary openings in the female.

Labor. The process a woman's body goes through when giving birth, consisting of the contractions of the uterus, the dilatation of the cervix, and the final expelling of the child.

Labor Pains. Discomfort caused by the contractions of the uterus in its attempt to expel the baby.

Laceration. A tear; as a baby passes through the birth canal, this may happen to the tissues near the vagina. Episiotomy is performed as a precaution to a large or uneven tearing. Superficial tears in this area heal easily.

Lactation. The production of milk by the mammary glands.

Lamaze Classes/Course. Classes for expectant parents in the techniques of Dr. Fernand Lamaze. *See* natural childbirth, psychoprophylaxis.

Lanugo. The soft, downy hairlike growth that appears on the body of the newborn infant which eventually falls out.

Let-Down Reflex. The involuntary ejection of milk that occurs during breast-feeding as a result of stimulation, hormone secretion, and muscle contractions around the milk ducts.

Libido. More narrowly, the drive for sexual gratification, i.e., sex drive. In general psychoanalytic terms, the constructive instinctual drive, the basic energy of life, generally sexual in nature.

"Lightening." During late pregnancy, a dropping of the uterus as the fetus engages its head in the upper birth canal in preparation of labor.

"Lithotomy" Position. The standard hospital delivery position in which the woman lies on her back with her legs up in stirrups.

Lochia. Vaginal discharge occurring for five to six weeks after delivery. The color is initially red, changing to pink, to brown, and finally to white.

Masturbation. Generally referring to stimulation of one's own genitals; can also refer to sex play (mutual masturbation) that is not specifically intercourse but involves stimulating one's partner's genitals.

Matricentric. Mother-centered, the emphasis being placed on the mother's role and experiences.

Meconium. A baby's first stool, consisting of waste materials usually normally suspended in the amniotic fluid, passed within the first twenty-four hours. It is extremely sticky and greenish black in color.

Midwife. Traditionally women, now anyone, who delivers

babies and is not a medical doctor. Today midwives are usually nurses who received special obstetrical training. There are still lay midwives.

Midwifery Centers. Often a special section of a hospital where labor and delivery is attended by midwives rather than medical doctors. Many of them have a more comfortable homelike setting.

Miscarriage. *See* spontaneous abortion.

Molding. The process of adjusting the shape of the baby's head to fit the size and shape of the birth canal.

Morning Sickness. The nausea experienced by many women in the first trimester of pregnancy.

Mucous Membranes. The thin mucus-secreting tissue that lines body cavities connecting with the outside air, including the alimentary canal, respiratory tract, vagina, etc.

Mucous Plug. The heavy mucus that blocks the opening of the cervix during pregnancy.

Mucus. The clear viscous secretion of the mucus membranes that serve to keep the membranes moist.

Multigravida. A woman who has had more than one pregnancy.

Multiparous. A woman who has given birth more than once.

Natural Childbirth. A term that has come to be applied to any method of training and preparation for labor that reduces the need for anesthesia. *See* psychoprophylaxis, Lamaze classes/course, "husband-coached" birth.

"Nesting" Behavior. A need among expectant parents to put their environment in order, or create a place for the baby, much as animals build a nest.

Nurturing. Engaging in those activities that promote development or growth in another, such as feeding and caring for a baby.

Obsession. An intrusive or recurring thought and its associated emotional state, which are experienced as irrational and uncontrollable.

Ontogeny. The biological development of a single individual organism; as contrasted to *phylogeny*.

Os. The (opening) passageway from the cervix to the uterus. *See* cervix.

Ovary. The female reproductive gland in which the ova are developed and released. The gland is responsible for the secretion of the hormones estrogen and progesterone.

Overcompensating Behavior (overcompensation). A defense mechanism to relieve anxiety about uncomfortable feelings by exaggerating desirable feelings and behavior.

Ovulation. The release of a mature egg from the female.

Ovum. The mature egg cell produced by the ovaries that contain one-half of the chromosomes necessary for a complete cell. The other half will be supplied by a sperm cell during fertilization.

Palpation. A technique of medical examination in which the physician uses his/her hands to feel for certain signs of the condition of the baby.

Pelvic, or "Internal," Examination. An examination of the female internal organs, i.e., vagina, uterus, and ovaries.

Pelvic Organs. Those organs contained within the ring of the pelvic bones, including the uterus, ovaries, vagina, fallopian tubes, bladder, and rectum.

Pelvis. The bony ring in the lower torso that supports and transfers weight of the body to the legs. It consists of the two hip bones joined in front by the pubic bone and in the back by the sacral vertebra. In the female this ring forms the walls of the birth canal.

Perineal Muscle. The floor of the pelvis through which the urethra, vagina, and rectum pass. Covers the same area as the perineum and supports the pelvic organs. *See* perineum.

Perineum. The area between the anus and the base of the vulva (in females) or scrotum (in males).

Peripheral Nervous System (PNS). Bundles of sensory and motor nerves that radiate from the brain and spinal cord and reach all parts of the body.

Phylogenetic/Phylogeny. The evolutionary development of a species.

Pitocin. A hormone of the pituitary gland that is often injected to stimulate the uterus to contract and deliver the placenta.

Placenta. A broad flat organ partially surrounding the baby. It attaches to the uterine wall and the baby's umbilical cord and is responsible for the exchange of nutrients and wastes between mother and child. *See* afterbirth.

Placenta Previa. Meaning ''placenta first,'' when the placenta is attached to the walls of the uterus in such a position that it covers the cervical opening and blocks the baby's passage through the birth canal. May indicate a Caesarean procedure.

Postpartum. Refers to the time after the birth of the baby.

Postpartum Depression. Feelings of depression after the birth of the child.

"Preemy." A baby delivered prematurely, i.e., before the ninth month. *See* premature.

Premature. The birth of an infant between the seventh month (twenty-ninth week) and the thirty-sixth week of pregnancy and/ when a newborn weighs under five pounds. Survival may require extra medical provisions.

Prenatal. The expectancy period (after conception and before the birth of the child), i.e., pregnancy.

Prepped. The procedure performed at the hospital to prepare the woman for childbirth.

Presentation. The position the baby's body is in when she/he first appears at the external opening of the birth canal, i.e., breech, vertex, posterior, and anterior.

Primipara. A woman who is pregnant for the first time.

Procaine. A local anesthetic; trade name Novocaine (name literally means ''instead of cocaine'').

Progesterone. A female hormone secreted by the ovaries that is responsible for the building up of the endometrium (lining of the uterus) to receive the fertilized egg and for maintaining the lining during the pregnancy.

Projection. A defense mechanism in which one's own unacceptable wishes, feelings, desires, or characteristics are attributed to someone else.

Psychoanalytic Theory. A psychological theory originated by Freud emphasizes the role of the unconscious and instinctual drives in our conscious actions.

Psychogenesis. Something created in or by the mind (that is, by a psychological process, such as the ability to tolerate stress) rather than from somatic origins.

Psychoprophylaxis. The methods of preparation for labor and delivery brought to the West by Dr. Fernand Lamaze. The mother is taught the physiological and psychological processes of childbirth along with exercises and breathing techniques to help her participate effectively in the labor and delivery.

Psychosexual Stages. In psychoanalytic theory, the child goes through five developmental stages: oral, anal, phallic, latency, genital. In each stage, a different part of the body dominates in interest and sensual gratification. The way a child resolves conflicts at each stage will effect basic personality traits.

Pubic Bones. The front bones of the pelvic girdle that join the two hip bones.

Puerperium. The six weeks following delivery.

Quickening. The first movements of the fetus in utero that are felt by the mother, generally around the fifth month of pregnancy.

Regression. A psychological defense mechanism intended to reduce anxiety in times of conflict by retreating to the aims, desires, and behavior of an earlier age.

Repression. A defense mechanism that bars from consciousness an unacceptable impulse, memory, emotion, or desire, as a protection from anxiety.

"Ripe." A descriptive term for the condition of the cervix when it is ready for labor to begin.

"Ripening" of the Cervix. A prelabor process involving slight contractions that serve to prepare the cervix for the actual delivery by effacing and dilating it.

Rooming-In. A method of postdelivery care in which the infant stays in the same room as its mother, rather than in the nursery.

Rooting Reflex. Present in newborn infants, it is the instinctual movements of the head and mouth toward a touch on the cheek or mouth area.

Scrotum. In the male, it is the sac of skin in which the testes are suspended.

Second Stage of Labor. The point of labor in which the baby is actually born. Contractions are from two to five minutes apart and last forty-five to ninety seconds.

Seminal Fluid. The fluid produced by the seminal vesicles in the male and which serve as a transport medium for the sperm cells.

Sex Roles. The general behavior patterns and attitudes that are considered differentially appropriate for men and women in any given society.

Show. *See* "bloody show."

Sperm. The male reproductive cell. Like the egg (ovum) it contains twenty-three chromosomes. It unites with the ovum in the fallopian tubes to cause conception.

Sperm Count. The number of sperm per milliliter of semen. The average ejaculate contains 200–500 million sperm.

Sperm Motility. The ability of the sperm to travel through the vagina and cervix to the fallopian tubes where they can fertilize the ovum.

Sphincter Muscle. A muscle in the shape of a ring that in its normal state of contraction closes an opening. For example, the anal sphincter closes the rectum.

Spontaneous Abortion. The premature delivery of the embryo, generally occurring during the first trimester, also called miscarriage.

Striae. "Stretch marks"; the pinkish purple lines appearing on a woman's abdomen, thighs, buttocks, and breasts due to the overstretching of the skin during pregnancy. They later fade to white scars or disappear.

Sympathy Pains. *See* couvade syndrome.

Term. The completed cycle of pregnancy, full term being forty weeks.

Testicles. The sperm-producing organs in the male. They also produce the male hormone testosterone. The testicles are suspended in the scrotal sac below the penis.

Third Stage of Labor. Expulsion of the placenta, occurring after the baby has been delivered.

Toxemia. A metabolic disorder of pregnancy. Symptoms are hypertension, swelling, and albumin in the urine.

Transition. The last and most intense period of the first stage of labor that accomplishes full cervical dilatation (ten centimeters). Contractions are two minutes apart and last about ninety seconds.

Trimester. One-third of the time span of the pregnancy, or a three-month period. There are three trimesters in the pregnancy, each having its characteristic changes.

Umbilical Cord. The three blood vessels that transport oxygen and nourishment to the fetus and take wastes back to the mother's blood stream while in utero. The navel, or belly button, is what remains after it is cut.

Umbilicus. *See* umbilical cord.

Urethra. The canal between the bladder and the outside world through which urine passes.

Uterus. A hollow muscular pear-shaped organ located in the pelvis of the female in which the embryo develops to a child; womb.

Vagina. The canal leading from the uterus to the outside of the body; part of the birth canal.

Varicose Veins. Abnormally swollen blood vessels, generally in the legs. *See* hemorrhoids.

Vernix Caseosa. A whitish, cheeselike substance covering the baby's skin while in the uterus that acts as protection from constant exposure to the amniotic fluid.

Version. An obstetric procedure in which the doctor attempts to turn the baby in the birth canal to the most advantageous position for delivery.

Vertex. The top or crown of the head; in childbirth, the baby is usually born in the vertex position, that is, head down.

Viable. The point of development at which the child or fetus can survive outside the uterus.

Bibliography

Abenheimer, K. M. "A Note on the Couvade in Modern England (and Scotland)." *British Journal of Medical Psychology* 20 (1945–46): 376–377.

Alexander, L. "Fathers in the Delivery Room." *American Baby* 34 (January 1972): 24–25.

American Journal of Nursing. "Babies Have Fathers Too." *American Journal of Nursing*, October 1971, pp. 1980–1981.

Anthony, J. E. and Benedek, T., eds. *Parenthood: Its Psychology and Psychopathology.* Boston: Little, Brown, and Company, 1970.

Arms, S. *Immaculate Deception: A New Look at Women and Childbirth in America.* Boston: Houghton, Mifflin Company, 1975.

Arnstein, H. S. "The Crisis of Becoming a Father." *Sexual Behavior* 2 (April 1972): 43–47.

Bean, C. *Methods of Childbirth.* New York: Doubleday, 1972.

Benedek, T. "Parenthood as a Developmental Phase." *Journal of the American Psychoanalytic Association* 7 (1959): 389–417.

Benson, L. *Fatherhood: A Sociological Perspective.* New York: Random House, 1968.

Bernstein, R. and Cyr, F. E. "A Study of Interviews with Husbands in a Prenatal and Child Health Program." *Social Casework* 38 (1957): 473–480.

Bibring, G. "Psychological Processes in Pregnancy." *Psychoanalytic Study of the Child* 14 (1959): 113–119.

Biller, H. B. "Include the Father in Pregnancy." *Sexual Behavior* 2 (1972): 47.

Biller, H. and Meredith, D. *Father Power.* New York: David McKay, 1974.

Bing, E. and Colman, L. *Making Love During Pregnancy.* New York: Bantam Books, 1977.

Boston Women's Health Book Collective. *Our Bodies, Ourselves.* 2d ed. New York: Simon and Schuster, 1976.

Bradley, R. "Father's Presence in Delivery Rooms." *Psychosomatics* 3(6): 474–479.

Bradley, R. *Husband-Coached Childbirth.* New York: Harper & Row, 1965.

Brewer, G. *What Every Pregnant Woman Should Know.* New York: Random House, 1977.

Brown, J. et al. *Two Births*. New York: Random House/Book Works, 1972.

Bucove, A. "Postpartum Psychoses in the American Male." *Bulletin of the New York Academy of Medicine* 40 (1964): 961–971.

Burlingham, D. "The Preoedipal Infant-Father Relationship." *Psychoanalytic Study of the Child* 28 (1973): 23–47.

Burr, W. R. "Satisfaction with Various Aspects of Marriage over the Life Cycle: A Random Middle Class Sample." *Journal of Marriage and Family Living* 32 (1) (February 1970): 29–37.

Caplan, G. "Patterns of Parental Response to the Crises of Premature Birth." *Psychiatry* 23 (1960): 365–374.

Cogan, R. "Comfort During Prepared Childbirth As a Function of Parity, Reported by Four Classes of Participant Observers." *Journal of Psychosomatic Research* 19 (1) (1975): 33–37.

Cohen, A. *Childbirth is Ecstasy*. San Francisco: Aquarius Publishing Company, 1971.

Coley, S. B. and James, B. E. "Delivery: A Trauma for Fathers?" *Family Coordinator*, October 1976, pp. 359–363.

Colman, A. D. and Colman, L. *Pregnancy: The Psychological Experience*. New York: Seabury Press, 1971.

Cronenwett, L. R. and Newmark, L. R. "Father's Responses to Childbirth." *Nursing Research* 23 (1974): 210–217.

Curtis, J. A. "A Psychiatric Study of 55 Expectant Fathers." *U.S. Armed Forces Medical Journal* 6 (1955): 937–950.

Dawson, W. R. *The Custom of Couvade*. Manchester, Eng.: Manchester University Press, 1929.

Despres, M. "Favorable and Unfavorable Attitudes Towards Pregnancy in Primipara." *Journal of Genetic Psychology* 51 (1937): 241.

Deutscher, M. "Brief Family Therapy in the Course of First Pregnancy: A Clinical Note." *Contemporary Psychoanalysis* 7 (1970): 21–35.

Dick-Read, G. *Childbirth Without Fear*. 4th ed. New York: Harper & Row, 1944.

Disbrow, M. A. "Meeting Consumer Demands for Maternity Care." Proceedings of a Conference, September 16, 1972. Contact: Maternal-Child Health Nursing, University of Washington, Seattle, Washington.

Dobbyn, D. "A Feminist's Case for Homebirth." *Women: A Journal of Liberation* 4 (3) (1975): 20–23.

Dovavon, B. *Caeserean Birth Experience*. Boston: Beacon Press, 1977.

Dyer, E. "Parenthood as Crisis: A Re-Study." *Marriage and Family Living* 25 (1963): 196–201.

Edwards, M. E. "Unattended Home Births." *American Journal of Nursing* 73 (8) (August 1973): 1332.

Eloesser, L.; Galt, E. H.; and Hemingway, I. *Pregnancy, Childbirth and the Newborn: A Manual for Rural Midwives*, 1959. Available from: Istituto Indigenista Interamericano, Ninos Heroes, 139 Mexico 7, D.F.

English, O. Spurgeon, and Foster, C. J. *Fathers Are Parents Too: A Constructive Guide to Successful Fatherhood*. New York: Putnam, 1951.

Enoch, M. D.; Trethowan, W. H.; and Barker, J. C. *Some Uncommon Psychiatric Syndromes*. Bristol: John Wright, 1967.

Evans, W. "Simulated Pregnancy in a Male." *Psychoanalytic Quarterly* 20 (1951): 165–178.

Fein, R. "Men's Entrance to Parenthood." *Family Coordinator* 25 (4) (October 1976): 341–348.

Freeman, T. "Pregnancy As a Precipitant of Mental Illness in Men." *British Journal of Medical Psychology* 24 (1951): 49–54.

Genne, W. *Husbands and Pregnancy.* Rev. ed. St. Meinrad, Ind.: Abby Press, 1970.

Gilles, P. "Violence and Pregnancy: A Note on the Extent of the Problem and Needed Services." *Family Coordinator* 24 (4) (January 1975): 81–86.

Ginath, Y. "Psychoses in Males in Relation to Their Wives Pregnancy and Childbirth." *Israel Annuals of Psychiatry and Related Disciplines* 12 (1974): 227–237.

Goodrich, F. W., Jr. *Preparing for Childbirth: A Manual for Expectant Parents.* Englewood Cliffs, N.J.: Prentice-Hall, 1966.

Greenberg, N. and Morris, N. "Engrossment: Newborn's Impact on the Father." *American Journal of Orthopsychiatry* 44 (1974): 520–531.

Hartman, A. and Nicolay, R. "Sexually Deviant Behavior in Expectant Fathers." *Journal of Abnormal and Social Psychology* 71 (1966): 232–234.

Hazell, L. *Birth Goes Home,* 1975. Available from: International Childbirth Education Association Supplies Center, P.O. Box 70258, Seattle, Washington 98107.

Hazell, L. *Commonsense Childbirth.* New York: Putnam, 1969.

Hazlett, W. B. "The Male Factor in Obstetrics." *Child and Family*, Fall 1967, pp. 3–11.

Helper, M. M.; Cohen, R. R.; Beitsenman, E. F.; and Eaton, L. F. "Life-Events and Acceptance of Pregnancy." *Journal of Psychosomatic Research* 12 (3) (1960): 183–184.

Hines, J. D. "Father—The Forgotten Man." *Nursing Forum* 10 (1971): 176–200.

Hobbs, D. F. "Parenthood As Crisis: A Third Study." *Journal of Marriage and the Family* 27 (1965): 367–372.

Hobbs, D. "Transition to Parenthood: A Replication and an Extension." *Journal of Marriage and the Family* 30 (August 1968): 413–417.

Hogenboom, P. "Man in Crisis: The Father." *Journal of Psychiatric Nursing* 5 (September-October 1967): 457–464.

Hott, J. R. "The Crisis of Expectant Fatherhood." *American Journal of Nursing* 96 (9) (1976): 1436–1440.

Howells, J. G., ed. *Modern Perspectives in Psycho-obstetrics.* New York: Brunner/Mazel, 1972.

Inman, W. S. "The Couvade in Modern England." *British Journal of Medical Psychology* 19 (1941-43): 37–55.

Illsley, R. "The Sociological Study of Reproduction and its Outcome." In *Childbearing Its Social and Psychological Aspects*, edited by S. A. Richardson and A. F. Gittmacher. Baltimore: Williams and Wilkins Company, 1967.

Jacobson, E. "Development of the Wish for a Child in Boys." *Psychoanalytic Study of the Child* 5 (1950): 139–159.

Jacoby, A. "Transition to Parenthood: A Reassessment." *Journal of Marriage and the Family* 31 (4) (1969): 720–727.

Jarvis, W. "Some Effects of Pregnancy and Childbirth on Men." *American Psychoanalytic Association Journal* 10 (1962): 689–700.

Kaplan, E. H. and Blackman, L. H. "The Husband's Role in Psychiatric Illness Associated with Childbearing." *The Psychiatric Quarterly* 43 (3) (1969): 396–409.

King, E. "The Pregnant Father." *Bulletin of the American College of Nurses and Midwives* 13 (February 1968): 19–25.

Kitzinger, S. *Experience of Childbirth*. Baltimore: Penguin Books, 1972.

Lacoursiere, R. "The Mental Health of the Prospective Father: A New Indication for Therapeutic Abortion?" *Bulletin of the Menninger Clinic* 36 (1972): 645–650.

Lacoursiere, R. A. "Fatherhood and Mental Illness: A Review and New Material." *Psychiatric Quarterly* 46 (1972): 109–124.

Lamaze, F. *Painless Childbirth: The Lamaze Method*. Chicago: Henry Regnery Company, 1970.

Lamb, M. E. and Lamb, J. E. "The Nature and Importance of the Father-Infant Relationship." *Family Coordinator*, October 1976, pp. 379–385.

Landis, J. T.; Poffenberger, T.; and Poffenberger, S. "The Effects of First Pregnancy Upon the Sexual Adjustment of Couples." *American Sociological Review* 15 (1950): 766–772.

Lang, R. *Birth Book*. Palo Alto, Calif.: Genesis Press, 1972.

Leboyer, F. *Birth Without Violence*. New York: Alfred A. Knopf, 1975.

LeMasters, E. E. "Parenthood as Crisis." *Marriage and Family Living* 19 (1957): 352–355.

Levin, P. and Berne, E. "Games Nurses Play." *American Journal of Nursing* 72 (March 1972): 483–484.

Liebenberg, B. "Expectant Fathers." *American Journal of Orthopsychiatry* 37 (1967): 358–359.

Liebenberg, B. "Expectant Fathers." *Child and Family* 8 (3) (Summer 1969): 265–277.

Lynn, D. B. *The Father: His Role in Child Development*. Monteray, Calif.: Brooks and Cole Publishing Company, 1974.

Marquart, R. K. "Expectant Fathers: What Are Their Needs?" *American Journal of Maternal Child Nursing* 1 (1) (January/February 1976): 32–36.

Marzollo, J., compiler. *Nine Months, One Day, One Year: Guide to Pregnancy, Birth and Baby Care*. New York: Harper Colophon Books, 1976.

Masters, W. H. and Johnson, V. E. *Human Sexual Response*. Boston: Little, Brown and Company, 1966.

May, I. and the Farm Midwives. *Spiritual Midwifery*. Summertown, Tenn.: The Book Publishing Company, 1975.

Mead, M. "Cultural Patterning." In *Childbearing, Its Social and Psychological Aspects*, edited by S. A. Richardson and A. F. Guttmacher. Baltimore: Williams and Wilkins Company, 1967.

Meikle, A. and Gerritse, R. "A Comparison of Husband-Wife Responses to Pregnancy." *Journal of Psychiatry* 83 (1) (January 1973): 17–23.

Meyerowitz, J. and Feldman, H. "Transition to Parenthood." *Psychiatric Research Reports* 20 (1966): 78–84.

Meyerowitz, J. "Satisfaction During Pregnancy." *Journal and Marriage and the Family* 32 (1): 78–84.

Milinaire, C. *Birth*. New York: Harmony Books, 1974.

Miller, J. "Fathers in the Delivery Room." *Child and Family* 3 (1964): 3–11.

Mishler, C. "Birthing at Home." *Mother Earth News* 9 (May 1971): 54.

Morris, N. "The Frequency of Sexual Intercourse During Pregnancy." *Archives of Sexual Behavior* 4 (5) (September 1975): 501–507.

Munroe, R. L. and Munroe, R. H. "Male Pregnancy Symptoms and Cross-Sex Identity in Three Societies." *Journal of Social Psychology* 84 (1971): 11–25.

Munroe, R.; Munroe, R.; and Nerbove, S. "Male Pregnancy Symptoms and Cross-Sex Identity: Two Replications." *Journal of Social Psychology* 89 (1) (February 1973): 147–148.

New Interest in Home Deliveries. Maternal-Child Health Information, 29 (1972). Available from: Maternal-Child Health Services, Health Services and Mental Health Administration, Health, Education and Welfare, Rockville, Maryland 20852.

Nillson, L.; Furuhjelm, M.; Ingelman-Sundberg, A.; and Wirsen, C. *A Child Is Born.* New York: Delacorte Press, 1977.

Obrzut, L. A. J. "Expectant Fathers Perception of Fathering." *American Journal of Nursing* 96(9)(1976): 1440–1442.

Parke, R. and Sauvin, D. B. "The Father's Role in Infancy: A Re-Evaluation." *Family Coordinator*, October 1976, pp. 365–371.

Pederson, F. and Robson, K. "Father Participation in Infancy." *American Journal of Orthopsychiatry* 39 (3) (April 1969): 466–472.

Price, R. *Abnormal Behaviour, Perspectives in Conflict.* New York: Holt, Rinehart and Winston, 1972.

Pryor, K. *Nursing Your Baby.* New York: Pocket Books, 1973.

Reik, T. *Ritual: Psychoanalytic Studies.* 2d ed. New York: Farrar, Straus, 1946. 1st ed. London: Hogarth Press, 1931.

Rendina, I. and Dickerscheid, J. B. "Father Involvement with First Born Infants." *Family Coordinator*, October 1976, pp. 373–378.

Retterstöl, N. "Paranoid Psychoses Associated with Impending or Newly Established Fatherhood." *Acta Psychiatrica Scandinavica* 44 (1968): 51–61.

Riker, B. "Childbirth at Home." *Los Angeles Times*, February 28, 1971.

Rossi, A. "Transition to Parenthood." *Journal of Marriage and the Family* 30 (1968): 26–40.

Schaefer, G. "The Expectant Father: His Care and Management." *Postgraduate Medicine* 38 (December 1965): 658–663.

Schaefer, G. *The Expectant Father.* New York: Barnes and Noble, 1972.

Senn, M. and Hartford, C. *The Firstborn: Experiences of Eight American Families.* Cambridge, Mass.: Harvard University Press, 1968.

Sousa, M. *Childbirth at Home.* Englewood Cliffs, N.J.: Prentice-Hall, 1976.

Spock, B. *Baby and Child Care.* New York: Pocket Books, 1970.

Starr, J. "Home Delivery of Babies, Rewards Versus Risks." *Mother Earth News* 9 (May 1971): 50–52.

Stender, F. *Husbands in the Delivery Room.* Bellevue, Washington: International Childbirth Education Association (I.C.E.A.), Supplies Center, 1971.

Tanzer, D. and Block, J. R. *Why Natural Childbirth? A Psychologists' Report on the Benefits to Mothers, Fathers, and Babies.* Garden City, New York: Doubleday and Company, 1972.

Towne, R. D. and Afterman, J. "Psychosis in Males Related to Parenthood." *Bulletin of the Menninger Clinic* 19 (January 1955): 19–26.

Trethowan, W. H. "The Couvade Syndrome—Some Further Observations." *Journal of Psychosomatic Research* 12 (1968): 107–115.

Trethowan, W. H. and Conlon, M. F. "The Couvade Syndrome." *British Journal of Psychiatry* 111 (January 1965): 57–66.

van Leeweun, K. "Pregnancy Envy in the Male." *International Journal of Psychoanalysis* 47 (1966): 319–324.

Vaughn, V. C. and McKay, R. J. *Textbook of Pediatrics.* 10th ed. Philadelphia: W. B. Saunders Company, 1975.

Wainwrite, W. H. "Fatherhood As a Precipitant of Mental Illness." *American Journal of Psychiatry* 123 (July 1966): 40–44.

Ward, C. and Ward, F. *The Home Birth Book.* Washington, D.C.: Inscape Corporation, Publishers, 1976.

Weiss, K. "Birth: Suffering for Science." *Off Our Backs*, September-October 1975, pp. 14–17.

Wente, A. S. and Crockenberg, S. B. "Transition to Fatherhood: Lamaze Preparation, Adjustment Difficulty and the Husband-Wife Relationship." *Family Coordinator*, October 1976, pp. 351–357.

White, G. J. *Emergency Childbirth.* Franklin Park, Illinois: Interstate Printers and Publishers, 1973.

Wonnell, E. B. "The Education of the Expectant Father for Childbirth." *Nursing Clinics of North America* 6 (4) (December 1971): 591–603.

Zilboorg, G. "Depressive Reactions Related to Parenthood." *American Journal of Psychiatry* 87 (1931): 927–962.

Index